Scope English   Level Five

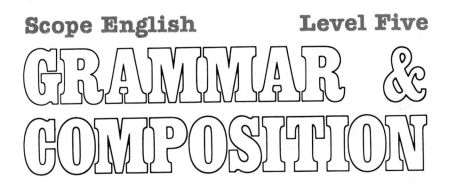

GRAMMAR &
COMPOSITION

CONSULTANTS

Dr. Joanna McKenzie
Professor of English Education
Department of Secondary Education
California State University at Northridge
Northridge, California

Professor Charles R. Duke
College of Humanistic Studies
Department of English
Murray State University
Murray, Kentucky

CURRICULUM CONSULTANTS

Nora Forester
Reading Coordinator
Northside Independent School District
San Antonio, Texas

William Horst
Teacher
Robert E. Lee High School
Springfield, Virginia

Barbara Krysiak, Ed. D.
Principal
North Hampton Elementary School
North Hampton, New Hampshire

Nancy McHugh
Teacher
Grant High School
Van Nuys, California

Scope English Level Five

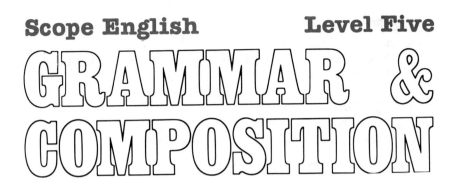

GRAMMAR & COMPOSITION

SCHOLASTIC INC.

STAFF

Project Editor: Stella Sands
Level Five Authors: Richard Foerster, Michael Adams, Dale Donovan
Level Five Editor: Karl Weber
Production Editors: Judy Susman and Ann Craig
Senior Art Director: Mary Mars
Design and Art Production: Canard Design, Inc.
Cover Design and Photograph: Jack George Tauss

LEVEL FIVE READERS

Mary Ann Brock
Teacher
Bell High School
Hurst, Texas

Marlene McDaniel
Teacher
Northside High School
Roanoke, Virginia

Gregory Wojcik
Chairperson
English Department
T. F. North High School
Calumet City, Illinois

ACKNOWLEDGMENTS

Grateful acknowledgment is made for the use of copyrighted material.

Joan Daves Agency for excerpts from Chapter 5 of *Good Old Boy* by Willie Morris. Copyright © 1971 by Willie Morris.

Photo Credits: Roe DiBona, pp. 28–29, 100–101, 138–139, 188–189, 228–229, 268–269, 312–313, 364–365, 416–417, 482–483; Wide World Photo, p. 57 (top); Jacques Demareceaux, p. 57 (bottom); Wide World Photo, p. 115; Canadian Government Office of Tourism, p. 205 (top); UPI, p. 205 (bottom); David Schroeder, Scholastic/Kodak Photography Award, 1982, p. 435 (top left); Scott Sedlik, Scholastic/Kodak Photography Award, 1982, p. 435 (top right); Fiona Entwistle, Scholastic/Kodak Photography Award, 1982, p. 435 (bottom left); Maura Stewart, Scholastic/Kodak Photography Award, 1982, p. 435 (bottom right).

Grateful acknowledgement is made to the Brooklyn Museum for permission to take the photo on pages 138–139 in the Brooklyn Museum Sculpture Garden, Brooklyn, NY.

ISBN 0-590-07700-7

12 11 10 9 8 7 6 5

Level Five

Contents

Unit Six

Writing a Composition 140

Unit Seven

Phrases 164

Unit Eight

Writing a Comparison 190

Unit Fifteen

Using Pronouns and Modifiers Correctly 336

Unit Sixteen

Writing a Review 366

Unit Seventeen

Punctuation 380

Unit Eighteen

Writing an Autobiographical Narrative 418

Unit Nineteen

Vocabulary and Spelling 438

Scope English   Level Five

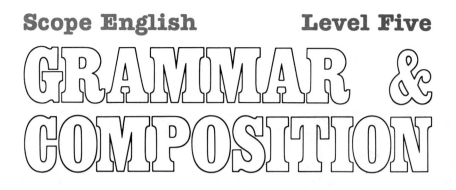

GRAMMAR & COMPOSITION

Unit One
Understanding Sentences

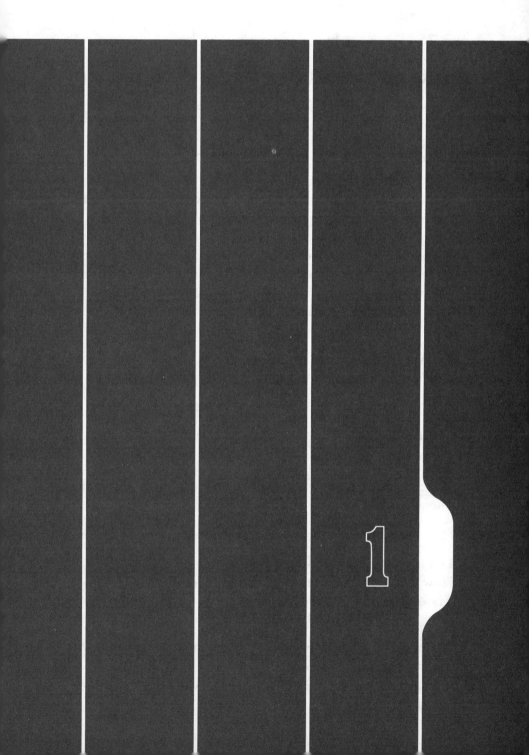

Understanding Sentences

Lesson One

Sentences and Sentence Fragments

Suppose you come home from school and find the following note from your brother:

Hired! Working. Pick up dinner. Mom—call.

Lou

You are the only person at home, and you don't understand what your brother is trying to tell you. Who has hired your brother? Where is he working? Are you supposed to pick up dinner, or will your brother do it? Are you supposed to call Mom, or is she going to call you? The note is confusing because none of the words or groups of words express complete thoughts.

You would have no trouble understanding the note if it were written like this:

Vic Adams, the gas-station owner, just hired me! I am working until 9 p.m. Can you pick up the dinner? Call Mom at work.

Lou

This second note is easy to understand because it is written in *sentences*.

● A <u>sentence</u> is a group of words that expresses a complete thought.

Here are more examples of sentences:

Lou is working at Vic's gas station.
How can I make my car's engine run more smoothly?
Try our new Superblend gasoline.
Wow, the engine is really humming now!

Notice that a sentence begins with a capital letter and ends with a punctuation mark. Look again at the first note. The four words or groups of words begin with capital letters and end with

4

punctuation marks. But they are not sentences because they do not express complete thoughts. They are called *sentence fragments*.

Here are more examples of sentence fragments:

At half past eight.
If you want to.
In Mike's car.

There isn't enough information in any of these fragments for you to understand what the writer is trying to communicate. People sometimes use sentence fragments when they speak. In a conversation, sentence fragments are usually understandable, since the rest of the conversation can help to explain what the fragments mean. Also, listeners can ask questions if they don't understand something. Here are the sentence fragments from above used as part of a conversation. They are easily understood.

"When will you be leaving for the movie?"
"At half past eight."
"May I come along?"
"If you want to."
"How will we get there?"
"In Mike's car."

However, in writing, sentence fragments are usually confusing. There is often no conversation to help supply the missing information. Sentences are clearer than fragments. Use sentences in your writing so that your reader will be able to understand what you are trying to express.

PRACTICE A

The following groups of words have no capital letters or end punctuation. Number your paper from 1 to 10. If a group of words is a sentence, write it as a sentence: begin with a capital letter and end with a period. If a group of words is a fragment, copy the words on your paper and write *fragment* after them.

Examples: twenty crates of apples fell from the truck
            Twenty crates of apples fell from the truck.

            on the busiest street in town
            on the busiest street in town   fragment

1. apples rolled everywhere
2. under the wheels of passing cars
3. people stumbled and fell
4. as the apples were crushed
5. by heavy trucks and buses
6. the sweet smell of apple juice filled
7. some people picked up the loose apples
8. bags were filled with fresh fruit
9. apple sauce clogged
10. that was a funny

PRACTICE B

The paragraph below contains some sentence fragments. Rewrite the paragraph so that there are no fragments. You may need to add words to form new sentences.

Example: My parents aren't sure. Whether they want to buy a new car.
My parents aren't sure whether they want to buy a new car.

Last Friday night, our class held a dance called "Space Hop." In the school gym. The gym was decorated like a space station. Black and silver "control panels" with flashing lights. There were murals on the walls. Showing the blackness of space speckled with stars and planets. The band members wore metallic jump suits and helmets. Which made them look like robots. The drummer wore a pair of antennas. Bounced on his head as he played. The band played such songs as "Ten Thousand Light Years from Home," by the Rolling Stones. And the theme from *Star Wars*.

PRACTICE C

Write five sentences on any one of the topics on the following page. Be sure that each sentence expresses a complete thought.

Example: A Well-Trained Dog
A Well-Trained Dog
A well-trained dog can be more than a friend. It can be a lifesaver, too. Last summer, my friend Barbara's German shepherd helped save a person from

drowning. The dog was the only one to hear the girl's call for help. It barked at Barbara's window until she came outside and spotted the little girl, just in time.

Topics:
A Disappointing Movie
An Unpleasant Job
A Dream Vacation
A Perfect Friend
A topic of your own choice

Lesson Two

Kinds of Sentences

Suppose your sister wants you to clean up your half of the bedroom. There are several ways she could let you know what she wants.

She might say, "If you start now, you can get your half of the room cleaned by dinnertime."

She might ask, "When are you going to clean your half of the room?"

She might exclaim, "Your half of the room is a complete wreck!"

Or she might demand, "Get your half of the room cleaned up now!"

Depending on what kind of person your sister is, she might use any of these four sentences to get across her message. The first sentence makes a statement. The second asks a question. The third expresses strong feeling. The fourth is a command. Each of these four sentences represents one of the four kinds of sentences—*declarative, interrogative, exclamatory,* and *imperative.*

● **A <u>declarative sentence</u> makes a statement. It ends with a period (.).**

Kim visited her grandparents last year.
There will be a soccer game this Saturday afternoon.
Movies are too expensive.

- An <u>interrogative sentence</u> asks a question. It ends with a question mark (?).

  Who is going with us?
  Have the astronauts for the next space flight been chosen yet?
  How can you afford to buy that jacket?

- An <u>exclamatory sentence</u> expresses strong emotion. It ends with an exclamation point (!).

  We're the champions!
  The bell won't stop ringing!
  That was some accident!

- An <u>imperative sentence</u> gives a command or makes a request. It can end with a period (.) or an exclamation point (!).

  Use a period if a sentence expresses a simple request.

  Tell me your good news.
  Don't forget to take your medicine.
  Remember to call your mother.

  Use an exclamation point if a request or command is expressed with strong emotion.

  Stop that noise!
  Throw him the life preserver!
  Don't bother me now!

  Use the correct end punctuation in your writing. It will help your readers understand what you are saying.

PRACTICE A

The following groups of words lack end punctuation marks. Copy each group of words on your paper, and add the correct end punctuation. After each sentence, write the kind of sentence it is—*declarative, interrogative, imperative,* or *exclamatory.*

Example: When will you call me
          When will you call me?   *interrogative*

1. New York City is called the "Big Apple" by many people
2. Have you ever visited New York City
3. The city is an exciting place to visit

4. Visit the city and see how great it is
5. Ride the elevator to the observation deck of the World Trade Center
6. What a breathtaking view
7. Did you know that New York City is the financial capital of the nation
8. It is also the home of the major TV networks
9. New York has been labeled the fashion capital of America
10. Be sure to visit New York's Seventh Avenue, also called Fashion Avenue

PRACTICE B

Change each of the following sentences into the kind of sentence called for in parentheses. You may need to add or take away words. Write the new sentence on your paper. Be sure to use the correct end punctuation.

Example: Joe likes to go fishing.   (interrogative)
   Does Joe like to go fishing?

1. I'd like you to close the door.   (imperative)
2. Were you saying something?   (declarative)
3. You should use safety belts when driving.   (imperative)
4. Adam will get a summer job.   (interrogative)
5. Is Scott home?   (declarative)
6. It was a great game.   (exclamatory)
7. Does Lorraine know about the surprise party?   (declarative)
8. You shouldn't do that.   (imperative)
9. Liz is sure that she is right.   (interrogative)
10. Do you think that Bob Marley's music will continue to be popular?   (declarative)

PRACTICE C

Choose one of the following five topics. Write at least four sentences about the topic. Write at least one of each of the four kinds of sentences. Label your sentences *declarative, interrogative, exclamatory,* or *imperative.*

Example: A Sport I Like
   Ice hockey is my favorite sport.   *declarative*

Have you ever seen an ice hockey game?   interrogative

What an exciting game it is!   exclamatory

Go to a game and see for yourself.   imperative

Topics:

A Sport I've Played

My Dream Car

The Worst Day of My Life

Where I'd Like To Be Right Now

A topic of your own choice

Lesson Three

Subjects

Can you fill in the blank below?

_____ live in the deserts of North Africa.

Here are some possible answers:

Camels

Nomadic tribes

Several kinds of poisonous snakes

Each sample answer that fits in the blank is the *subject* of the sentence.

● **The subject of a sentence tells who or what is doing something or who or what is being spoken about.**

The word or words that fit in the blank space above tell *who* or *what* lives in the deserts of North Africa.

To find the subject of a sentence, ask yourself :

1. Who or what is doing something?

or

2. Who or what is being spoken about?

Simple and Complete Subjects

What is the subject of the sentence at the top of page 11?

His thin, freckled face brightened at the good news.

If you say that *his thin, freckled face* is the subject, you are correct. *His thin, freckled face* is the complete subject. However, you are also correct if you say that *face* is the subject. *Face* is the most important word in the complete subject. *Face* is the *simple subject* of the sentence.

- The <u>simple subject</u> is the most important word in the subject.

- The <u>complete subject</u> includes the simple subject and all the words nearby that give more information about it.

For example, the complete subject of the following sentence is in boldface type:

My sixty-year-old aunt jogs two miles each day.

The most important word in the complete subject, *aunt,* is the simple subject. The other words in the complete subject, *my sixty-year-old,* give information about the simple subject.

Here are some other examples:

This old car gets only twelve miles per gallon of gas.

The simple subject is *car.* The complete subject is *this old car.*

My cousin from Puerto Rico is sixteen today.

Cousin is the simple subject. *My* and *from Puerto Rico* are details that give information about the simple subject.

What are the simple and complete subjects of the sentence below?

Dinner was served by Bill.

The complete subject is *dinner.* The simple subject is also *dinner.* If no nearby words give information about the simple subject, the complete subject and the simple subject are the same.

Note: From now on in this book, the word *subject* will be used to mean the *simple subject* of a sentence.

The Position of the Subject in a Sentence

The subject does not always come first in a sentence. Notice the positions of the subjects in the sentences on the next page.

Do **you** know how to repair that engine?
After breakfast **Lorene** took her brother to the park.
Softly and silently fell the **rain.**

The subject of an imperative sentence is not always stated.

Close the door, please.

The subject is understood to be *you.*

PRACTICE A

Copy each of the following sentences on your paper. Underline the complete subject in each sentence. Then put a second line under the simple subject. If the subject is understood to be *you,* write *you* after the sentence on your paper.

Example: The brown dachshund barked noisily.
           The brown dachshund barked noisily.

1. I found a bunch of bananas in the package.
2. Six sausage pizzas were served at the party.
3. A hot breakfast provides a good start for the day.
4. Do you eat soup on cold days?
5. John's favorite sandwich is ham and cheese.
6. After football practice, he ate a thick steak with onions.
7. Have some potato salad with your sandwich.
8. My Uncle Sal's special chili is famous all over town.
9. Rosa's favorite fruit is oranges.
10. Al sliced the pineapple with a sharp knife.

PRACTICE B

Below is a list of words. Choose any five words. Use each word as the simple subject in a sentence of your own. Add words that give information about each simple subject. Underline the complete subject of each sentence.

Example: eyes
           Her large brown eyes filled with tears.

| birds | song | football | kitten | homework |
| car | city | peanuts | trees | swimmer |

Lesson Four

Predicates

Imagine a bicycle without wheels, an automobile without an engine, and an airplane without wings. You couldn't travel very far with any of them.

In the same way, the subject of a sentence isn't very useful by itself. To express a complete idea, a subject must be joined to a *predicate*.

● **The predicate expresses some action done by or done to the subject, or it expresses the state of being of the subject.**

Look at the following sentences. The predicate of each sentence is all the words that are not part of the complete subject. The predicates are in boldface type.

My sixty-year-old aunt **jogs two miles each day.**
Dinner **was served by Bill.**
My cousin from Puerto Rico **is sixteen today.**

In the first sentence, *aunt* is the subject. *Jogs two miles each day* tells what the subject does. *Jogs two miles each day* is the predicate.

In the second sentence, *dinner* is the subject. *Was served by Bill* is the predicate. The predicate tells what was done to the dinner.

In the third sentence, *my cousin* is the subject. *Is sixteen today* is the predicate. The predicate expresses the state of being of *my cousin*.

Simple and Complete Predicates

Just as a complete subject contains a simple subject, a complete predicate contains a *simple predicate*. The simple predicate is also called the *verb*.

● **The simple predicate, the verb, is the most important word or words in the predicate.**

Find the most important word in the complete predicate below.

My sixty-year-old aunt **jogs two miles every day.**

Jogs is the most important word. The sentence wouldn't make

13

any sense without it. However, if you dropped *all* the words in the complete predicate *except* the verb, the sentence would still make sense:

My sixty-year-old aunt **jogs.**

Jogs, then, is the simple predicate, the verb.

Note: From now on in this book, the simple predicate will be called the *verb.*

The verb in a sentence does one of two things:

1. Some verbs express action. They tell what the subject did or what was done to the subject. The action may be either physical or mental. (See Unit Three, Lesson Three.)

My sixty-year-old aunt **jogs** two miles every day.
Dinner **was prepared** by Bill.
Elena **stumbled** in the darkened theater.
Sal **thought** about his science project.

2. Some verbs do not express action. They express the state of being of the subject. These kinds of verbs are called *linking verbs.* (See Unit Three, Lesson Three.)

My cousin from Puerto Rico **is** sixteen today.
Manny and Liz **were** late.
This electronic music **sounds** weird.
Pete **seems** tired this morning.

Helping Verbs and Main Verbs

A verb can include more than one word. When a verb has more than one word, it is called a *verb phrase.*

In the examples below, the verb phrases are in boldface type:

Rachel **is working** two nights a week at the library.
She **will work** there every week until June.
She **has worked** in the library since September.

In each of these sentences, a *helping verb* has been added to the main verb, *work.* A helping verb helps the main verb show the time of the action.

In the first sentence, *is* is the helping verb. It helps show that the action is happening now.

14

In the second sentence, *will* is the helping verb. It helps show that the action is going to happen in the future.

In the third sentence, *has* is the helping verb. It helps show that the action happened in the past.

Here is a list of common helping verbs:

have	has	had
do	does	did
am	are	is
was	were	
be	been	
shall	will	

The words *not* and *never* are not part of a verb or verb phrase.

Rachel **has** never **worked** so hard before.
She **is** not **working** in the same library as Ed.

In an interrogative sentence, the subject often comes between the helping verb and the main verb.

Does Rachel **work** in the children's room at the library?

You will learn more about verb phases in Unit Three.

PRACTICE A

Copy each of the following sentences on your paper. In each sentence, draw a vertical line between the complete subject and the complete predicate. Underline the verb or verb phrase in each sentence.

Example: A castle is a house or tower with thick stone walls for protection.

   A castle|is a house or tower with thick stone walls for

   protection.

1. Many castles were built in the Middle Ages for use in warfare.
2. The walls of medieval castles were usually from five to fifteen feet thick.
3. The windows were protected by strong iron grills.
4. Most castles had moats around them.
5. A movable drawbridge went across the moat.
6. The most heavily guarded part of the castle was the keep.

15

7. The keep was located in the center of the castle.
8. The top of a steep hill was usually chosen as the site for a castle.
9. A castle in a high location was safe from enemy attack.
10. Extensive castle-building occurred in Europe, the Middle East, China, and India.

PRACTICE B

Below are five groups of words that can be used as complete subjects of sentences. Think of three complete predicates that fit in each blank. Write these fifteen complete sentences on your paper. Underline the verb in each sentence.

Example: The yellow sailboat _____ .
The yellow sailboat belongs to my cousin.
The yellow sailboat is at the dock.
The yellow sailboat sails very fast.

1. Taxicabs _____ .
2. Wild animals _____ .
3. Spaghetti _____ .
4. A strong wind _____ .
5. My cousin Harriet from Tulsa _____ .

PRACTICE C

On the following page is a list of topics. On your paper write seven to ten sentences about one of the topics. Underline the verb or verb phrase in each sentence.

Example: Summer

Summer

Like many people, I enjoy summer more than any other season. I have several reasons. I wear light, comfortable clothes in the summer. There are more hours of daylight for sports and recreation. And on July Fourth, my family always has an all-day picnic. In the morning, we swim in the lake. In the afternoon, we play a wild game of softball. In between, we eat mountains of ribs, hamburgers, and corn on the cob. My family has enjoyed a July Fourth picnic every year since 1971. The picnic has become a family tradition.

Topics:
Winter
A Person I'll Never Forget
Horror Movies
A Good Way for a Teenager to Earn Money
A topic of your own choice

Lesson Five

Compound Subjects and Verbs

Some things come in pairs: salt and pepper; a cup and a saucer; Popeye and Olive Oyl. Other things come in groups: a knife, a fork, and a spoon; Moe, Larry, and Curly; the *Niña,* the *Pinta,* and the *Santa Maria.* When a pair of words or a group of words is used as the subject of a sentence, it is called a *compound subject.*

● **A underline{compound subject} is two or more subjects that share the same verb. Compound subjects are usually joined by the connecting word underline{and} or underline{or}.**

The compound subjects and connecting words below are in boldface type. The verbs are in italics.

The **salt and pepper** *are* on the table.
Popeye or Olive Oyl *will watch* the baby.
Chemistry and math *are* my favorite subjects.
The yellow **truck and** the blue **bus** *were* parked near the bus station.

In the last example above, only the simple subjects and the connecting word are in boldface type. The modifying words *yellow* and *blue* are not included in the compound subject.

When a compound subject contains three or more subjects, put a comma after each subject except the last one. Also put the connecting word *and* or *or* before the last subject. Here are some examples:

Moe, Larry, and Curly *locked* themselves in the broom closet.
Carbon, hydrogen, and oxygen *are* essential for living things.

17

Like subjects, verbs can also come in pairs or groups: You can eat and drink; you can sink or swim; you can hop, skip, and jump. When verbs are used in pairs or groups, they form a *compound verb*.

- **A <u>compound verb</u> is two or more verbs that share the same subject. The verbs are usually joined by the connecting word *and* or *or*.**

The star of the movie **sang and danced.**
Miguel **will sell or keep** his motorcycle.
The pelican **soared, swooped, and dived** into the water.

The last example contains three verbs. When a compound verb contains three or more verbs, put a comma after each verb except the last one. Also put the connecting word *and* or *or* before the last verb.

A sentence can have both a compound subject and a compound verb. Here are some examples:

The **robin and** the **sparrow** *snatched* the bread *and flew* away.
The **Caseys and** the **Smiths** *danced and sang* at the party.
Juanita and her **parents** *have flown or have driven* across the country three times.

PRACTICE A

Copy the sentences below on your paper. Underline the subjects with one line. Underline the verbs with two lines. Circle all connecting words.

Example: Todd, Sharon, and Bill bought flowers for Jane.
           Todd, Sharon, (*and*) *Bill bought flowers for Jane.*

1. Blue, red, and yellow are the primary colors.
2. With credit cards, customers buy now and pay later.
3. Sue walks or rides to work.
4. Firefighters and police rushed to the scene of the accident.
5. During our vacation, we biked, jogged, and swam.
6. Henry signed and sealed the letter.
7. The principal or the dean reads and signs every announcement.
8. According to a poll, baseball, football, and basketball are still the most popular sports in the United States.

9. Justine sketches and paints skillfully.
10. The mayonnaise looks and tastes fresh.

PRACTICE B

Some of the sentences below have no subjects. Others have no verbs. If a sentence has no subject, fill in the blank with a compound subject. If a sentence has no verb, fill in the blank with a compound verb. Then write the completed sentences on your paper.

Example: _____ are my favorite singers.
            Diana Ross and Melissa Manchester are my favorite singers.

1. _____ are two nearby cities.
2. The cook _____ in the kitchen.
3. _____ cost more than a dollar now.
4. Juan _____ on weekends.
5. _____ are easy games to learn.
6. The branches _____ in the wind.
7. _____ are going to the movies.
8. Many people _____ during the summer.
9. Kelly and Mike _____ at the picnic.
10. _____ are sitting in the hall closet.

PRACTICE C

On the following page is a list of topics. Choose one and write three sentences about it. Include the following:

1. one sentence with a compound subject
2. one sentence with a compound verb
3. one sentence with both a compound subject and a compound verb

Example: Flowers
            1. *Roses and tulips are my favorite flowers.*
            2. *Flowers grow and bloom in greenhouses all year.*
            3. *Dandelions and chicory have spread and now flourish by the highway.*

Topics:
Wild Animals
The Most Unusual Place I've Visited
Space Travel
This Year's Fashions
A topic of your own choice

Lesson Six

Simple and Compound Sentences

All of the sentences you have studied so far in this unit have been *simple sentences.*

- **A simple sentence has one subject and one verb, both of which may be compound.**

Notice the various kinds of simple sentences. The subjects are underlined with one line. The verbs are underlined with two lines.

The logs rolled into the river.   (simple sentence with a single subject and a single verb)

Pierre and Gaston balanced on top of the logs.   (simple sentence with a compound subject)

The logs bobbed and bounced on the waves.   (simple sentence with a compound verb)

Pierre and Gaston lost their footing and fell into the water. (simple sentence with both a compound subject and a compound verb)

A simple sentence can have a single subject, a single verb, a compound subject, a compound verb, or both a compound subject and a compound verb. A compound subject is considered *one subject* and a compound verb is considered *one verb.*

A simple sentence may be any of the four kinds of sentences that you learned about in Lesson Two. Here are some examples:

Bill and Mary are at the beach.   (declarative sentence with a compound subject)

Have you won or lost the game? (interrogative sentence with a compound verb)

Will you or Peter set the table and make a salad? (interrogative sentence with a compound subject and a compound verb)

The team won the game and captured the championship! (exclamatory sentence with a compound verb)

Lock and bolt the door! (imperative sentence with a compound verb)

All of these sentences are simple sentences because each has one subject and one verb.

Just as there are compound subjects and compound verbs, there are also compound sentences.

● A <u>compound sentence</u> is made up of two or more simple sentences joined by a comma and a connecting word such as *and, or, but,* or *for.*

The simple sentences in a compound sentence may also be joined by a semicolon with no connecting word.

Here are some examples. The simple sentences in each compound sentence below are in boldface type.

The public loved the film, and **it was nominated for an Academy Award.**

I will visit my cousins next week, but **I will see my aunt and uncle tomorrow.**

The President will visit Germany next year, or **the German chancellor will travel to the United States.**

The storm lasted two days; **flooding destroyed more than twenty houses.**

You must decide which of the two ways of joining sentences to use. The first method, which includes a connecting word, is more common. Use the second method only if the ideas expressed in the two sentences are clear without a connecting word.

Be careful to avoid creating *run-on sentences.*

● A <u>run-on sentence</u> is two or more sentences that are separated by only a comma or by no punctuation at all.

Here are some examples of run-on sentences and possible ways to correct them:

Incorrect: I enjoy ice-skating it is my favorite sport.
Correct: I enjoy ice-skating. It is my favorite sport.

Incorrect: I learned to skate when I was six Dad taught me.
Correct: I learned to skate when I was six; Dad taught me.

Incorrect: Come skating with me, I'll teach you how.
Correct: Come skating with me, and I'll teach you how.

As you can see, a run-on sentence can be corrected in three ways: by changing it into two sentences, by adding a semicolon between the two sentences, or by adding a comma and a connecting word between the two sentences.

PRACTICE A

Copy the following sentences on your paper. After each sentence, write whether it is a *simple* or a *compound* sentence.

Example: Ed and Tom perform in a rock band.
          Ed and Tom perform in a rock band.   simple

1. Leslie screamed, but her warning was too late.
2. Linda and Fran can speak and write in Spanish and French.
3. Bean sprouts and chick peas make a salad more interesting.
4. Did you answer her question, or did Adam answer it?
5. Rachel found the book; Vicki had not missed it.
6. Ann and Dot took care of the puppies and their mother.
7. I usually eat in the cafeteria, but in warm weather I eat outdoors.
8. Tony calls or visits me every day.
9. Lorraine applied for the job in May, but she wasn't hired until December.
10. Mark and Jeff are learning jujitsu, judo, and karate.

PRACTICE B

Here are five pairs of simple sentences. Make each pair into a compound sentence by adding a comma and an appropriate connecting word. Put the comma before the connecting word.

Example:　I baby-sit for my younger brother.
My sister Sue rarely baby-sits.
I baby-sit for my younger brother, but my sister Sue rarely baby-sits.

1. Tom bought a new truck.
Victor remodeled his car.
2. Sandy will get her hair trimmed.
She will keep it long.
3. Tod has never visited Washington.
Randy has been there five times.
4. The dog approached the cat.
The cat hissed at the dog.
5. Frank's handwriting is hard to read.
His printing is quite clear.

PRACTICE C

Below are ten simple sentences. To each one, add another simple sentence to make it a compound sentence. You may add a comma and a connecting word to join the two sentences, or you may use a semicolon without a connecting word. In either case, be sure the meaning of the compound sentence is clear.

Example:　Jane finally arrived at the beach.
Jane finally arrived at the beach, but she could not find her friends.

1. My job doesn't pay well.
2. The weather forecaster predicts rain.
3. Juan studies art at the museum on Saturdays.
4. London's subways are very clean.
5. Some people like their cooked vegetables crisp.
6. Many pets require a lot of attention.
7. Joe cannot make a quick decision.
8. The average height of an adult male is five feet ten inches.
9. I prefer peaches to nectarines.
10. Sharon's mother is from Texas.

Review Exercises

I. Copy each group of words on your paper. If the words are a sentence, capitalize the first word and add the proper end punctuation. If the words are a fragment, add your own words to make the fragment a sentence. (Lesson One)

Examples: she arrived on the noon flight
She arrived on the noon flight.

after the movie
After the movie, we went home.

1. no one knew the answer
2. my brother is going to the grocery store
3. under the bed
4. the painting on the wall is crooked
5. because Darren loves the Beatles' music
6. rabbits are sometimes pets
7. when we go
8. if the ground is wet
9. my grandparents just celebrated their fortieth anniversary
10. watching the birds

II. Copy each of the following sentences on your paper. Capitalize the first word in each sentence, and add the correct end punctuation. Then identify the sentence as *declarative, interrogative, imperative,* or *exclamatory.* (Lesson Two)

Example: what kind of flower is that
What kind of flower is that?   interrogative

1. that was a close call
2. have you ever had the measles
3. salute when the general passes
4. the little boy was lost in the department store
5. don't ever do that again
6. he will not be playing in today's game
7. please straighten up your room
8. what a beautiful sunset
9. why is Sharon crying
10. we won

III. Copy each of the following sentences on your paper. Draw one line under the complete subject. Draw two lines under the complete predicate. (Lessons Three and Four)

Example: Our math teacher gives us a quiz every week.
           Our math teacher gives us a quiz every week.

 1. Donna finished her work early.
 2. The rest of the class took ten more minutes for the quiz.
 3. June got the highest grade.
 4. My friend David didn't finish the quiz.
 5. Peter received a grade of 80 on the quiz.
 6. The members of the band left class early today.
 7. They were excused from today's quiz.
 8. The music director was grateful.
 9. Our teacher seemed pleased with our work.
10. Everyone in class passed the quiz.

IV. Copy the sentences below on your paper. Draw one line under the simple subject. Draw two lines under the verb or verb phrase. (Lessons Three and Four)

Example: My dog chases birds.
           My dog chases birds.

 1. The humpback whale is an endangered species.
 2. Many northern birds migrate south in the autumn.
 3. Sharks rarely attack human beings.
 4. I am the youngest member of my family.
 5. The bus will seat thirty-nine passengers.
 6. Too much greasy food can give you a stomachache.
 7. Saturday is my favorite day of the week.
 8. I like Monday least.
 9. My family eats dinner together every night.
10. Helen has practiced for the concert every day this month.

V. Below are ten groups of words that can be used as compound subjects. Use each group as the compound subject in a sentence of your own. Write the completed sentences on your paper. (Lesson Five)

Example: cream and sugar
           The cream and sugar are on the table.

25

1. Harriet and Loretta
2. ice, sleet, and snow
3. Mom and Dad
4. spring and summer
5. trains or planes
6. oil and vinegar
7. my brother and my sister
8. Arthur, Michael, and Frank
9. tennis and swimming
10. Washington and Lincoln

VI. Think of a compound verb that will fit in each blank space. If you want, add other words to make the sentences interesting. Write the completed sentences on your paper. (Lesson Five)

Example: Kate _____ .
           Kate talks and laughs with her friends.

1. My old car _____ .
2. Our school band _____ .
3. Frank and Anna _____ .
4. The police officer _____ .
5. The sports announcer _____ .
6. My brother or my sister _____ .
7. His aunt _____ .
8. The fire in the abandoned barn _____ .
9. My best friend _____ .
10. The skier _____ .

VII. Below are simple sentences grouped in pairs. Combine each pair to form a compound sentence. You may use a comma and a connecting word, or a semicolon without a connecting word. (Lesson Six)

Example: The hurricane destroyed property.
           No one was hurt.
           The hurricane destroyed property, but no one was hurt.

1. The actress was not well known before this movie.
   She has now been nominated for an Academy Award.

2. Champion figure skaters must practice daily.
   They lose their strength and stamina.
3. A thunderstorm is expected.
   The Collinses went fishing anyway.
4. I made pancakes for breakfast.
   My family ate them all.
5. Gasoline costs less than two dollars a gallon in the United States.
   In Europe it costs over three dollars a gallon.
6. I loved the movie *Grease*.
   Henry hated it.
7. Sailing is John's favorite sport.
   He spends many hours taking care of his boat.
8. Herb's mother will roast a turkey for Thanksgiving.
   She will bake a ham.
9. Tara's cousin lives in California.
   Her grandparents live in Massachusetts.
10. Alaska is the largest state in the United States.
    Rhode Island is the smallest.

VIII. Below is a list of topics. Choose one topic, and write five to ten sentences about it. Include each of the following:

1. one simple sentence with a compound subject
2. one simple sentence with a compound verb
3. one simple sentence with both a compound subject and a compound verb
4. one compound sentence

When you finish, read over your sentences. Do they express complete thoughts? Do they begin with capital letters and end with the correct punctuation marks? If not, go back and make the necessary corrections. (Lessons One to Six)

Topics:
A Recent News Event
My Plans for Next Summer
My Town in the Year 2000
My Family
A topic of your own choice

Writing Paragraphs

Lesson One

The Main Idea

Imagine this. You are home alone. It's a gray, rainy Saturday. You have nowhere to go and nothing to do. Suddenly you remember a jigsaw puzzle someone gave you for your last birthday. You didn't open it then, thinking that it would be a perfect pastime for a rainy day.

You pull the puzzle down from a shelf. On the cover of the box is a photograph of a lake. Reflected in its surface is a thick forest of evergreens. A chain of snow-capped mountains rises in the background. The box promises "Hours of fun with 1,500 interlocking pieces." A perfect way to spend the rainy day!

You open the box and dump the pieces onto the table. There are hundreds of tiny pieces, each a different shape. How can you turn this jumble of separate pieces into one picture? You move the pieces, trying to fit them together. It seems hopeless.

Suddenly, you realize that some of the pieces seem to belong together. There are many dark green pieces, for example, that you recognize as parts of the evergreen forest. There are light blue pieces that are parts of the sky, and white pieces that are parts of the snowy mountain peaks. Maybe if you sort the pieces by color you'll be able to put together the pieces that belong together.

You soon realize that putting the puzzle together is easy when you work in an organized way. By gathering the puzzle pieces that form each main part of the puzzle — the lake, the mountains, the sky, and so on — you gradually turn a confusing pile of 1,500 pieces into a picture just like the one on the cover of the box.

When you are getting ready to write, you may have many ideas in your mind. These ideas may be in a jumble, like unconnected pieces of a jigsaw puzzle. If you write your ideas that way, your readers will feel as you do when you first look at a puzzle — confused! But just as you can organize the pieces of a jigsaw puzzle by color, you can organize your ideas when you write. To organize your thoughts, group them into *paragraphs*.

- **A <u>paragraph</u> is a group of sentences that relate to a single main idea.**

Just as all the green pieces of the puzzle form a picture of a forest, the separate sentences of a paragraph express one main idea. The main idea is the point of the paragraph.

The information below includes four main ideas. Therefore, it has been divided into four paragraphs. Notice how the sentences in each paragraph work together to express a single main idea. Also notice that the first line of a paragraph is always indented; that is, there is a small blank space before the first word on the line.

For over 100 million years, dinosaurs were the most powerful creatures on earth. These huge reptiles lived in nearly every place in the world. Some were over 80 feet long and as tall as two-story houses. Some were fierce hunters, with teeth as long as kitchen knives. Dinosaurs ruled the earth.

Yet suddenly, around 70 million years ago, the dinosaurs vanished. No one really knows why, although scientists have suggested many possible explanations. Some say that an ice age brought cold temperatures that killed the dinosaurs. Others blame some unknown disease. Still others say that the dinosaurs were killed off by the earliest mammals, who ate the dinosaurs' eggs. None of these explanations has been proven true.

Now, however, a new and startling explanation has been put forth. According to a few scientists, a giant meteor — a rock, ten miles across, flying through space — may have crashed into the earth. The force of the crash stirred up great clouds of dust all over the earth. A thick layer of such dust hanging in the air for a year or more could have blocked many of the sun's rays. Without these rays, many of the plants in the earth's jungles and forests may have died. And the plant-eating dinosaurs, who needed a vast amount of food to support their large bodies, may have starved as a result.

This new explanation of the death of the dinosaurs is not accepted by most scientists. But some think it is worth further study. Scientists are now studying the rocks and fossils of 70 million years ago, looking for clues that may prove or disprove the meteor theory.

The first five sentences of the passage tell how dinosaurs once ruled the earth. The first sentence states the main idea, and the other sentences show the importance and power of the dinosaurs. Therefore, this group of five sentences makes one paragraph.

The next sentence begins a new idea — the disappearance of the dinosaurs. Six sentences discuss possible reasons for the dinosaurs' disappearance. This group of sentences forms the second paragraph of the passage.

The third main idea is about a new theory concerning the death of the dinosaurs. The next six sentences describe this new theory. They make up the third paragraph of the passage.

Finally, the last three sentences of the passage discuss another main idea — that some scientists are now looking for clues to determine whether or not the meteor theory is true. These three sentences make up the fourth and final paragraph of the passage.

Dividing the passage into four separate paragraphs makes it easy to read. The main ideas stand out clearly because each is in a separate paragraph.

EXERCISE ONE

Below are five short paragraphs, followed by a list of five main ideas. Number your paper from 1 to 5. Write the main idea next to the number of its paragraph.

Example: The next time you pass a playground or schoolyard, stop and watch the children. Do you realize that they are hard at work? According to social scientists, play is a child's "work." It is through games that children first learn many of the social and physical skills they will need as adults.
Main idea: *Children learn by playing.*

1. Games teach children about living with others. By learning to follow the rules of a game, a child comes to understand the need for rules in society. Games teach children the need for fair play, taking turns, and good sportsmanship. And team games help children to learn the importance of cooperation in working toward a common goal.

2. Games also help children to develop their physical skills. Ball games help children to develop sharp eyes and agility. Races and

tag games help children develop speed. And games like marbles, mumblety-peg, and cat's cradle foster coordination and dexterity.

3. When you were a child, you probably played games like leap-frog, hide-and-seek, and blindman's buff. You may be surprised to learn that these same games have been played by children for thousands of years. The ancient Egyptians, for example, are known to have played blindman's buff, as did the early Greeks and Romans. A Roman book written in the first century A.D. describes boys playing leapfrog in the same way that children do today.

4. Many children's games are found the world over. For instance, children throughout Europe play games with marbles just as many children in the United States do. Marbles are also used in India, China, South America, and Africa. In Middle Eastern countries such as Turkey and Syria, marbles made from the knucklebones of sheep are used; in other countries, polished pebbles or balls of baked clay are used. The materials used vary, but the games themselves are the same.

5. Those who study human behavior say that the games of modern children often imitate the ancient customs and beliefs of adults. The game of "Here We Go 'Round the Mulberry Bush," for example, resembles the spring festival dances of ancient Europe. And the game of tag may be based on a belief of primitive peoples that one could escape evil spirits by fleeing to a "safe" place, such as a magic wood.

Main Ideas:
Some children's games have been played for thousands of years.
Games help children to develop their physical skills.
Marbles is one game that is played all over the world.
Some children's games resemble ancient customs and beliefs.
Games teach children about getting along with others.

EXERCISE TWO

The following passage contains four main ideas. However, it has not been divided into paragraphs. Read it through carefully. Then copy it on your paper, dividing it into paragraphs. Start each paragraph on a new line and indent the first word. Then write the main idea of each paragraph below that paragraph. You may either put the main idea in your own words or find a sentence in the paragraph that expresses the main idea. The first paragraph of the article has been done for you, so you will only write three paragraphs and three main ideas.

Suppose someone invented a vehicle that used no fuel, could be stored almost anywhere, rarely broke down, and was cheap and easy to drive. It would be a great achievement, wouldn't it? Well, there already is such a vehicle. Its inventor was Kirkpatrick Macmillan of Scotland, and it is called the bicycle. Actually, two-wheeled vehicles similar to bicycles were used as early as the 1700's. However, these machines, called "hobbyhorses," had no pedals or chains. Riders had to push against the ground with their feet in order to move. Hobbyhorses were a popular fad in London in the early 1800's, but they were not very practical. It was easier and faster to walk! In 1839, Macmillan made the first real bicycle. He took an old-fashioned hobbyhorse and added pedals for the rider's feet. The pedals did not turn in a circle like modern bicycle pedals. Instead, they moved forward and backward, turning the rear wheel through two metal rods. Macmillan's bicycle was not as efficient as the bicycle of today. But it was a great advance over the original hobbyhorse. Later inventors added other improvements. In 1861, the Michaux brothers in Paris changed Macmillan's back-and-forth pedals into the cranking pedals used today. Another French company created the first chain-driven bicycle in 1869. In 1888, John Dunlop of Ireland invented inflatable rubber tires. By the 1890's, companies in Europe and the United States were making bicycles almost the same as those we ride today.

Example: *Suppose someone invented a vehicle that used no fuel, could be stored almost anywhere, rarely broke down, and was cheap and easy to drive. It would be a great achievement, wouldn't it? Well, there already is such a vehicle. Its inventor was Kirkpatrick Macmillan of Scotland, and it is called the bicycle.*
Main idea: The invention of the bicycle was a great achievement.

34

EXERCISE THREE

Think of five topics to write about. You can choose from the topics listed below, or come up with topics of your own. Then think of a main idea for a paragraph about each of the five topics you choose. Write the main idea on your paper in a complete sentence.

Example: Topic: *Modern Machines*
            Main Idea: *In America today, computers can be seen almost everywhere.*

Topics:

Modern Machines	Movies
Cooking	A Hobby
Heroism	Looking for a Job
A Pet	Music
Sports on Television	My Favorite Month

Lesson Two

The Topic Sentence

As you learned in Lesson One, a paragraph is a group of sentences about one main idea. Can you find the main idea of the following paragraph?

You can swim in the cold, clear water of Evergreen Lake. You can spend an afternoon hiking up Mt. Sydney. There are beautiful scenes of nature to photograph or sketch. At night, the only sound is the lapping of the waves near your tent. You can tell stories by the fire or count the thousands of stars overhead.

These five sentences contain a number of facts and ideas. They all seem to be about the same topic. But it's hard to tell exactly what the main idea of the paragraph is, because the main idea is not stated in any sentence.

Notice the difference between the group of sentences above and the one on the same topic that follows.

North Ridge State Park is a great place for a summer camping trip. You can swim in the cold, clear water of Evergreen Lake. You can spend an afternoon hiking up Mt. Sydney. There are beautiful scenes of nature to photograph or sketch. At night, the only sound is the lapping of the waves near your tent. You can tell stories by the fire or count the thousands of stars overhead.

The first sentence of this paragraph states the main idea of the paragraph. The first sentence of this paragraph is a *topic sentence.*

● **A topic sentence states the main idea of a paragraph.**

A topic sentence helps a reader grasp the main idea of a paragraph easily. Like a sign on the highway saying, "Mt. Sydney— 21 kilometers" or "Highway 164 to Evergreen Lake," a topic sentence lets your readers know exactly where they are going.

A topic sentence can be placed at the beginning of a paragraph, in the middle, or at the end.

1. A topic sentence can come at the beginning of a paragraph to introduce the subject. Here is an example:

Many people don't know about the important activities that take place behind the scenes in zoos. Some zoos are centers for biological research. The diets, diseases, and behavior of animals can often be studied best in a zoo. Some zoos help spread information about animal life through classes, books, films, and magazines. And many zoos are important centers for the breeding of all kinds of animals.

2. A topic sentence can come at the end of a paragraph to sum up the ideas of the paragraph. Here is an example:

Wen Wang, who ruled China almost 3,000 years ago, is said to have built one of the earliest zoos. The Bible says that King Solomon kept a collection of animals from many lands. Alexander the Great sent animals back to Greece from the lands that he conquered. In the 1500's, the Aztecs of Mexico had a zoo so enormous that it needed a staff of 300 workers. **Zoos have been around for thousands of years.**

3. A topic sentence may appear in the middle of a paragraph to build suspense. Here is an example:

What do the Hawaiian goose, the European bison, and Père David's deer have in common? All are animals that were saved from extinction through breeding in zoos. **In addition to preserving endangered species, breeding in zoos serves several other purposes.** Zoos breed animals partly to have animals for display. Zoos often swap zoo-bred animals with other zoos to keep the collections varied and complete. Breeding also does away with the need for expensive expeditions to capture animals in the wild.

As these three examples show, the topic sentence does *not* have to be the first sentence of the paragraph. In most cases, however, a paragraph is clearer if the topic sentence is first. The reader is immediately aware of the main idea.

EXERCISE FOUR

Find the topic sentence in each paragraph below. Write the topic sentence on your paper next to the number of the paragraph.

Example:　The best vacation spot my family ever found was the mountain cabin we stayed in last summer. The mountains that surrounded the cabin had many miles of trails. We went hiking or horseback riding every day. A clear, cold mountain lake near our cabin was filled with fish eager to bite. My sister caught a big striped bass, and I caught a pickerel. The beauty of the mountains added to our fun.
Topic Sentence: *The best vacation spot my family ever found was the mountain cabin we stayed in last summer.*

1. It wasn't easy to reach our cabin. First, we had to leave the main highway and drive north along a narrow gravel road marked "Elk Mountain Lane." Turning left at a white stone marker, we drove down a winding dirt road to a fork. To the right, the road went steeply uphill, but to the left, it led gently down to the driveway of our cabin.

2. The deep blue water of the mountain lake was completely calm. The dark green trees around the cabin made me feel peaceful and secure. There were no sounds of cars, planes, or boats. There were only the songs of birds. It was a quiet, relaxing place.

3. One day, we rowed across the lake and climbed up Lookout Hill for a view of the surrounding country. In the distance, mountaintops reached toward the sky. The forest of pine and spruce trees looked like a gigantic evergreen carpet. Our cabin, which was big enough to sleep eight people, was just a tiny dot across the lake. The view made us realize how small we are compared to the creations of nature.

EXERCISE FIVE

The paragraphs below need topic sentences. Read each paragraph and decide what the main idea is. Write it in a clear topic sentence. Then copy each paragraph on your paper, putting the topic sentence where you feel it belongs. Underline your topic sentence.

Example: Southern City High has won eleven games in a row. Two players on the team were chosen for this year's All-State Basketball Team. The center, Billy Floyd, led the Lakeside Conference in scoring and rebounds. Five players have been offered basketball scholarships by colleges.

Southern City High has a fabulous basketball team. *Southern City High has won eleven games in a row. Two players on the team were chosen for this year's All-State Basketball Team. The center, Billy Floyd, led the Lakeside Conference in scoring and rebounds. Five players have been offered basketball scholarships by colleges.*

1. The stands were packed with excited fans. They were waiting to cheer on their team. Brightly colored banners had been hung from the ceiling of the gym. The powerful lights had been turned on. The crowd had joined in the singing of the national anthem. All eyes turned to the gleaming floor of the gym.

2. With feet spread about shoulder width, stand directly behind the foul line, or about ten feet from the basket. Place one hand lightly under the ball, supporting it. Place the other hand behind the ball, cupping it in your fingers. Bring the ball directly over your head. Then, using the wrist and elbow of your shooting arm for power, send the ball smoothly toward the basket. Follow through by pointing your hand and arm toward the basket.

3. Basketball is one of the few sports that has almost continuous action. Also, the fans are close to the action, which adds to the excitement. Basketball requires disciplined teamwork, but it also allows individual stars to shine. There is usually a lot of scoring, so fans on both sides have plenty of chances to cheer.

Lesson Three

Paragraph Unity

Read the following paragraph, and see if it sounds strange to you.

There are four main types of instruments in the modern orchestra: woodwinds, brass, strings, and percussion. The composer Berlioz wrote one musical work that called for an orchestra of more than 200 musicians and 300 singers. The gamelan orchestra, found in the Pacific islands of Bali and Java, includes gongs, flutes, and xylophones. The composer Haydn first made the clarinet a regular member of the woodwind section of the orchestra.

What is wrong with this paragraph? Its first word is indented. Each sentence makes sense, and there are no sentence fragments. The facts are all correct. Yet the paragraph as a whole is confusing. It contains so many unrelated ideas that it is like an orchestra in which each musician is playing a different melody. The result is not music; it's noise!

A good paragraph has *unity*. Unity means that every sentence relates to the main idea stated in the topic sentence. In the paragraph above, each sentence goes off in a different direction. There is no one main idea, and there is no topic sentence.

If you use a topic sentence in every paragraph you write, you will probably never write a paragraph as confusing as the one above. But even if you do have a main idea and a topic sentence, you may not have paragraph unity. The following paragraph does not have paragraph unity. Can you tell why?

Today's orchestras include a wide variety of percussion instruments. Several types of drums are used, including the bass drum, the tom-tom, the snare drum, and the bongo. My cousin Ed is taking drumming lessons and hopes to play in a band next year. Some percussion instruments can play definite notes and melodies. These include the xylophone, marimba, and chimes. Other percussion instruments do not play definite notes. These include cymbals, the triangle, gongs, and such Latin American instruments as maracas, timbales, and claves.

The topic sentence of this paragraph is the first sentence: *Today's orchestras include a wide variety of percussion instruments.* Most of the sentences in the paragraph give examples of the percussion instruments used in orchestras. But one sentence stands out. The third sentence of the paragraph deals with an unrelated topic: Cousin Ed's drumming lessons. Paragraph unity has been lost because the writer included a sentence unrelated to the main idea.

This type of error is easy to correct. After you write a paragraph, reread it. If you find an unrelated sentence, remove it. Can you find the sentence that is not related to the main idea in the following paragraph?

The traditional music of India is played by small groups of musicians using various native instruments. There are drums and cymbals of several kinds. The tabla is a set of two drums that can be tuned to play high notes or low notes. Indian wind instruments include the bamboo flute and a trumpet which may be over six feet long. Many European composers have written music for small groups of wind instruments, such as the woodwind quintet. Two stringed instruments used in India are the tambura, which makes a steady droning sound, and the sitar, which plays melodies. Americans became familiar with the sitar when the Beatles and other rock groups used it in some of their recordings.

The sentence that does not relate to the main idea is the fifth sentence: *Many European composers have written music for small groups of wind instruments, such as the woodwind quintet.* It should be removed from the paragraph.

After writing a paragraph, always reread it to make sure that every sentence deals with the same main idea. Make any changes needed to give your paragraph unity.

EXERCISE SIX

Each of the following paragraphs contains one sentence that is not related to the main idea of the paragraph. Number your paper from 1 to 4. Next to each number, copy the sentence from that paragraph that does not relate to the main idea.

Example: The best job I've ever had was working as a waiter at Meyer and Bloom's coffee shop. I had enough to do to keep from getting bored. But the work was never too hard. Sometimes when I'm doing chores at home, I'm so bored I could scream. The other workers were friendly and fun. My boss, Charlie, was kind-hearted and loved to tell jokes and stories. Best of all, I earned a lot of tips with a smile and a little hustle. *Sometimes when I'm doing chores at home, I'm so bored I could scream.*

1. Meyer and Bloom's is an old restaurant, but it's beautiful. The floor is made of old tiles. The tops of the tables are black marble, and the counter is a big piece of dark, polished wood. There are mirrors everywhere, some with stained-glass borders. The drugstore and shoe-repair shop on the same block are about as old as Meyer and Bloom's. Two old ceiling fans turn slowly on summer days.

2. Charlie's way of running the restaurant is old-fashioned, too. He makes his own ice cream with a big, noisy, ancient machine in the back room. Charlie taught me to make fresh whipped cream the old-fashioned way, with a wire whisk. Charlie even bakes his own cakes and grinds his own beef for hamburgers. On busy days, at lunch time, the demand for hamburgers keeps Charlie busy tossing them onto the grill.

3. I worked at Meyer and Bloom's after school for almost a year. When I joined the school soccer team, I had to quit so that I could attend workouts. My coach once played for a professional team in Brazil. I often visited Meyer and Bloom's after quitting. I even took the soccer team there for sandwiches one day. But I just heard that Meyer and Bloom's is going to be torn down to make way for a new department store. Charlie says he'll retire and live in the South. It makes me sad to think that soon I'll be visiting Meyer and Bloom's for the last time.

Lesson Four

Developing a Paragraph

As you've seen, the most important sentence in a paragraph is the topic sentence. It lets the reader and writer know where the paragraph is going.

A topic sentence, however, isn't enough to make a good paragraph. A topic sentence can express a main idea. But to make the main idea come to life, you must *develop* the paragraph by adding details and specific ideas to explain and support the main idea.

Paragraphs can be developed in several ways. The way you choose will depend on your purpose in writing. Here are some of the ways a paragraph can be developed.

1. A paragraph can give *reasons* to support the main idea. Here is an example:

There are many reasons why California has become our nation's most populated state. The climate in California is pleasant all year round. It is not too cold in the winter or too hot in the summer. Because of the ocean and the mountains, Californians can enjoy almost every kind of recreation, from swimming and surfing to skiing and tobogganing. Many businesses in quickly growing fields, such as electronics and communications, are located there, so that many jobs are available.

The topic sentence of this paragraph is the first sentence. Each of the other sentences helps develop the topic. Each sentence gives a reason for California's growth in population.

2. A paragraph can relate *an incident or story*. The story could be something that happened to you. It could be something that happened to someone else. Here is an example:

The highlight of our trip to California was a tour of the studios of one of the television networks. While Sharon and I were visiting the sets where shows are made, we saw Rick Sutter, the young star of our favorite soap opera, studying a script. No one else in the tour group recognized Rick, because he was wearing a long white beard for his role in a new TV movie. We were excited and were about to point him out to the others when he came over and said quietly, "Listen, I'm too busy right now to say hello to a lot of people, so please don't say who I am. If you promise not to give me away, I'll give you both an autographed picture. Just come by my dressing room behind Stage Number Seven in an hour." We agreed, and later we got the pictures—signed, "With love, Rick"!

The first sentence of this paragraph is the topic sentence. The other sentences develop the topic by telling an incident that took place during a trip to California.

3. A paragraph can give *facts*. A fact is information that can be proved true. Here is an example:

Factories in California produce over 60 billion dollars' worth of products each year. Farming and fishing are major industries there as well. California produces over four billion dollars' worth of gas and oil each year. Tourism is a 12-billion-dollar business. The economy of California is larger than that of many entire nations.

The topic sentence is the last sentence of the paragraph. The other sentences give facts to help show the size of the economy of California.

4. A paragraph can give *examples*. An example is a specific instance that illustrates a general idea. Here is a paragraph that gives examples:

In recent years, politicians from California have become well known all over the United States. Former President Nixon is one example. He was born and raised in California. Jerry Brown is another example. While governor of California, he ran for the Democratic presidential nomination in 1976. Ronald Reagan is a third example. After two terms as governor of California, and two tries for the presidency, he was elected President in 1980.

Here, the first sentence is the topic sentence. Each of the other sentences gives an example that supports the topic sentence.

The paragraphs above have different purposes, and they are developed with different kinds of details. However, each paragraph has a topic sentence expressing one main idea and several sentences that develop that idea.

Complete each topic sentence below. Then, write the method you would use to develop the topic sentence—*reasons, incident, facts,* or *examples.* Finally, write some notes on the specific information you would include in each paragraph. You do not have to write paragraphs, only notes of ideas.

Example: Ten years from now I hope to be _____ .
Ten years from now, I hope to be a news photographer.
Reasons:
I enjoy taking pictures.
I'm already a good photographer.
I like to develop pictures myself.
I would like to travel and witness dramatic events and meet famous people.

Topic Sentences:
1. Ten years from now, I hope to be _____ .
2. Crime in our community _____ .
3. The best part of my last vacation was _____ .
4. The best (or worst) thing about being a teenager is _____ .
5. A balanced diet and exercise _____ .

Lesson Five

Organizing Your Ideas

Before you write a paragraph, you may feel as confused as a person trying to put together a jigsaw puzzle. You may have lots of ideas, facts, and opinions to use in your paragraph. But you may not know how to fit them together. You need a plan in order to get your jumble of ideas into a logical order.

If you write without a plan to guide you, you may end up with a paragraph like this one:

Last Saturday was one of the worst days of my life. The car wouldn't start, so I had to walk two miles to the football game. When I woke up, it was pouring. My dog had decided to play with my slippers outside. Then I discovered we were out of soap and toothpaste. I had to march at the football game in a soaking wet band uniform. Breakfast was awful, and I didn't have time for lunch. I learned at the game that my date for the dance that night was home in bed with the flu. What a day!

The writer of this paragraph had a good main idea and topic sentence. There are plenty of ideas to support the main idea. But instead of taking the time to plan the paragraph, the writer just put down whatever came to mind. The result is a confusing paragraph.

The paragraph could be made into a good one by arranging the sentences in an order that makes sense. Since the paragraph describes the events of a day, it might be useful to arrange the events in the order in which they happened. The rearranged paragraph would look like this:

Last Saturday was one of the worst days of my life. When I woke up, it was pouring. My dog had decided to play with my slippers outside. Then I discovered we were out of soap and toothpaste. Breakfast was awful, and I didn't have time for lunch. The car wouldn't start, so I had to walk two miles to the football game. I had to march at the game in a soaking wet band uniform. Finally, I learned at the game that my date for the dance that night was home in bed with the flu. What a day!

Following a plan changed a confusing paragraph into a clear one.

When writing a paragraph, use a plan to organize your ideas. Here are three basic methods of organization for a paragraph:

1. **Chronological order.** When you write a paragraph that describes an event or incident, it's a good idea to organize your ideas in the order in which they happened. The paragraph about the rainy Saturday made sense when it was written in chronological order.

Putting ideas in chronological order is also useful for giving directions or instructions. By using chronological order, you make it easy for your reader to follow your instructions step by step.

2. **Spatial order.** When putting together a jigsaw puzzle, you might start with the border and work your way to the middle of the picture. When painting a wall, you might start at the top and work your way down. These are examples of spatial order. Spatial

order can be useful when writing paragraphs, too. Spatial order is especially useful when writing a descriptive paragraph in which you want to create a word-picture of a person, place, or thing.

If you are describing a person's appearance, for example, you might begin at the top, with the way the hair looks, and work your way down to the shoes—or vice versa. Or, when describing the view from your window, you might begin with what is closest to you (the tree right outside) and end with what is farthest away (the hills on the horizon). Or you might begin with what is farthest to the left and work your way to the right. There is no one spatial order that is correct. Any order that makes sense to you can be effective.

3. Order of importance. This method of organization is especially useful when writing paragraphs of opinion or facts. You can present your most important fact or opinion first, then add the others one by one. Or you can start with facts and opinions of lesser importance and build up to the most important. If you start with the most important idea, your paragraph will make a strong first impression on your reader. If you end with the most important idea, you'll leave your reader with a strong impression of your point of view. Either method can be effective.

Putting ideas in an order of importance can also be used in writing a description. In describing a person, for example, you might begin by describing that person's most striking feature. If the first thing you notice is big, piercing brown eyes, you might describe them first and then go on to describe the person's other features in their order of importance.

Whatever plan you choose, stick to it. Follow the plan that you feel will best express your ideas.

EXERCISE EIGHT

On the next page are five possible topics for a paragraph. Choose one. Write a topic sentence for your topic. Be sure that it is a complete sentence and states a main idea about the topic. Decide which method of organization you think would be best: chronological order, spatial order, or order of importance. Write five to eight supporting sentences that develop the main idea of the topic sentence. Arrange the supporting sentences according to the method of organization you think is best. Write your sentences as a paragraph.

Example: Topic: How to Prepare a Wonderful Breakfast
Topic Sentence: *It's easy to make my favorite breakfast—oatmeal pancakes with blueberries.*

How to Prepare a Wonderful Breakfast
It's easy to make my favorite breakfast—oatmeal pancakes with blueberries. You need two eggs, milk, oil, uncooked oatmeal, and flour. Of course, the amounts you use will depend on how many pancakes you want to make. First, blend the oatmeal and the flour together. Beat the eggs and mix them with the milk and the oil. Stir this mixture into the oatmeal and flour until you have a thick batter that's not too lumpy. Pour a spoonful of batter at a time onto a hot, buttered pan, and cook the pancakes until they're slightly brown. I like to put a spoonful of creamy plain yogurt on my pancakes, with the blueberries on top. You can use frozen blueberries, as I do, or get fresh ones if they are in season.

Topics:
How to Prepare a Wonderful Breakfast
My Neighborhood
A Typical Weekday Afternoon
Why I Want to Work This Summer
A topic of your own choice

Lesson Six

Transitional Words and Phrases

When you fit together the pieces of a jigsaw puzzle, you get some help from the puzzle maker. The shapes of the puzzle pieces are designed so that pieces which belong together will lock into one another, notch to tab.

To help you write unified paragraphs, there are special types of words and phrases which can serve the same purpose as the notches in a jigsaw puzzle. These are called *transitional words and phrases.* Like the notches on puzzle pieces, transitional words help hold together the "pieces," or sentences, of your paragraph.

There are several kinds of transitional words. All of them help to link the ideas in a paragraph. Here are some of the kinds of transitional words you can use in your writing:

1. Words or phrases that show <u>spatial</u> relationships

The quiet lake was a mirror for the sky, clouds, and mountains. **At the edge** of the lake was a tiny cabin looking out on it all.

The phrase *at the edge* connects the second sentence to the first. It places the cabin next to the lake, so that the reader "sees" where one is in relation to the other.

Here is a list of some words and phrases that indicate direction or location. They can serve as transitions to help connect ideas in a paragraph.

above	beside	inside	outside
around	between	near	over
at the end of	in	next to	under
behind	in front of	on	

These words and phrases are useful in paragraphs of description.

2. Words or phrases that show <u>chronological</u> relationships

When painting a room, you must **first** move all the furniture to the middle of the room. **Next,** cover the furniture with a canvas drop cloth to keep it clean. **Then** you are ready to begin preparing the walls for painting.

The words *first, next,* and *then* connect the sentences above to one another. They show the reader that the three sentences describe three steps in a process.

Here are some words and phrases that can be used to show time relationships in a paragraph:

after that	earlier	meanwhile	the next step
at first	finally	next	until
at the same time	first	second	while
before	later	then	

These words are useful in paragraphs giving directions, giving an explanation, or telling an incident.

3. Words or phrases that show <u>cause and effect</u> relationships

It rained and snowed for three hours on the morning of the big football game. **As a result,** the field was wet and slippery. **So** it was hard for either team to gain many yards by rushing. **Therefore,** Coach Warren decided to try using short passes instead.

The phrase *as a result* and the words *so* and *therefore* make it easy for the reader to see how one event led to another.

Here are some of the words that can show cause-and-effect relationships:

as a result	due to	since
because	if	so
caused by	resulted from	therefore

These words and phrases are useful in paragraphs of opinion or explanation.

4. Words or phrases that show <u>differences</u> or <u>contrasts</u>

My family has two cars. One is twelve years old. It drives well, never needs repairs, and has plenty of room for people and cargo. **In contrast,** the other car is one year old. My family can barely squeeze into it, and it has already broken down several times. Maybe there really were "good old days"!

The phrase *in contrast* connects two parts of the paragraph. It clearly shows the reader that two different cars are being described. It calls the reader's attention to the differences.

Here are some of the common transitional words that can be used to show contrast:

although	even so	on the contrary
but	however	on the other hand
by contrast	nevertheless	yet

These words and phrases are useful in paragraphs that show contrasts.

5. Words or phrases that show <u>similarities</u>

When I was learning to play the piano, I wasn't sure where the keys were. I had to watch my hands and the keyboard.

When I didn't, I hit some sour notes. **In the same way,** when I was learning to type, I had to watch the typewriter keys. When I didn't, I typed some very strange-looking words.

The phrase *in the same way* connects the sentences of the paragraph. It shows that learning to play the piano was similar to learning to type.

Here are some transitional words that can be used to show similarities:

also	in the same way	same
as well	like	similar
just as	likewise	similarly

These words and phrases are useful in paragraphs showing comparisons.

Practice using transitional words and phrases in the paragraphs you write. They will help to make your paragraphs unified and easy to follow.

EXERCISE NINE

Most of the transitional words have been removed from the paragraph below. Copy the paragraph on your paper. Fill in appropriate transitional words from the list provided. You will not use all the words on the list. There may be more than one word or phrase that could be correctly used in a particular sentence. The first word has been filled in for you.

Transitional words:

As a result	First	On the other hand	When
But	However	So	
Finally	Next	Then	

My parents and I left my uncle's cabin at 3 p.m., hoping to drive home in less than two hours. ___However___, our plans were ruined. It began to snow. _____ we had to reduce our speed to twenty miles per hour. _____ we hit an icy patch and skidded off the road into a guard rail. Luckily, no one was hurt. _____ we got the car back on the road, the snow was even heavier. _____, we had to turn on our headlights and drive even slower. _____, at 10 p.m. we staggered into our home in the city, tired, hungry, and cold.

Lesson Seven

Writing and Revising

In this unit, you have studied some ideas for writing a good paragraph. You have learned about the importance of using a topic sentence and the need for unity in a paragraph. You have seen some of the different ways in which paragraphs may be developed, and you've learned ways in which the details in a paragraph may be organized. Finally, you've learned about the importance of using transitional words and phrases to unify your paragraphs.

All of these ideas will help you in writing paragraphs. But knowing these ideas is not enough. Like building a chair, baking a pie, or painting a picture, writing a paragraph is a *process*, a job with several steps. The only way to learn to do it is to practice the process from start to finish.

In this lesson, you will study five steps in the process of writing a paragraph: choosing a topic, jotting down your ideas, getting organized, writing, and revising. You will have a chance to practice writing a paragraph of your own. And you will check your work to see whether you have written a paragraph that is clear, well-organized, and unified.

Choose a Topic

Sometimes, you do not have a choice of writing topics. For example, when you take a test, you must answer the questions that you are asked.

However, in many cases, you are able to choose your own topic. When you have this opportunity, take the time to choose carefully. A topic that is right for you will make writing easier and more pleasant. What you write will probably be interesting, too. Here are some suggestions for choosing a topic:

1. *Write about something you know.* If you choose a topic that is familiar to you, you will have something to say about it. You may choose a topic from your personal experience—an event from your life, for instance, or a job or hobby you have enjoyed. Or you may choose a topic you know about from your reading.

2. *Write about something that interests you.* If you find your

topic interesting, you will enjoy writing about it. Your interest will show in your writing.

3. *Choose a topic that is not too narrow or too broad.* When choosing a topic, think about the amount of writing you plan to do. Choose a topic that fits the amount of space you have. If you choose a topic that is too narrow, you will run out of things to say. You may begin to repeat ideas or bring in unrelated ideas as you try to fill up space. If the topic you choose is too broad, you will not be able to cover it. You may have to leave out important facts or ideas. You may not have enough space to include an interesting example or detail.

For example, if you are writing one paragraph, a topic such as "How to Pack the Mustard for a Picnic in the Park" is probably too narrow. There is not enough to say for more than one or two sentences. On the other hand, a topic such as "How to Have Fun in the Summer" is too broad for one paragraph. You would only have enough space to mention one or two ways to have fun. A topic such as "My Favorite Foods for a Picnic in the Park" is probably an appropriate one for one paragraph. It can be covered fully in one paragraph without your running out of things to say or having too much to say.

EXERCISE TEN

Look at the two photographs on page 57. Choose the one you find more interesting. Think of five possible topics for a paragraph based on that photograph. Here are some kinds of topics the photograph may suggest:

1. a description of the scene in the photograph
2. an incident or event that could have taken place in the scene in the photograph
3. your opinion about a topic related to the photograph
4. a description of an activity that could take place in the scene in the photograph
5. facts about a topic which the photograph suggests

Jot down your five possible topics in a few words or in complete sentences. Then, read them over. Are any of them too broad or too narrow? For example, suppose one possible topic is *activities that are fun at the beach.* You might make that topic less broad

52

by changing it to *how to build a sand castle* or *how to eat a sandwich at the beach without getting sand in it.*

Work on your five choices until each one is narrow enough to be covered in one paragraph. Then choose the topic you like best. Write this topic in a few words or in a complete sentence at the top of a new piece of paper. Save this paper for use in the next exercise.

Jot Down Your Ideas

After choosing a topic, the second step in writing a paragraph is to think of specific ideas that can be used to develop the topic. The best way to do this is to write down any ideas you have about the topic. Include everything that comes to mind: facts, opinions, examples, even words and phrases that are related to the topic.

EXERCISE ELEVEN

Look at the topic you wrote for Exercise Ten. Jot down on your paper as many ideas about your topic as you can. If you are writing a description, you might write down as many details about the various parts of the scene as you can. If you are writing an opinion, jot down all the ideas you can think of that relate to your opinion.

Each thought you write down can help you think of others. Try to write without stopping for at least five minutes. Don't worry about grammar and spelling. These notes are for your use only in exploring ideas to include in your paragraph.

Get Organized

The third step in writing a paragraph is to organize your ideas. To do this, you work with the notes you have already written. Here are some guidelines that will help you:

1. *Write a topic sentence.* Look over your notes and try to find the most important idea or the idea that sums up most of the other ideas. This can be used as the main idea of your paragraph. Write it as a complete sentence. This sentence will be your topic sentence.

2. *Choose the ideas to include in your paragraph.* Look over your

notes again, keeping your topic sentence in mind. Choose the notes that are related to the topic sentence. Cross out any that are unrelated. If you think of ideas that could be added, write them down. You should now have a list that includes all the ideas you want your paragraph to contain.

3. *Plan your paragraph.* Decide on an order for the ideas you want to include. You can use chronological order, spatial order, or order of importance. Choose a plan that makes sense to you. You can number the ideas on your list in the order in which you want to present them. This list with numbers can serve as a simple outline for your paragraph.

At any time, you may decide to change your main idea. If you do, change the topic sentence to fit your new main idea. Make sure that everything to be included in your paragraph relates clearly to your new main idea.

EXERCISE TWELVE

Look over your notes from Exercise Eleven. Does one idea seem more important than the others? Does one idea summarize all the other ideas? If so, turn that idea into a complete sentence. This will be the topic sentence of your paragraph.

If none of your ideas would work as a topic sentence, look over your notes again. Write a sentence that will introduce or summarize most of your ideas. This will be your topic sentence.

When you have a topic sentence, select ideas from your notes to use in developing the paragraph. Choose ideas that are interesting to you and that relate directly to the topic sentence. Turn those ideas into complete sentences. You can change your ideas or add others if you want.

Next, decide on a plan for your paragraph. You may choose to arrange your ideas in chronological order, in spatial order, or in order of importance. Number your ideas in the order you have decided on. This is the order in which they will appear in your paragraph.

Write Your Paragraph

After jotting down the ideas for your paragraph and organizing them, you are ready to write your paragraph. Write your ideas in complete sentences in the order you planned. Include the topic sentence in a place that seems appropriate to you. Use appropriate transitional words or phrases to help unify the paragraph.

EXERCISE THIRTEEN

Write your paragraph, using your notes from Exercise Twelve as a guide. Include the topic sentence in a place that seems appropriate to you.

Turn to pages 47–50 and review transitional words and phrases. Try to use these or other words to link the ideas expressed in your sentences.

Revise Your Paragraph

Even after you have written a paragraph, your job is not finished. The paragraph you have written is probably not the best you can write. You must reread and revise it. This will give you the chance to find and correct any mistakes you have made and any places where the paragraph could be made clearer. Revision helps you make your paragraph the best it can be.

Revision is a crucial step. Students are not the only writers who need to revise their work. The world's greatest authors revise their work. Writing is a challenging job. No one can be expected to do it perfectly the first time.

When you are writing a paragraph, take the time to reread your work at least twice. The first time, concentrate on the ideas in the paragraph. Make sure you have stated your main idea clearly. Make sure that the details, examples, or facts in the paragraph are related to the main idea. Make sure you have said what you meant to say.

The second time you reread your paragraph, check the grammar, punctuation, and spelling. Make sure each sentence expresses a complete thought and ends with the right punctuation mark. Use a dictionary to check the spelling of any word you aren't sure about. Make sure your corrections are neat, so that they will be easy to read when you are making your final copy.

Here is one more suggestion about revision. If you can, put aside your paragraph after writing it and reread it the next day. After a day has passed, you will probably notice errors that you didn't catch the day before. You may also think of a new detail or fact to include in your paragraph. It isn't always possible to set your work aside for a day. But if you can, do it.

EXERCISE FOURTEEN

Reread your paragraph carefully or exchange papers with a classmate. Use the Checklist below to evaluate the paragraph. If your paragraph is weak in any way, revise it as needed. Work on your paragraph until it is the best you can do.

Checklist

1. Does the paragraph contain a topic sentence that states the main idea of the paragraph?
2. Is every sentence related to the main idea expressed in the topic sentence?
3. Are the sentences arranged in a clear, logical order?
4. Have appropriate transitional words and phrases been used to help unify the paragraph?
5. Does each sentence contain a subject and verb and express a complete thought?
6. Does each sentence begin with a capital letter and end with the correct punctuation mark?
7. Are all words spelled correctly?
8. Is the first line of the paragraph indented?

Unit Three
The Parts of Speech

3

The Parts of Speech

Lesson One

Nouns

Imagine that you are a world traveler. You have just landed in a faraway country. Everything you see—the people, the buildings, the clothing—is new to you.

"Who are those people there?" you might ask.

"They are **fellahin,** who work on the farms near the village," someone might reply.

"Where are they going?"

"To the **bazaar,** where all kinds of goods are bought and sold."

"What is that long cloak one of the fellahin is wearing?"

"It is called a **burnoose.**"

The words in boldface type are *nouns*.

● A <u>noun</u> is a word that names a person, place, thing, or idea.

Here are more examples of nouns:

Persons: teacher, redhead, Aunt Angela, Ronald Reagan
Places: village, park, Mount Kisco, South Pole
Things: desk, dragonfly, Bill of Rights, Golden Gate Bridge
Ideas: democracy, happiness, power, love

Compound Nouns

Most nouns consist of only one word, but some nouns are made up of more than one word. These nouns are called *compound nouns*.

● A <u>compound noun</u> is made up to two or more words that name one person, place, thing, or idea.

Some compound nouns are written "solid," as one word: **dragonfly, battlefield, tabletop.**

Other compound nouns are written with one or more hyphens: **sister-in-law, self-control, city-state.**

60

Still others are written in "open style," as separate words: **ice cream, free enterprise, United States of America.**

Use a dictionary to help you spell and learn the meanings of compound nouns.

Common and Proper Nouns

If you say to a friend, "I live in a white house," your friend will probably say, "So what?" But if you say, "I live in the White House," your friend might be quite surprised.

The difference between *a white house* and *the White House* is the difference between a *common noun* and a *proper noun.*

● **A common noun names a category of people, places, or things.**

● **A proper noun names a specific person, place, or thing.**

A proper noun begins with a capital letter. A common noun does not.

Here are some examples:

People

Common Nouns	*Proper Nouns*
singer	Barbra Streisand
poet	Carl Sandburg
athlete	Julius Erving

Places

Common Nouns	*Proper Nouns*
park	Central Park
village	Bedford Village
country	Mexico

Things

Common Nouns	*Proper Nouns*
short story	"The Tell-Tale Heart"
building	Independence Hall
battle	Battle of Britain

Singular and Plural Nouns

All nouns are either *singular* or *plural* in number. A singular noun refers to one person, place, thing, or idea. A plural noun refers to more than one person, place, thing, or idea.

Singular	Plural
firefighter	firefighters
farm	farms
frankfurter	frankfurters
friendship	friendships

PRACTICE A

Number your paper from 1 to 10. Write the nouns from each of the following sentences next to the number of the sentence. Draw a circle around each compound noun. Underline each proper noun.

Examples: We read about the history of glass in our textbook.

history, glass, (*textbook*)

Mr. Vere, who is our teacher, showed us a movie about the subject.
Mr. Vere, teacher, movie, subject

1. The art of glassmaking began more than 3,500 years ago in Mesopotamia and the Fertile Crescent.
2. The first glassmakers heated sand and crushed limestone in simple furnaces.
3. The sand melted quickly and mixed with the lime.
4. The hot mixture was glass.
5. Glassblowers cooled and shaped the glass into jugs, plates, or jars.
6. Today glassworks produce many kinds of objects.
7. Most glassware is now produced by machines.
8. Ohio, New York, New Jersey, and Nevada are among the leaders in the production of glass in the United States.
9. Along with its many uses in the home, glass is important in business and industry.
10. Glass is used in making lenses, fabrics, and parts for machines.

PRACTICE B

Rewrite the following sentences. Replace the twenty underlined common nouns with proper nouns. You may need to change some words that come before the nouns.

Example: A senator serves on a committee.
          Senator Cutler serves on the Budget Committee.

1. A person lives on a street.
2. A president helps govern a country.
3. We took a taxi from an airport to a city.
4. On this day, we will climb a mountain.
5. The singer performed at a building in a benefit performance.
6. A team played poorly at a stadium.
7. A man bought a car.
8. An actress won an award.
9. A student directed a play.
10. A company bought a store.

PRACTICE C

Write a short story using at least ten of the nouns below. Use them in any order you wish.

Nouns:

campground	Yellowstone National Park
fear	Hilary
hiker	backpack
moose	food
mountain lion	journey
wild flowers	cliff
heat	ranger
river	weather
trail	water
Yellowstone Falls	days

Lesson Two

Pronouns

Suppose you receive the following note in the mail:

Dear Maria,

Does Maria have the two books Jane and Maria were assigned to read for English class? Jane needs to read part of *The Scarlet Letter* and part of *Huckleberry Finn*. If Maria isn't using the two books that Jane and Maria were assigned for English class, may Jane borrow the two books? Meet Jane at Jane's locker at three o'clock tomorrow. Bring the two books Jane and Maria were assigned for English class. Thanks.

Jane

This note sounds strange. Certain words and phrases are repeated over and over. As a result, the note is awkward and confusing.

Jane's message would be clearer if she wrote it this way:

Dear Maria,

Do **you** have the two books **we** were assigned to read for English class? **I** need to read part of *The Scarlet Letter* and part of *Huckleberry Finn*. If **you** are not using **them,** may **I** borrow **them?** Meet **me** at **my** locker at three o'clock tomorrow, and bring **them.** Thanks.

Jane

The words in boldface type above, which make the second note easier to read, are all *pronouns*.

● **A** <u>pronoun</u> **is a word that is used in place of one or more nouns.**

The following examples show pronouns used in place of nouns:

Ted baked the cupcakes, and then Ted decorated the cupcakes.
Ted baked the cupcakes, and then **he** decorated **them.**

(The pronoun *he* is used in place of the noun *Ted.* The pronoun *them* is used in place of the noun *cupcakes.*)

After Ana painted Ana's car, Ana was able to sell the car for a higher price.
After Ana painted **her** car, **she** was able to sell **it** for a higher price.

(The pronoun *her* is used in place of the noun *Ana's.* The pronoun *she* is used in place of the noun *Ana.* The pronoun *it* is used in place of the noun *car.*)

● **The word or group of words to which a pronoun refers is called its** <u>antecedent.</u>

64

Look at the following example. The arrow from each pronoun points to its antecedent:

Ted baked the cupcakes, and then **he** decorated **them.** (*Ted* is the antecedent of the pronoun *he. Cupcakes* is the antecedent of the pronoun *them.*)

In some sentences, the antecedent consists of more than one word:

Fran and Tony ate lunch before **they** left. (*Fran* and *Tony* are the antecedents of the pronoun *they.*)

After choosing a blouse and skirt, Susan paid for **them.** (*Blouse* and *skirt* are the antecedents of the pronoun *them.*)

Sometimes, the pronoun may come before its antecedent:

Before **they** left, Fran and Tony ate lunch.

Because **he** was sleepy, Angel took a nap.

Sometimes, the antecedent of the pronoun appears in an earlier sentence:

Joe is a good swimmer. **He** is an excellent skater, too.

Please bring me my lunchbox. **It** is on the kitchen table.

Kinds of Pronouns

There are several kinds of pronouns—*personal pronouns, possessive pronouns, reflexive pronouns, relative pronouns, interrogative pronouns, demonstrative pronouns,* and *indefinite pronouns.* Each one does a different job in a sentence.

A *personal pronoun* indicates the person speaking, the person being spoken to, or the person or thing being spoken about.

	Singular	Plural
First Person:	I, me	we, us
Second Person:	you	you
Third Person:	he, him, she, her, it	they, them

She and **I** gave the dog a bath.
Will **they** come to the party with **her?**
We told **him** about **you.**

A personal pronoun that is used to show ownership or possession is called a *possessive pronoun.*

	Singular	Plural
First Person:	my, mine	our, ours
Second Person:	your, yours	your, yours
Third Person:	his, her, hers, its	their, theirs

Here are some examples of possessive pronouns. The arrows point to the pronouns' antecedents.

Larry forgot **his** gloves.

Life has **its** ups and downs.

We will bring **our** car to the party.

A *reflexive pronoun* refers back to a noun or pronoun already stated.

	Singular	Plural
First Person:	myself	ourselves
Second Person:	yourself	yourselves
Third Person:	himself, herself, itself	themselves

Sarah hurt **herself** during the competition.

The dog is scratching **itself** because it has fleas.

The reflexive pronouns are called *intensive pronouns* when they are used for emphasis.

Merry **herself** built the scenery for the play.

A *relative pronoun* introduces an adjective clause. (You will learn about adjective clauses in Unit Nine.) The relative pronouns are *who, whom, whose, which,* and *that.*

Erica is the runner **who** won today's race.
I voted for the candidate **whose** beliefs were most similar to mine.
Ants at a picnic are a nuisance **that** I cannot tolerate.

An *interrogative pronoun* is used to introduce a direct or indirect question. The interrogative pronouns are *who, whom, whose, which,* and *what.*

What did he say?

The coach asked **who** could help him after practice.

Which will you read for your first assignment?

A *demonstrative pronoun* is used to point out a specific person, place, thing, or idea.

Singular	Plural
this	these
that	those

That is a very expensive diamond.

The prettiest stamps in my collection are **these**.

This is no time for foolishness.

An *indefinite pronoun* is used to refer to an unspecified person, place, thing, or idea.

Something is wrong with my radio.

Each is a different color.

No one dares to run against him in the race.

The chart below lists the most common indefinite pronouns.

Singular

another	either	neither	somebody
anybody	everybody	nobody	someone
anyone	everyone	no one	something
anything	everything	nothing	
each	much	one	

Plural

both	several
few	two, three (etc.)
many	

Either Singular or Plural

all	most
any	none
more	some

You will learn more about the use of indefinite pronouns in Unit Eleven.

PRACTICE A

Copy the following sentences onto your paper. Underline all the pronouns in each sentence. Then draw an arrow from each pronoun to its antecedent(s). If the antecedent is not stated in the sentence, write *not stated.*

Example: After painting the model, Tom showed it to his sister.

After painting the model, Tom showed it to his sister.

1. Jessica wrote John a ten-page letter, but she forgot to mail it to him.
2. Although they like to eat out, Jeremy and Alice don't like to pay high prices.
3. The streetlight burned all day until the electrician brought her tools and repaired its switch.
4. You yourself are responsible for finishing the assignment and getting it in on time.
5. The ibis, which is native to Japan, may soon become extinct.
6. Children learn best when they solve problems themselves.
7. Who told her about the surprise party?
8. Jake told everyone about his new guitar.
9. Most arrived early and left late.
10. That was only the beginning.

PRACTICE B

Number your paper from 1 to 20. Complete the following story by supplying the kind of pronoun specified.

Example: Gina went to the gym yesterday to practice the gym-

nastics routine (1) _____ (2) _____
                        relative   personal
had learned the day before.
(1) *that*
(2) *she*

After Gina fell from the parallel bars, she felt a pain in

(1) _____ left ankle. Gina realized that (2) _____
        possessive   personal
could not put weight on (3) _____ when (4) _____
                            personal   personal
stood.

Gina limped painfully to the medical station. (5) _____ <u>indefinite</u> told Gina to wait. About ten minutes later, (6) _____ <u>personal</u> was helped into Dr. Baker's office. Gina showed (7) _____ <u>personal</u> the injured ankle and asked (8) _____ <u>interrogative</u> she should do. The doctor looked at the ankle and responded, "(9) _____ <u>demonstrative</u> does not appear to be serious. Athletes often injure (10) _____ <u>reflexive</u> in this way. The best remedy for a sprained ankle is to rest (11) _____ <u>personal</u> . (12) _____ <u>possessive</u> ankle will heal in a few days."

Dr. Baker taped Gina's ankle and told (13) _____ <u>personal</u> to come back in a week. During that week, Gina wanted to practice (14) _____ <u>possessive</u> gymnastics routine, but she knew that (15) _____ <u>demonstrative</u> would be a mistake. She felt bored and frustrated, but she knew she couldn't do (16) _____ <u>indefinite</u> about it.

Finally, it was time for (17) _____ <u>personal</u> to visit the medical station again. Dr. Baker removed the tape and tested Gina's ankle. The doctor announced, "(18) _____ <u>personal</u> are completely healed. You can go back to gymnastics now. That wasn't so bad, was it?"

Gina was already halfway out the door. "It was the longest week of (19) _____ <u>possessive</u> life!" (20) _____ <u>personal</u> replied.

PRACTICE C

Write seven to ten sentences describing a friend, but do not mention the person's name. Use pronouns to describe how your friend looks, acts, and thinks. Include examples of at least five kinds of pronouns. Underline each pronoun you use.

Example: *The person <u>whom</u> <u>I</u> am describing is sometimes shy.*
<u>She</u> often stays by <u>herself</u> in the lunchroom and the

study hall at school. When people <u>whom</u> <u>she</u> doesn't know try to make friends with <u>her</u>, <u>she</u> blushes and doesn't know what to say. But when <u>she</u> is with <u>her</u> close friends, <u>she</u> is a lot of fun. At parties, <u>she</u> laughs, sings, and tells funny stories. <u>Her</u> green eyes sparkle with happiness, and dimples appear in <u>her</u> cheeks. <u>That</u> is <u>her</u> true self. Whenever <u>I</u> feel sad, <u>I</u> call <u>her</u> up, because <u>she</u> always has <u>something</u> cheerful to say to <u>me</u>.

Lesson Three

Verbs

Imagine that you are in Mexico with Professor von Kranken and Professor von Schlegel. You are helping the professors as they study the ruins of the ancient Mayan civilization. They are seeking clues to the cause of the mysterious decline of the Mayan cities in the tenth century. After many months of digging, the professors find several flat stones carved with words. But some of the words have been rubbed away, and can no longer be read. Here is what the stones say:

After the fourth moon, the rains _____ . The crops _____ . The priests _____ with the gods in the temples. Thousands of our people _____ and _____ in the streets. Happiness _____ .

As you look on, the two professors study these stones for several minutes. Then Professor von Kranken announces, "I have it! The message on these stones explains the decline of the Mayan cities. The mystery is solved!" He explains that he has been able to understand the message by filling in the words that cannot be read. Proudly, he reads aloud the completed message:

"After the fourth moon, the rains *stopped.* The crops *failed.* The priests *pleaded* with the gods in the temples. Thousands of our people *starved* and *died* in the streets. Happiness *disappeared.*"

"Nonsense!" declares Professor von Schlegel. "The words you have put into the message are all wrong. I, too, have filled in the blank spaces, and I think that the message is this:

"After the fourth moon, the rains *came*. The crops *grew*. The priests *rejoiced* with the gods in the temples. Thousands of our people *danced* and *celebrated* in the streets. Happiness *returned*."

The two professors begin to quarrel. Is it possible to figure out the decline of the Mayan civilization from the message on the stones? It probably is not, but you can figure out one thing: The words that cannot be read in the message on the stones are all *verbs*. A group of words without a verb cannot express a complete thought.

● A <u>verb</u> expresses action done by or to the subject, or it expresses the state of being of the subject. The action expressed may be either physical action or mental action.

As you can see, verbs are extremely important. They convey a large part of the meaning of any sentence.

Transitive, Intransitive, and Linking Verbs

The three main kinds of verbs in English are *transitive verbs, intransitive verbs,* and *linking verbs.*

A *transitive verb* expresses action that passes from the subject to an object of the verb. Here is an example:

The gardener **planted** the flowers.

The action, *planted,* is performed by the subject, the *gardener.* This action "passes" from the gardener to the *flowers.*

The word that is affected by the action of a transitive verb is called the *object* of the verb. In this example, *flowers* is the object of the verb *planted.* (You will learn more about objects in Unit Five.)

An *intransitive verb* does not have an object. The action of an intransitive verb ends with the verb itself.

The sun **shone.**
The rain **fell** gently.
The weeds **grew** faster than the flowers.

Some verbs can be used as either transitive or intransitive verbs. In the last example above, the verb *grew* does not take an object. Therefore, it is an intransitive verb. However, in the following sentence, the same verb is used as a transitive verb.

The gardener **grew** vegetables, too.

The object of the transitive verb *grew* is *vegetables.*

A *linking verb* expresses a state of being. It is used to "link" or show a connection between the subject and another word in the sentence. The most common linking verb is *be.* Here are its forms:

am
is
are
was
were
(will) be
(is) being
(has) been

Dr. Jekyll and Mr. Hyde **is** a good movie.   (The verb *is* links *Dr. Jekyll and Mr. Hyde* with *movie.*)

The movie **was** a box-office hit in the 1930's.   (The verb *was* links *movie* with *hit.*)

It **is** still popular today.   (The verb *is* links *it* with *popular.*)

Notice that the linking verb connects the subject to another word that describes or gives information about the subject.

Besides the verb *be,* some other verbs may also be used as linking verbs:

act	remain
appear	seem
become	smell
continue	sound
feel	stay
grow	taste
look	turn

Here are some examples of these linking verbs in sentences:

Dr. Jekyll **became** Mr. Hyde.

He **looked** hairy and ferocious.

He **remained** a monster until the potion wore off.

72

Some of the verbs that can be used as linking verbs can also be used as transitive or intransitive verbs:

Linking: Dr. Jekyll's potion **tasted** bitter.   (*Tasted* is a linking verb. It links *potion* with *bitter*.)

Transitive: He **tasted** the potion eagerly.   (*Tasted* is a transitive verb. The object of the verb is the word *potion*.)

Linking: Dr. Jekyll's face **grew** fierce.   (*Grew* is a linking verb. It links *face* with *fierce*.)

Intransitive: His hair **grew**.   (*Grew* is an intransitive verb. The action it describes ends with the verb.)

Verb Phrases

Some verbs contain more than one word. These verbs are known as *verb phrases*. A verb phrase consists of a *main verb* and one or more *helping verbs*.

The *main verb* is the word in a verb phrase that expresses action or state of being. The other word or words in a verb phrase are the *helping verbs*. Some helping verbs help to show the *time* that the action or state of being occurred. Others show the *possibility* of the action or state of being, or a *wish* that it would occur.

Here are some common helping verbs:

am	have	can
are	has	could
is	had	may
was	do	might
were	does	must
be	did	should
being	shall	would
been	will	

Here are some examples of verb phrases:

The sun **will shine** tomorrow.
The rain **has been falling** all day.
The weeds **are growing** faster than the flowers.
The rake **must be kept** in the toolshed.

The parts of a verb phrase can be separated by other words. Sometimes a negative word, such as *not* or *never,* breaks up a verb phrase. The parts of a verb phrase in a question are often separated by the subject. Other words can divide a verb phrase.

Joanna *should* **not** *have been* invited.
Can **the challenger** *win* the title?
The challenger *will* **probably** *win* the title.

You will learn more about verb phrases in Unit Seven, Lesson One.

Principal Parts of Verbs

A verb occurs in four forms, called the *principal parts* of the verb. The principal parts of a verb are the *base form* (or the *infinitive*), the *present participle*, the *past*, and the *past participle*.

Here are the principal parts of the verbs *dance* and *swim*:

Base Form (Infinitive)	Present Participle	Past	Past Participle
(to) dance	(is) dancing	danced	(has) danced
(to) swim	(is) swimming	swam	(has) swum

The base form and the past-tense form of a verb can be used alone, as the only verb in a sentence:

You **dance** very gracefully.
We **swam** in Cheryl's pool all afternoon.

The present participle and the past participle cannot be used alone in a sentence. Each must be used with a helping verb. The present participle must be used with a form of the helping verb *be*. The past participle must be used with a form of the helping verb *have*.

The elephants **were dancing** around the circus tent.
I **have swum** two miles in the last hour.

You will learn more about the use of verbs in Unit Thirteen.

PRACTICE A

Number your paper from 1 to 10. Write the verb or verb phrase in each sentence next to the number of the sentence. Write whether the verb is a *transitive* verb, an *intransitive* verb, or a *linking* verb.

Examples: Last year the school held the crafts fair in the gym.
held   transitive

The crafts fair has been a popular event for several years.
has been   linking

1. This year the school moved the crafts fair outdoors to the parking lot.
2. The fair attracted a crowd of several thousand.
3. Many local people displayed their crafts.
4. The pottery objects were beautiful.
5. In one booth a weaver was spinning wool.
6. The woodcarving exhibit was also popular.
7. At a food booth we bought some *sashimi,* a Japanese dish.
8. We ate under a striped umbrella.
9. By two o'clock, rainclouds were filling the sky.
10. In a moment heavy rain was drenching the crowd.

PRACTICE B

The sentences below need verbs or verb phrases. Rewrite each sentence on your paper. Fill in each blank with a verb or verb phrase.

Example: German _____ a difficult language to learn.
German is a difficult language to learn.

1. Mice _____ in the attic of my aunt's house.
2. Janet and Tom _____ across the lake.
3. The movers _____ the dresser down two flights of stairs.
4. Jack _____ a letter to his cousin in Australia.
5. I _____ to Mexico for a visit next year.
6. The sound of a piano _____ from the apartment next to ours.
7. My chemistry teacher _____ the experiment in the front of the class.
8. Ruth _____ a fire for cooking hamburgers at the picnic.
9. Ed _____ faster than anyone else on the team.
10. The doctor _____ Stanley's broken ankle.

PRACTICE C

Below is a list of verbs. Write a short story using ten of them. Use them in any order you wish. In at least three sentences, use the verb as part of a verb phrase. Underline the ten verbs or verb phrases you use.

Verbs:

be	blow	see	crash	lie
say	hit	pull	sink	appear
swim	grab	save	try	look
fall	seem	sail	hold	feel

Lesson Four

Adjectives

Imagine that your cousin Lydia is coming to visit you. You plan to meet her at the airport. Since you have never seen her before, she has sent you a description of herself. The description says:

I'll be wearing a hat, a coat, and a pair of gloves.
I will carry a bag.

You arrive at the busy airport just as the passengers are leaving Lydia's plane. There are at least six young women in the crowd wearing coats, hats, and gloves. They are all carrying bags! Which one is Lydia? You realize, too late, that the description she sent is not very useful.

It would have been easy to recognize Lydia in the crowd if she had written this:

I'll be wearing a **long green** coat, a **white fur** hat, and **knitted** gloves. I will carry a **red vinyl overnight** bag.

The words that make this description clearer are called *adjectives*.

● An <u>adjective</u> is a word that modifies a noun or a pronoun.

In grammar, to *modify* means to *describe* or *limit the meaning of*. In the second description above, the words in boldface type modify nouns.

long green coat
white fur hat
knitted gloves
red vinyl overnight bag

Each adjective gives information about the noun it modifies. The adjectives make the description clearer and more specific.

Adjectives often answer one of these questions:

1. What kind?
2. Which one or which ones?
3. How much or how many?

Notice how these questions can be used to find the adjectives in the following sentence:

I threw away those two broken cups.

What kind of cups? *Broken* cups. *Which* cups? *Those* cups. *How many* cups? *Two* cups. All three adjectives modify the one noun, *cups,* and all three adjectives come before the noun.

An adjective can come after the noun or the pronoun that it modifies:

The cups, **chipped** and **cracked,** finally broke.
She seemed **tired** yet **happy.**

In the first sentence, the adjectives *chipped* and *cracked* modify the noun *cups.* In the second sentence, *tired* and *happy* modify the pronoun *she.*

Proper Adjectives

Adjectives formed from proper nouns are called *proper adjectives.* (For a review of proper nouns, see Lesson One of this unit.) Compare these two sentences:

Shakespeare wrote many sonnets.
Shakespearean sonnets end with two lines that rhyme.

In the first sentence, *Shakespeare* is a proper noun. It is the name of a specific person. In the second sentence, *Shakespearean* is a proper adjective. It modifies the noun *sonnets* by telling *what kind* of sonnets.

Here are examples of proper adjectives formed from proper nouns. Notice that proper adjectives, like proper nouns, begin with capital letters.

Proper Nouns	Proper Adjectives
France	**French** cheese
Jefferson	**Jeffersonian** democracy
Asia	**Asian** history

Nouns and Pronouns Used as Adjectives

A word that is used as a noun or a pronoun in one sentence can be used as an adjective in another sentence. Compare the ways *television* is used in the sentences below.

Television and radio are two of the mass media.
I watched my favorite **television** program last night.

In the first sentence, *television* is a noun; it is the name of a thing. In the second sentence, *television* is an adjective that modifies the noun *program*. It tells *what kind* of program.

Here are more examples of nouns used as adjectives:

Nouns	Adjectives
automobile	**automobile** insurance
school	**school** activities
California	**California** climate

Many of the pronouns that you studied in Lesson Two can be used as adjectives. They are considered adjectives when they are used to modify nouns.

Pronoun: **Which** of the three stories did you like best?
Adjective: **Which** story did you like best?

Pronoun: **This** is my favorite dress.
Adjective: **This** dress is my favorite.

Pronoun: We saw two movies. **Neither** was very good.
Adjective: **Neither** movie was very good.

As you saw in Lesson Two of this unit, words such as *my, your, his, her, its, our,* and *their* are called possessive pronouns.

78

Because a possessive pronoun modifies the noun that follows it, it is sometimes called a *possessive adjective*.

Her office is down the hall.

Is this **his** bicycle?

The dog cut **its** paw on the sharp stones.

However, in this book, *my, your, his, her, its, our,* and *their* will be called possessive pronouns.

Articles

The three most common adjectives are *the, a,* and *an*. They are called *articles*. *A* is used before a word beginning with a consonant sound. *An* is used before a word beginning with a vowel sound.

PRACTICE A

Copy the following sentences on your paper. Underline all adjectives. Do not underline articles or possessive pronouns. Then draw an arrow from each adjective to the noun that it modifies. Draw a circle around every proper adjective.

Example: For his homework assignment, Leonard read about several Spanish painters.

For his homework assignment, Leonard read about several Spanish painters.

1. The first hockey game of the season ended in a scoreless tie.
2. The oil tanker foundered in the rough seas.
3. Within twenty minutes after takeoff, the American spacecraft was flying over Europe.
4. The artist painted a lovely portrait.
5. The careless use of chemical sprays threatens plants, animals, and people.
6. Before he filled a deep cavity, the kind dentist tuned in some pleasant music.
7. The point of the long speech was lost on the restless audience.
8. The small, furry creature moved closer to the warm embers of the campfire.
9. The youthful mayor led the colorful parade.
10. After a difficult trial, the judge was ready for a long vacation.

PRACTICE B

Rewrite each sentence below on your paper. Fill in each blank with an adjective.

Example: There was a _____ line of people waiting to buy tickets for the _____ game.
There was a long line of people waiting to buy tickets for the football game.

1. I like _____ movies better than any other kind.
2. On a(n) _____ day, a(n) _____ drink is refreshing.
3. The _____ runner was presented with a(n) _____ trophy.
4. Eric drives a(n) _____ car with _____ seats and a(n) _____ engine.
5. This sweater is too _____ for me.
6. Since _____ weather is predicted for Election Day, a(n) _____ turnout of voters is expected.
7. _____ lifeguards are on duty at the beach.
8. Through the window of the _____ house, _____ music could be heard.
9. The _____ museum has _____ displays from all over the world.
10. The baby was wrapped in a(n) _____ blanket.

PRACTICE C

Write five sentences describing where you live. Include at least five adjectives in your description, not counting articles. Underline all the adjectives. Draw arrows from the adjectives to the nouns or pronouns they modify.

Example: *I live in a tall building on a crowded city street. My neighborhood is noisy. Laughing children, busy shoppers, and strolling couples fill the sidewalks. It's a friendly place. Whenever I walk down the street, I see familiar faces.*

Lesson Five

Adverbs

One of the great moments in sports history took place during the 1954 World Series. The New York Giants were playing the Cleveland Indians in New York City. With the Indians at bat, Vic Wertz hit a line drive deep to center field. It looked like trouble for the Giants, but Willie Mays was playing center field. Here are two paragraphs that describe what happened next. Which do you think describes the action more vividly?

Paragraph A
Mays turned and ran toward the center-field wall. As the ball began sinking, Mays stretched out his arm, without looking, and stuck out his glove. The ball dropped. Mays had made a catch that baseball fans would remember.

Paragraph B
Mays immediately turned and ran, incredibly fast, straight toward the center-field wall. As the ball began sinking, Mays stretched out his arm, without looking back, and suddenly stuck out his glove. The ball dropped in. Mays had made a catch that baseball fans would always remember.

The second paragraph contains words that make it a more vivid description than the first: *immediately, incredibly, fast, straight, back, suddenly, in,* and *always.* These important words are *adverbs.*

- **An _adverb_ is a word that modifies a verb, an adjective, or another adverb.**

Adverbs usually answer one of the following questions: *When? Where? How? To what degree?* or *How often?* Adverbs usually modify verbs:

Mays **immediately** turned. (The adverb *immediately* tells *when* Mays turned. It modifies the verb *turned.*)

Sara stopped **here.** (*Here* tells *where* Sara stopped. It modifies the verb *stopped.*)

Candy sang **powerfully.** (The adverb *powerfully* tells *how* Candy sang. It modifies the verb *sang.*)

81

Mr. Lem gave a quiz **weekly**.   (The adverb *weekly* tells *how often* the quiz was given. It modifies the verb *gave*.)

Adverbs can also modify adjectives:

The librarian is **usually** helpful.   (The adverb *usually* modifies the adjective *helpful*. It tells *when* the librarian is helpful.)

I bought a **very** interesting book.   (The adverb *very* modifies the adjective *interesting*. It tells *to what degree* the book is interesting.)

Adverbs can also modify other adverbs:

Mays ran **incredibly** fast.   (The adverb *incredibly* modifies the adverb *fast*. It tells *how* fast Mays ran.)

Our dog Taurus barks **too** loud.   (The adverb *too* modifies *loud*, which is an adverb. It tells *to what degree* Taurus barks loud.)

The word *not* is one of the most commonly used adverbs. When *not* is used with a verb phrase, it usually comes between the main verb and the helping verb or verbs. However, *not* is not part of the verb phrase. It is an adverb and modifies the verb phrase. Sometimes *not* appears as the contraction *n't*. Like *not*, *n't* is an adverb, not part of the verb.

Steve has **not** decided what book he will read.
The winner of the contest will **not** be announced until tomorrow.
My car was**n't** damaged in the accident.

The adverbs *never, often,* and *probably* also separate the main verb from the helping verb or verbs in many sentences. Remember that they are adverbs, not parts of the verb.

Fernando has **never** visited Disneyland.
Walter has **often** gone to the movies with Katie.
The bus is **probably** waiting at the station.

PRACTICE A

Copy the following sentences on your paper. Then underline all the adverbs in each sentence. Draw an arrow to the word that each adverb modifies. The number in parentheses following each sentence tells how many adverbs are in that sentence.

Example: The accountant worked hard.   (1)

    The accountant worked hard.

1. The inn opened yesterday.   (1)
2. The fire spread rapidly.   (1)
3. The students carefully performed the experiment.   (1)
4. The skater completed the triple jump twice.   (1)
5. The award for the most exciting adventure story was won by my grandmother.   (1)
6. Sandy attends dance practice less often in the summer.   (2)
7. The dog ate its dinner hungrily.   (1)
8. The test pilot landed the new plane safely and smoothly.   (2)
9. The boy did not break the window.   (1)
10. The patrol responded immediately to the red alert signal.   (1)

PRACTICE B

The sentences below could use adverbs. Copy each sentence on your paper. Fill in each blank with an adverb.

Example: The fireworks exploded _____ .

    The fireworks exploded overhead.

1. Ellen _____ displayed her prize-winning painting.
2. The new skating rink will open _____ .
3. At the hunter's approach, the rhino snorted _____ .
4. Patrick leaped _____ and made the catch.
5. The fire engine raced across town _____ .
6. The students listened _____ to Mrs. Diaz.
7. Mark _____ watched his younger brother playing the guitar.
8. The historic decision was made _____ .
9. Elissa lifted the heavy package _____ .
10. The old car climbed the hill _____ .

PRACTICE C

Number your paper from 1 to 15. Use each of the fifteen adverbs on the following page in a separate sentence.

Example: yesterday

    The rock concert was held yesterday.

1. hungrily
2. never
3. happily
4. very
5. always
6. carefully
7. not
8. anywhere
9. once
10. skillfully
11. quite
12. overhead
13. silently
14. somewhat
15. firmly

Lesson Six

Prepositions

Imagine that tomorrow is your younger sister's twelfth birthday. You have bought her a catcher's mitt that she has wanted for months. Now all you have to do is hide it until tomorrow. But where? Should you hide it **in** the linen closet, **on** your father's workbench, or **among** the old newspapers in the garage?

All the boldfaced words show a relationship between the gift you want to hide and the places you might hide it. The boldfaced words are *prepositions.*

- A <u>preposition</u> shows the relationship between a noun or pronoun (called the object of the preposition) and another word in the sentence.

Look at these examples. In each sentence below, the preposition is in boldface type.

The catcher's mitt is hidden **in** the umbrella stand.
A picket fence runs **near** the garden.
The book **on** the shelf is overdue.
Tom scored twenty points **for** Seldon High.
He scored thirty-one points **in** the game **against** Morrison High.

As you can see, prepositions are extremely useful words. They can help you express many kinds of relationships.

Here is a list of common prepositions.

about	beneath	in	past
above	beside	inside	since
across	besides	into	through
after	between	like	to
against	beyond	near	toward
along	by	of	under
among	despite	off	until
around	down	on	up
at	during	onto	upon
before	except	out	with
behind	for	outside	within
below	from	over	without

Some prepositions consist of more than one word. They are called *compound prepositions*. A compound preposition is considered one preposition.

Here is a list of compound prepositions.

according to	in place of
as of	in spite of
aside from	instead of
because of	on account of
by means of	out of
in addition to	owing to
in front of	prior to

According to experts, the Northeast will suffer from a shortage of water for three years.
The coach chose Carol **instead of** me as captain of the team.
The little girl danced **in front of** her friends.

The noun or pronoun that follows a preposition is called the *object of the preposition*. In the sentences below, the objects of the prepositions are in boldface type.

The snowstorm caused hardship throughout the **Midwest**.
The baby cried during the **night**.
The bicycle was standing outside the **gate**.

Because the object of the preposition is a noun or a pronoun, it can have modifiers. The preposition, its object, and any modifiers of the object are called a *prepositional phrase*.

Paper blew **around the empty schoolyard.**
Ed's family moved **into a new and larger apartment.**

There can be more than one prepositional phrase in a sentence.

We had a picnic **beneath the branches of the old oak tree.**
The pioneers traveled **over mountains, across plains,** and **through valleys.**

PRACTICE A

Write the following sentences on your paper. Underline each prepositional phrase. Draw a circle around each preposition. Some sentences contain more than one prepositional phrase.

Example: The bus traveled slowly because of the heavy snow.

The bus traveled slowly (because of) the heavy snow.

1. The teacher stood beside the map.
2. Despite the heavy rainfall, the water supply is low.
3. The tonsils in your throat help defend your body against infection.
4. The diner across the street serves dinner from five o'clock until nine o'clock.
5. According to the Nielsen ratings, millions of people watched the telecast of the World Series.
6. The new car, like the old one, was equipped with faulty brakes.
7. Every student except Clarisse attended the school play.
8. Throughout the stormy night, we waited for the rescue party.
9. Out of nowhere, another runner sped past me and crossed the finish line.
10. The teenager with the red cap will be your tour guide.

PRACTICE B

Number your paper from 1 to 20. Supply prepositions for the blanks in the following story. When you finish, read over the story to be sure it is clear.

Example: _____ many years of testing, the reusable space shuttle is finally a reality.

After

(1) _____ April 14, 1981, the space shuttle *Columbia* became the first spacecraft (2) _____ the history (3) _____ the U.S. space program to land (4) _____ dry ground rather than (5) _____ the water. Formerly, spacecraft had been carried (6) _____ earth (7) _____ enormous parachutes. They would plunge (8) _____ the ocean and become useless (9) _____ a single flight. In contrast, *Columbia* landed softly (10) _____ its own landing gear, (11) _____ an airplane.

Thousands (12) _____ people watched the 102-ton craft glide (13) _____ the skies and land (14) _____ California's Mojave Desert. The pilots (15) _____ the shuttle were delighted (16) _____ the performance (17) _____ the new spacecraft. (18) _____ the success of this first flight, many experts say the space shuttle will play a major role (19) _____ the future exploration (20) _____ space.

PRACTICE C

Choose one of the five topics below. Write seven to ten sentences about the topic. Include at least ten prepositional phrases. Underline each prepositional phrase. Draw a circle around each preposition.

Topics:
An Enjoyable Trip
How to Cook My Favorite Dish
My Favorite Place to Relax
A Frightening Experience
A topic of your own choice

Lesson Seven

Conjunctions

Have you ever taken a trip by train? If so, you may have changed from one train to another at a station where two or more railroad lines meet. This kind of station is called a *junction*, a word which means a place where two things join.

In grammar, the word *conjunction* refers to a different kind of joining.

● **A conjunction is a word that joins two or more other words.**

Conjunctions can join two or more single words.

Salt **and** pepper are on the table.
For exercise, Jenny jogs **or** swims every day.
After the race, Paul was tired **but** happy.

Conjunctions can also join two or more groups of words.

Buy a ticket from the man at the gate **or** the woman at the booth.
I walked through the kitchen **and** into the living room.
Susan parked the car **and** took her packages from the trunk.

A conjunction can be used to join the parts of a compound sentence. (See Unit One, Lesson Six for a review of compound sentences.)

Sal broke a dish, **but** he fixed it with some glue.
Marion directed the play, **and** Joshua designed the set.
The rain did not stop, **so** the game was cancelled.

Kinds of Conjunctions

There are three kinds of conjunctions. In this lesson, you will learn about two of them: *coordinating conjunctions* and *correlative conjunctions.* (The third kind, *subordinating conjunctions,* will be explained in Unit Nine.)

There are seven coordinating conjunctions: *and, but, or, nor, for, yet,* and *so.*

Coordinating conjunctions can be used to join two or more nouns, verbs, adjectives, or adverbs. They can also be used to join two or more prepositional phrases or the simple sentences that make up a compound sentence.

Nouns: Did you give Dana a hat **or** a scarf?
Verbs: The old car rattled **and** shook.
Adjectives: As the test began, Ali was nervous **but** hopeful.
Adverbs: Steve painted the model plane slowly **and** carefully.
Prepositional Phrases: The dog was not in the house **or** in the yard.
Simple Sentences: The team was glad, **for** they had won the game.

Correlative conjunctions always come in pairs. Here are the four most common correlative conjunctions:

both . . . and   neither . . . nor
either . . . or   not only . . . but also

The pair of words that make up a correlative conjunction always work as a team. Correlative conjunctions may be used to join words or groups of words.

Nouns: In Italy we visited **neither** Milan **nor** Genoa.
Verbs: Gina **both** repaired **and** painted the fence.
Adjectives: The drive to my aunt's house is **both** long **and** boring.
Adverbs: Tara solved the puzzle **not only** quickly **but also** correctly.
Prepositional Phrases: The letter is **either** on my desk **or** in the top drawer.
Simple Sentences: **Either** you will walk to the station, **or** Mr. Evans will take you there in his car.

PRACTICE A

Number your paper from 1 to 10. Write the conjunction or conjunctions from each sentence next to the number of the sentence.

Example: Technology and science have changed the world.
　　　　　and

1. The world is the same physical size, yet it is shrinking.
2. It is shrinking not only because of recent changes in transportation but also because of developments in communication.

3. We can now travel long distances in a short time and talk within seconds to people on other continents.
4. One hundred years ago, neither cars nor planes existed.
5. Before the Wright Brothers' flight in 1903, people flew only in gliders and balloons.
6. Today mass-produced automobiles roll off assembly lines throughout the world, and airplanes crisscross the globe.
7. The first transatlantic telegraph message was sent in 1901, and the first newsreels were shown in 1909.
8. Both radio and motion pictures became popular forms of communication and entertainment.
9. Thanks to satellites, words and pictures can now be sent around the globe in an instant.
10. No one can predict the technological changes of the future, but it is exciting to imagine the possibilities.

PRACTICE B

Combine the following sentences by using either coordinating or correlative conjunctions. You may need to add or take away words so that your new sentences will make sense. As you will see in the examples below, a sentence can be combined in more than one way.

Examples: I will join the swim team. I will go out for the track team.
I will either join the swim team or go out for the track team.

or

I will join the swim team and go out for the track team.

1. Elizabeth accepted the job. She reported for work at 8:00 a.m. the next day.
2. We chose the tan collie from the dog shelter. We took her home.
3. The game was in the final inning. We were still ahead.
4. The driving instructor did not explain the manual shift system. He did not explain the use of the parking brake.
5. Jenny and Peter canoed down the river. They camped along the riverbank.

Lesson Eight

Interjections

Imagine this: It is a cold, wet, snowy day. You've spent the morning outside cleaning off the sidewalk. Now you're tired and cold. You come inside, throw off your wet coat and boots, and sit down in a soft chair. Your mother brings you a steaming cup of hot chocolate.

"Ahhh!" you sigh.

Now imagine this: It is the Fourth of July. You're in a crowd at the park, waiting for the fireworks to begin. Suddenly, a rocket zooms towards the sky. It mounts higher and higher. Then it explodes with a bang, and streamers of every color burst forth.

"Oooh!" shouts the crowd.

There is a special name for the words that you use when you sigh and shout. They are called *interjections*.

● An <u>interjection</u> is a word that expresses a strong emotion. It is not connected grammatically to any other word in a sentence.

Here are some examples of interjections.

Wow! That was a great dive!
Oh no! I just dented my mother's car.
Ouch! That hurts!
Hey, stop that pushing!

As the examples above show, an interjection is followed by a comma or an exclamation point.

Interjections are common in speech but rare in writing. When you use an interjection in writing, be sure that the situation calls for the expression of strong emotion.

PRACTICE

Choose five interjections from the list below. Use each interjection in a sentence.

Example: Wow!
           Wow! That's a pretty hat.

Ugh   No   Oh   Great   Look out   Hurrah   Help

91

Lesson Nine

Determining Parts of Speech

In this unit, you have learned about the eight parts of speech: nouns, pronouns, verbs, adjectives, adverbs, prepositions, conjunctions, and interjections. As you have seen, some words can be used as more than one part of speech. For example, a word that is a noun in one sentence can be used as an adjective in another sentence. The best way to determine the part of speech of a particular word is to see how it is used in a sentence.

- **The way a word is used in a sentence determines its part of speech.**

Look at the several ways that *near* can be used in sentences:

Verb: As you **near** the lion's cage, don't make a sudden movement or loud noise.

Adjective: The astronauts landed on the **near** side of the moon.

Adverb: Come **near** so that I can see you better.

Preposition: The campers sat **near** the fire.

The chart below lists the eight parts of speech and their definitions. The examples show how each part of speech is used in a sentence. Use this chart to review what you have learned in this unit.

Part of Speech	Definition	Example
noun	A noun names a person, place, thing, or idea.	**Diane** sent many **postcards** from **Rome.**
pronoun	A pronoun is a word used in place of one or more nouns.	**Someone** will give **it** to **him.**
verb	A verb is a word that expresses action or state of being.	Lana **was** happy, so she **sang.**
adjective	An adjective is a word that modifies a noun or pronoun.	I returned **the three new** dresses.

92

adverb	An adverb is a word that modifies a verb, an adjective, or another adverb.	I **reluctantly** stopped eating, for my dessert was **much too** sweet.
preposition	A preposition is a word that relates a noun or a pronoun to another word in a sentence.	Give that book **with** the broken binding **to** me.
conjunction	A conjunction is a word that joins two or more words or groups of words.	I'll stay here, **and** you go for help.
interjection	An interjection is a word that expresses a strong emotion.	**Oh, no!** That's terrible news.

PRACTICE A

In the exercise below, there are twenty-five underlined words. Number your paper from 1 to 25. Write whether each underlined word is a *noun*, a *pronoun*, a *verb*, an *adjective*, an *adverb*, a *preposition*, a *conjunction*, or an *interjection*. (Articles should be listed as adjectives; possessive personal pronouns as pronouns.)

Example: The food of the future is being created today for the

use of travelers in space.

    1. preposition
    2. noun

Astronauts now enjoy better meals than those served to John Glenn on his orbital flight in 1962. He squeezed his food out of a toothpaste tube. It probably looked as appetizing as toothpaste. Yuck!

Later, researchers made a discovery. Astronauts could float weightlessly in their spacecraft and still eat food out of ordinary

containers. Moist food clung to spoons. It did not float around
     10   11   12
the ship.

Freeze-dried and precooked foods were prepared for the 1969
              13   14
flight to the moon. By the early seventies, in-flight food was
                        15
warmed in a specially designed heating tray. Because of these
                 16   17   18   19
improvements, travelers in space can enjoy tasty meals. Today's
     20   21   22
space meals look and taste better than food squeezed from tubes.
                 23   24   25

PRACTICE B

Number your paper from 1 to 10. Complete the following
passage by supplying the kind of word specified.

Example: Creative talent does not always appear _____
                                                        preposition
           the early years of one's life.
           during

Many readers today consider Walt Whitman the greatest poet

that America has (1) _____ produced. However, as a
                              adverb

young (2) _____ , Whitman did not (3) _____
                 noun   verb

poetry. He worked as a printer (4) _____ a newspaper
                                         conjunction

editor.

At the age of thirty, Whitman visited a phrenologist. According

to phrenology, a person's character can be discovered by studying

(5) _____ bumps (6) _____ that person's head.
         adjective   preposition
The phrenologist looked (7) _____ the bumps on Whitman's
                                 preposition
(8) _____ (9) _____ said that Whitman could be
         noun   conjunction
a great poet. Soon afterward, Whitman decided to devote

(10) _____ life to poetry.
          pronoun

Below are thirty words or phrases. Write a sentence for each, using the word or phrase as the part of speech listed.

Example: Noun: favor
          I finally repaid the favor.

Nouns:
  1. American
  2. direction
  3. library
  4. mud

Verbs:
  13. delivered
  14. had been waiting
  15. is
  16. will enjoy

Conjunctions:
  25. yet
  26. nor
  27. either . . . or

Pronouns:
  5. I
  6. their
  7. myself
  8. someone

Adverbs:
  17. slowly
  18. down
  19. earlier
  20. noisily

Interjections:
  28. ouch
  29. wow
  30. shh

Adjectives:
  9. thirteen
  10. an
  11. Italian
  12. squeaking

Prepositions:
  21. off
  22. after
  23. in addition to
  24. in spite of

Review Exercises

I. The story below contains thirty nouns. Number your paper from 1 to 30. Then copy each noun from the story next to a number. Write the nouns in the order in which they appear. The first noun is given as an example. You find the others, starting with number 2. (Lesson One)

Example: *1. century*

In the late nineteenth century, a small child named Maria was wandering in a dark cave near Altamira in Spain. She had gone exploring by herself while her father, a Spanish archeologist named Marcelino de Sautuola, worked nearby. Suddenly he heard his daughter shouting to him from within the cave. Maria had found brilliantly colored pictures of bison on the ceilings and walls. When the discovery was made known, archeologists thought the pictures had been forged, because their colors were so well preserved. Twenty years passed. Then, four boys found similar artwork in a cave in France. Archeologists realized that the Altamira paintings had indeed been made by ancient artists. Today, the 20,000-year-old paintings are famous throughout the world.

II. In each of the following sentences, one or more nouns are repeated one or more times. Rewrite each sentence, replacing the repeated nouns with pronouns. (Lesson Two)

Example: Dave dropped ice into the glass, and Dave handed the glass to me.
Dave dropped ice into the glass, and he handed it to me.

1. Jo Ann bought some jeans for Jo Ann.
2. Randy found Randy's socks and shoes in the bottom of Randy's locker.
3. Last winter Jill had a cold, and the cold bothered Jill for weeks.
4. The damaged plane lay on the plane's side in the middle of the runway.
5. Deborah learned to play golf two years ago, and Deborah has already won two tournaments.
6. Jeffrey said that Jeffrey could not leave the house until Jeffrey's father arrived.
7. The art gallery had to close after the art gallery lost a dozen paintings in a robbery.
8. Joe lent Joe's sister Joe's camera.
9. Linda watched Pete as Pete carefully clipped Pete's poodle's hair.
10. The orchestra members tuned up the orchestra members' instruments while the orchestra members waited for the orchestra members' conductor to arrive.

III. The following sentences have no verbs. Rewrite each sentence, filling in each blank with a verb or a verb phrase that completes the thought of the sentence. (Lesson Three)

Example: The speaker _____ her talk by 9:30 p.m.
          The speaker had finished her talk by 9:30 p.m.

1. Leslie _____ the new family car.
2. A strand of hair _____ stronger than a strand of copper of the same size.
3. The swimmer _____ off the high, rocky cliff into the water.
4. Jessica _____ the huge Victorian house.
5. Cottonseed bread _____ a nutlike taste.
6. The mountain climbers _____ after sundown.
7. Our galaxy _____ many millions of stars.
8. Late at night, Gina _____ the sounds of footsteps in the attic.
9. Next week, this stereo _____ fifty dollars less than it does now.
10. Please _____ this book by Friday.

IV. Copy the adjectives from each sentence below onto your paper. Include nouns used as adjectives; do not include articles or possessive pronouns. After each adjective, write the word that it modifies. (Lesson Four)

Example: The Milky Way galaxy contains about a trillion stars.
          Milky Way   galaxy
          trillion   stars

1. The tired child swung lazily on a swing.
2. The new American cars are selling very well.
3. Her office was located on the twelfth floor.
4. A large black ant slowly climbed up the porch railing, carrying a green leaf.
5. The overdue library book was returned by a tall blond man in a black raincoat.
6. That meeting was held yesterday.
7. The suitcase fell down six flights of stairs.
8. The fragile crystal arrived in a dozen small pieces.
9. Both books were written by George Orwell.
10. Some jobs require highly trained workers.

V. Copy the adverbs from each sentence below on your paper. The number in parentheses after each sentence tells how many adverbs it contains. (Lesson Five)

Example: Tomorrow Brian and his family will move far away.   (3)
        Tomorrow, far, away

1. The train left early.   (1)
2. If we travel quickly, we will arrive today.   (2)
3. Beth barely passed the exam.   (1)
4. John arrived at band practice unusually late.   (2)
5. The children left the room quietly.   (1)
6. Linda came too late for dinner.   (2)
7. Conrad slowly gathered his books.   (1)
8. We went to the early show once, but it was too crowded.   (2)
9. The carelessly dropped match eventually destroyed thousands of forest acres.   (2)
10. The commuters dashed madly for the subway doors.   (1)

VI. Use each prepositional phrase below in a sentence. (Lesson Six)

Example: into the sky
        The volcano threw hot rocks into the sky.

1. over the hurdle
2. around the bend
3. without her library card
4. under the front porch
5. beyond the mountains
6. until last summer
7. outside the window
8. because of the blizzard
9. in spite of the doctor's advice
10. near the lake

VII. The following sentences need conjunctions. Copy the sentences and add the necessary conjunctions. (Lesson Seven)

Example: _____ the table _____ the chairs will fit into the tiny room.
        Neither the table nor the chairs will fit into the tiny room.

1. _____ my sister _____ I are taking courses on outdoor survival.
2. We can go to Boston by train _____ by bus.
3. The awards banquet was over, _____ I had not received my trophy.
4. Jerry _____ Steve went swimming in the river.
5. _____ Rebecca _____ I wanted to cause any problems.
6. The school band _____ plays at football games _____ gives two concerts a year.
7. Many students signed up for the class every year, _____ the course was discontinued this fall.
8. Jason ordered roast beef, mashed potatoes, _____ salad for dinner.
9. The coach hasn't decided whether Joan _____ Eileen will run first in the track meet.
10. The papers were _____ sent to the main office _____ discarded.

VIII. Choose a topic from the list below and write a paragraph about it. Include in your paragraph at least one example of each of the following parts of speech: *noun, pronoun, verb, adjective, adverb, preposition, conjunction,* and *interjection.* After you have finished writing your paragraph, draw a line under one example of each of the parts of speech. (Lessons One to Seven)

Topics:
A Recent Event in the News
A Book I Am Reading
Buying a Bicycle
Dreams
A topic of your own choice

Writing Description

Lesson One

Sensory Details

"Well, I don't have a date for the dance yet. What is your cousin like?"

"Describe a typical New England village during the early colonial period."

"We think that car was the getaway car. Can you describe it?"

"Exactly what kind of shoes are you looking for?"

If you could give clear, detailed descriptions in answer to the questions above, you might be able to help a friend find a date for the junior prom, earn a high score on an American history test, help the police catch a bank robber, and find the perfect shoes to go with a new outfit.

A description is a picture in words of a person, place, or thing. A good description uses *sensory details* to create a vivid image of whatever is being described.

Sensory details are impressions that appeal to any of the five senses: sight, hearing, touch, smell, and taste. The best descriptions appeal to as many of the five senses as possible. Think of the last time you ate your favorite food. How would you describe that food to a person who had never eaten it? A vivid description would include many sensory details:

I ate one of the first apples of the fall from Mr. McNulty's orchard. The apple had a glistening, bright red skin flecked with tiny spots of yellow and white. On the top of the apple was a piece of brown stem with two dark green leaves growing from it. When I bit into the apple, it gave a crisp, crunching sound. A thin spray of cool juice splashed from the spot where my teeth had punctured the apple's skin, and a faint tangy smell filled the air. The white flesh of the apple was firm and crunchy, and the acid in the juice made my tongue sting a little. The apple was delicious, with a taste that was slightly tart, turning sugary sweet as I chewed and swallowed.

Someone who had never seen or tasted an apple would be able to imagine what it would be like after reading the description above. The description contains details that appeal to each of the five senses. Details such as "glistening, bright red skin flecked with tiny spots of yellow and white" and "two dark green leaves" appeal to the sense of *sight*. "It gave a crisp, crunching sound" appeals to the sense of *hearing*. "A thin spray of cool juice" and "the white flesh of the apple was firm and crunchy" appeal to the sense of *touch*. "A faint tangy smell" appeals to the sense of *smell*, and "slightly tart, turning sugary sweet" appeals to the sense of *taste*. The sensory details allow a reader to almost see, hear, feel, smell, and taste what a fresh, sweet apple is like.

Not every kind of description can include details that appeal to every sense. A description of a house, for example, probably wouldn't include details that appeal to the sense of taste. But the more sensory details a description includes, and the more senses the details appeal to, the more vivid the description will be.

EXERCISE ONE

Think of a favorite food. Try to remember that food as vividly as you can. List at least ten details that could be used to describe that food to someone who has never seen or tasted it before. Try to include details that appeal to each of the five senses.

EXERCISE TWO

Look closely at the picture on page 115. Imagine that you are in the place shown in the picture. Jot down as many sensory details that could be observed there as possible. Include details that you can see in the picture (the counters and trays, the people in the room) as well as details that you must imagine (the sounds and smells in the room). Try to write details that appeal to as many different senses as possible. List at least twenty different details.

EXERCISE THREE

Look back at the list of details you wrote for Exercise Two. For each detail, decide whether it appeals mainly to the sense of sight, hearing, touch, smell, or taste. Copy the details on a piece of paper with five columns headed *Sight, Hearing, Touch, Smell,* and *Taste.* If you have no details for one of the senses, try to think of one. Keep your paper for use later in this unit.

Lesson Two

Choosing a Central Theme

Have you ever heard the Indian fable about the five blind men and the elephant? According to the story, the five men came upon an elephant for the very first time. Each one tried to figure out and describe what the elephant was like.

The first man felt the elephant's leg and said, "An elephant is very much like a tree."

The second grabbed the elephant's tail and said, "No, you are wrong. An elephant is like a rope."

The third felt the elephant's trunk and told the others, "An elephant is something like a very large hose."

The fourth touched the huge, flapping ear of the elephant and said, "An elephant is like a fan."

The fifth man moved his hands along the elephant's side, and told the others, "An elephant is exactly like a big, rough wall."

Although each of the five men in the fable gave an accurate description of certain details about the elephant, none gave a good overall description of the animal. Sensory details are important for a good description. However, details will not add up to a good overall description unless they are united by a *central theme.*

The central theme of a description is the writer's main impression or most important idea about the thing being described. To decide on the central theme for a description, think about the sensory details you have noted about the person, place, or thing you want to describe. What is the main impression or feeling they suggest? What idea do they give you about the person, place, or thing? Try to sum up the main impression you have in a complete sentence. That sentence will state the central theme of your description. It will also be the topic sentence for the description. (For a review of topic sentences, see Unit Two, Lesson Two.)

Once you have written a sentence that states the central theme of your description, you can use the sentence to help you unify the sensory details you have noted. Look again at your list of details. Some of them will fit the theme you have stated. Others may not. Cross out the details that do not fit the theme you have chosen. The ones that remain will be the basis for your written description.

Here is a list of sensory details about an old house:

the house is very large — three stories tall
it has an enormous garden
the garden has many tall weeds and thorny bushes
the garden gate squeaks — it needs oil
big oak trees cast shade over the front porch .
the front of the house has twelve-foot-high windows
one window is broken
the windows are covered by dark shades
the house has wooden walls freshly painted dark green
small attic with peaked roof
attic windows have old wooden shutters that shake in the breeze
the attic looks dark and dusty

Here are two descriptions of the house by two different writers. Each writer has a different impression of the house, stated in the first sentence of the description. Notice how each writer has chosen details that fit the theme expressed in the topic sentence.

Description One

The house is the kind of big, rambling, old-fashioned house in which you could raise a large family. Looking at the house from the road, the first things you see are the big oak trees in front and the enormous garden. The windows in front of the house are twelve feet high. The walls are of wood and have been freshly painted. The house is very large and is three stories tall. It must contain many rooms. At the top of the house is an attic with a quaint peaked roof. The attic windows have old-fashioned wooden shutters that swing in the breeze. I love this old house.

Description Two

The house is huge, old, badly cared for, and a little spooky. As you walk through the garden gate, you hear the hinges squeak eerily. Big trees cast their dark shadows over the front porch. The windows along the front of the house are covered with dark shades; one window is broken. The wooden walls are painted dark green. At the top of the house is a small attic that looks dark and dusty. The wooden shutters on the attic windows rattle in the wind. The garden is filled with tall weeds and thorny bushes. This house makes me shiver.

Depending on how you feel about big, old houses, you could write either Description One or Description Two. Both are good descriptions. They are clear and interesting, and they use sensory details to express a particular impression of the house. As a writer, it is your job to decide on the central theme of your description and to choose the details that will fit that theme.

EXERCISE FOUR

The following list contains sensory details about a particular car. Read the list of details. Then choose one of the three possible topic sentences that follow. Find at least five details on the list that fit the topic sentence you chose. Copy the topic sentence and the appropriate details on your paper.

Sensory Details:
large dent on right front fender
engine hums quietly
bumper stickers from four camping trips on rear bumper
radio doesn't work
inside of car smells like pine needles from the time we drove home from the mountains with a fresh-cut Christmas tree
rear right window won't open
the car always starts quickly and easily
clouds of black smoke come from the exhaust pipe
trunk is large and roomy
trunk is filled with old camping gear and souvenirs
car is over twenty years old
glove compartment is filled with maps from places that we've visited all over America
seats are comfortable and soft
one door is painted a different color from the rest of the car
my brother and sister's beach toys are scattered all over the back seat

six people fit in the car comfortably
the upholstery in the back seat is torn
the car has new tires

Topic Sentences:
Our old car shows plenty of signs of wear and tear.
Our old car is filled with pleasant memories.
Our old car would be a good choice for someone who wants to buy a used car.

EXERCISE FIVE

Look again at the list of details about the picture on page 115 that you jotted down for Exercises Two and Three. Decide what your main impression of the picture is. Write a sentence that sums up that impression. Then choose at least five details from the list you wrote that fit the theme stated in your sentence. If your list does not include five details that fit your theme, add some. Write the sentence and the details on your paper. You do not have to write a description, just a list of details you could use in writing a description.

Lesson Three

Choosing Descriptive Adjectives and Adverbs

Here are two newspaper advertisements. Each one offers a brief description of the food served at a restaurant. Which advertisement do you think does a better job?

Advertisement One

We serve steaks.
Come in and try one.
STAN'S STEAK HOUSE

Advertisement Two

Our sizzling, flame-broiled steaks
are the thickest and juiciest in town.
Come in and try one.
FRED'S STEAK HOUSE

If you found Advertisement Two more appealing than Advertisement One, the reason is simple. The person who wrote the ad for Fred's Steak House understands one of the secrets of writing a vivid description: using specific adjectives.

As you learned in Unit Three, Lesson Four, an adjective is a word that modifies a noun or a pronoun. In Fred's ad, the words *sizzling, flame-broiled, thickest,* and *juiciest* are all adjectives. Each one gives more information about Fred's steaks. All together, they create a vivid word-picture of just how delicious Fred's steaks are.

When you are writing a description, try to think of adjectives that will give specific sensory information about the things you are describing. Notice how the following descriptions become more vivid when specific adjectives are added:

Harry's bicycle stood in a corner of the barn.
Harry's **rusty old** bicycle with its **patched** and **worn** tires and its **hard, springless** seat stood in a corner of the **dusty, dilapidated** barn.

The jewelry store's window was filled with necklaces, bracelets, and rings.
The **exclusive** jewelry store's window was filled with **glittering** necklaces, delicately **etched gold** bracelets, and **sparkling ruby, emerald,** and **diamond** rings.

The wind pushed open the front door, blowing a gust of snow into the parlor.
The **fierce winter** wind pushed open the front door, blowing a gust of **cold, wet** snow into the **cozy, firelit** parlor.

When writing a description, try to choose adjectives that convey your meaning exactly. For example, the adjective *red* tells something about the appearance of a thing. However, there are dozens of shades of red, and there are many adjectives to choose from in describing these different shades: *scarlet, crimson, maroon, brick red, cardinal, cherry, blood-red, fire-engine red, carmine,* and many others. Using the adjective that describes the exact shade of red you have in mind will make your description clear and vivid.

Like adjectives, adverbs can help to make your descriptions more vivid. As you learned in Unit Three, Lesson Five, adverbs modify verbs, adjectives, or other adverbs. Notice how different adverbs change the meaning of the following sentence:

The waves rocked the little houseboat **gently.**
The waves rocked the little houseboat **monotonously.**
The waves rocked the little houseboat **roughly.**
The waves rocked the little houseboat **furiously.**

The right adverb can help create the mood you want in your description.

Think back to the old house you read about in Lesson Two. As you saw, the same house could be described in different ways depending on the details chosen by the writer. The choice of adjectives and adverbs can also help to create a particular mood. The writer whose main impression of the house was of an old-fashioned, comfortable place could describe the oak trees in front of the house this way:

Large, stately oak trees tower above the house **protectively,** casting a **cool** shade on hot summer afternoons.

The writer whose main impression of the house was of a dark, spooky place could describe the very same trees in the following way:

Monstrous oak trees tower above the house **threateningly,** casting **black** shadows across the front porch.

When you are preparing to write a description, try writing down as many adjectives or adverbs as you can think of that could be used in your description. For example, if you were writing a description of your grandmother's homemade blueberry pie, you might list the following adjectives:

fresh	crisp
hot	steaming
fragrant	delicious
sweet	purple
juicy	crusty

When writing your description, you can then use as many of these adjectives as you wish.

EXERCISE SIX

Choose two nouns from the list below. Write at least ten adjectives that could describe each of the nouns you chose. Then write three or four sentences using the ten adjectives you wrote to describe the noun.

Example: guitar
1. *new*   6. *out of tune*
2. *electric*   7. *twanging*
3. *loud*   8. *powerful*
4. *white*   9. *expensive*
5. *glittering*   10. *sleek*

My sleek white electric guitar hangs on a nail in my closet.
My expensive new guitar is out of tune.
The rock star's glittering, powerful guitar pounded out the latest hit song.
The sound of my brother's loud, twanging guitar awoke my father.

Nouns:

watermelon	encyclopedia
motorcycle	turtle
dog	meadow
basement	salad
piano	tree

EXERCISE SEVEN

Choose two verbs from the list below. Write a sentence using each of the verbs you chose. Then write the same sentence three more times. Each time, add a different adverb to the sentence.

Example: swam
The girls in the pool swam.
The girls in the pool swam quickly.
The girls in the pool swam lazily.
The girls in the pool swam gracefully.

Verbs:

ran	ate	sang	fell	walked
jumped	laughed	spoke	swayed	slept

110

Lesson Four

Organizing a Description

Winston Churchill, a wartime leader of England, was a good amateur painter. Churchill once said that he enjoyed painting pictures because it reminded him of fighting a battle. Like a good general, a good painter begins with a battle plan. Without a plan, the battle may be lost, or the painting may be botched.

Churchill's idea can also be applied to the art of writing description. Painting a picture in words also calls for a battle plan. A plan can help turn a collection of details into a clear, well-organized description.

In Unit Two, you learned that a paragraph can be organized in any of several ways: according to *spatial order, order of importance,* or *chronological order.* Any of these methods of organizing a paragraph can be used to organize a description. Here are some suggestions and examples:

Spatial order is the most common way to organize a description. Depending on what you are describing, you can use many kinds of spatial order. If you were describing the appearance of a freight train, for example, you might start with the front of the train (the locomotive) and end with the rear of the train (the caboose). If you were describing a skyscraper, you might start at the ground floor and work your way up to the spire at the very top. In describing the view from your bedroom window, you might start with the parts of the landscape closest to you and end with the parts that are most distant. Any of these types of spatial order can be effective.

Order of importance can be a good way to organize a description. You can begin with the most important detail about the thing you are describing and end with the least important detail. Or you can begin with the least important and end with the most important. The choice is yours.

In describing an auditorium during a rock concert, for example, you might want to start with the detail that you consider most important: the deafening roar of the music. You could then go on to describe the other details in the order of their importance: the lighting effects, the appearance of the band, the behavior of the crowd, and so on.

Chronological order can also be used to organize a description. If you were describing the street where you live, you could use chronological order by tracing the sights, sounds, smells, and other details of your street over the course of a typical day. You would start by describing your street in the early morning, tell about how your street looks at the height of the morning rush hour, in the middle of the afternoon, and so on.

Whatever method of organizing your description you choose, follow it consistently. This will make it easy for your reader to understand your description.

EXERCISE EIGHT

Below is a list of six items that could be described in a paragraph. Choose one of them. Jot down at least ten sensory details to describe the item you chose.

Decide on a logical method for organizing the details. You can use any of the methods described in the lesson. Write a few words stating your method of organization.

Number the details you listed in the correct order for the method of organization you chose. You do not have to write a finished description.

Example: your room
            Sensory Details:
            10. ceiling painted dark blue with white "stars"
            8. old-time movie posters on the walls
            2. sports equipment piled in a corner
            7. stereo tape player, usually playing music by Earth, Wind and Fire
            1. a thick, soft red carpet on the floor
            5. desk covered with parts of a radio kit
            3. unmade bed with sheets and blankets in a tangle
            6. records and tapes neatly lined up on a shelf
            4. open window letting in warm air and street sounds
            9. mobile I made in art class hanging from the ceiling
            Method of Organization:
            Details in spatial order (bottom to top)

Items To Be Described:
your room

112

your favorite place to eat
the ideal car you would like to own someday
the tallest building in your hometown
your English classroom
your favorite place to swim

Lesson Five

Writing and Revising

Think of the one place you like to be more than any other place in the world. It might be someplace spectacular, like the top of a hill overlooking a breathtaking view of the countryside, or the most glamorous restaurant in town. It might be a more ordinary place, like the empty lot where you and your friends play football, or your special table at the library where you go for an hour of peace and quiet. No matter what kind of place you think of, it should have a special meaning for you.

In this lesson, you will put together a description of your special place that will allow your reader to feel as though he or she is really there.

EXERCISE NINE

Choose the place you want to describe. Make a list of all the sensory details you can think of about the place you want to describe. Try to include details that appeal to each of the five senses. List at least twenty different details.

Decide on the main impression that you have of the place. Is it peaceful, exciting, friendly, colorful, mysterious, noisy, private, or does it create some other feeling? Write a topic sentence that sums up your main impression.

Go back to your list of sensory details. Cross out any details that do not fit the theme expressed in your topic sentence. Add any other details you can think of that fit the theme.

Choose a method for organizing your description. You can use any of the methods discussed in Lesson Four. Number the details on your list in the correct order for the method of organization you chose.

Try to think of as many adjectives or adverbs as possible that could be used to describe your special place. List them on your paper. Try to list at least ten different adjectives or adverbs.

EXERCISE TEN

Using the numbered list of details you wrote for Exercise Nine, write your description in a paragraph. The paragraph should be at least ten sentences long. Include your topic sentence somewhere in the paragraph. Use as many of the adjectives or adverbs that you listed for Exercise Nine as possible. Add other descriptive adjectives or adverbs if you wish. Try to make your description as detailed and vivid as you can.

EXERCISE ELEVEN

Reread and revise your description, using the checklist below as a guide.

Checklist

1. Is there a topic sentence that states the theme of the description?
2. Do all the details in the description fit the theme?
3. Do the details in the paragraph appeal to as many of the five senses as possible?
4. Are the details presented in an order that makes sense?
5. Are descriptive adjectives and adverbs used to make the details vivid for the reader?
6. Does each sentence express a complete idea, begin with a capital letter, and end with the correct punctuation mark?

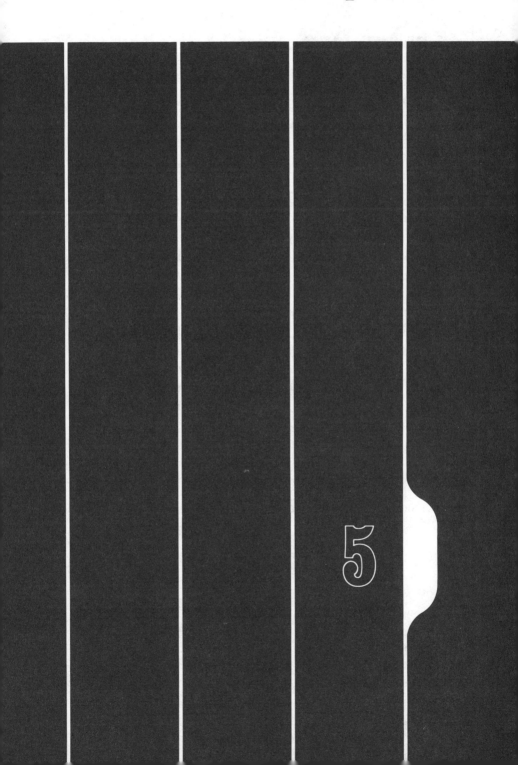

5

Complements

Lesson One

Recognizing Complements

Stan looked at himself in the mirror before leaving for school. He seemed pleased. He had chosen a pair of striped purple and gray slacks to go with a bright red plaid shirt and a blue polka-dot tie. Although it was a hot day, Stan had decided to top off the outfit with his gold and silver ski jacket because it was his favorite. As he looked in the mirror, Stan thought, "I look pretty good today. I'm sure that Anne will notice me in study hall."

When Stan arrived at study hall, he walked straight up to Anne. "Hi, Anne," he said, and he casually turned around once or twice to give her a good look at his outfit. "How do I look today?"

At first, Anne didn't know what to say. Then she said, "Well, Stan, you look — you look — that is, you look . . ."

"What's the matter?" Stan asked. "Is something stuck in your throat?"

"It's not that," Anne replied. "It's just that I want a *complement* to finish my sentence, and I can't think of one."

Stan was puzzled. "What do you mean?" he asked. "I'm the one who wants a *compliment!*"

Stan and Anne are both right. Stan wants a *compliment* (with an *i*) about the way he looks: "You look great!" or "You look super!" Anne wants a *complement* (with an *e*) for her sentence.

● A <u>complement</u> is a word or a group of words that completes the thought begun by the subject and the verb.

As you learned in Unit One, a sentence must contain a subject and a verb to express a complete thought. Anne's statement contains a subject and a verb:

You look

In some cases, however, a subject and a verb do not give enough information to express a complete thought. Anne's statement needs another word or a group of words to complete the thought:

118

You look **great.**
You look **weird.**
You look **interesting.**

The words *great, weird,* and *interesting* are complements.

Here are some other examples of subjects and verbs that need complements to express complete thoughts:

We wrapped
The guest of honor was
Pete's new car is

By adding a word or words to these fragments, you can turn them into sentences.

We wrapped the **presents.**
The guest of honor was **she.**
Pete's new car is **yellow.**

The words in boldface type are all complements. Notice that a complement can be a noun (*presents*), a pronoun (*she*), or an adjective (*yellow*).

There are five kinds of complements that you will learn about in this unit:

1. direct objects
2. indirect objects
3. predicate nominatives
4. predicate adjectives
5. object complements

PRACTICE

In the following sentences, the complements are in italics. Number your paper from 1 to 10. Write whether the complement is a *noun,* a *pronoun,* or an *adjective.*

Example: My favorite hobby is *philately.*
              noun

1. A philatelist collects *stamps.*
2. As a hobby, philately can be *fascinating.*
3. It is also *educational.*
4. After five years of collecting, I have six *albums.*
5. Stamps from South America are my *favorites.*

119

6. My collection of stamps from India is especially *good*.
7. Starting a collection is *easy*.
8. Buy an inexpensive *album*.
9. A package of assorted stamps costs very *little*.
10. Most local stamp dealers will gladly help new *collectors*.

Lesson Two

Direct Objects

How many different words can you think of to complete the thought begun by the subject and the verb below?

She discovered _____ .

Here are some possibilities.

She discovered a **secret**.
She discovered **it**.
She discovered the **treasure**.

The boldfaced words above are nouns and pronouns. As the examples below show, other parts of speech cannot complete the thought of the sentence.

She discovered *once*.   (adverb)
She discovered *beautiful*.   (adjective)
She discovered *across the floor*.   (prepositional phrase)

None of these sentences makes sense.
The complements (*secret, it, treasure*) that do make sense are called *direct objects*.

● **A direct object is a noun or a pronoun that receives the action of a transitive verb and therefore completes the meaning of the verb. A direct object answers the question *what?* or *whom?* after a transitive verb.**

We wrapped the **presents**. *(Wrapped what? Presents is the direct object of the transitive verb wrapped).*

Our team beat **them**. *(Beat whom? Them is the direct object of the transitive verb beat.)*

Did you leave the **tools** in the garage? *(Did you leave what? Tools is the direct object of the transitive verb phrase did leave.)*

A direct object is never the object of a preposition. (See Unit Three, Lesson Six.) Compare these two sentences:

Lena finished her **drawing.**
Lena finished **after midnight.**

In the first sentence, *drawing* is a direct object. It follows the transitive verb *finished* and answers the question *finished what?*

In the second sentence, *after midnight* is a prepositional phrase. *Midnight* is the object of the preposition *after*. A direct object is never the object of a preposition. The second sentence, then, does not have a direct object.

Direct objects can be compound. Here are examples of sentences with two or more direct objects.

Sal will buy a catcher's **mitt** or a **mask.** *(Will buy what?* The nouns *mitt* and *mask* form a compound direct object.)

Tina invited **Darla, Ray,** and **me** to her party. *(Invited whom?* The nouns *Darla* and *Ray* and the pronoun *me* form a compound direct object.)

Direct objects may be modified by other words, such as adjectives, articles, and possessive pronouns. The modifying word or words are not considered part of the direct object.

I wore a red cotton bowling **shirt.**

The noun *shirt* is the direct object of the verb *wore*. The article *a* and the adjectives *red, cotton,* and *bowling* modify the direct object.

Transitive Verbs and Direct Objects

As you learned in Unit Three, there are three types of verbs: transitive verbs, intransitive verbs, and linking verbs. Only transitive verbs have direct objects. Compare these two sentences:

Joanne walked the dog.
Joanne walked home.

Notice the difference in the way the verb *walked* is used in these two sentences. In the first sentence, *walked* is a transitive

121

verb. The noun that follows it, *dog,* receives the action of the verb *walked.*

In the second sentence, *walked* is an intransitive verb. It has no direct object to receive the action. The adverb *home* tells *where* she walked; it does not tell *what* she walked. A transitive verb always has a direct object; an intransitive verb never does.

Because linking verbs do not describe actions, they are never followed by direct objects. Compare these two sentences:

Edward sounded the alarm.
Edward sounded frightened.

In the first sentence, the verb *sounded* is a transitive verb. The noun *alarm* receives the action of the verb. *Alarm* is the direct object.

In the second sentence, the verb *sounded* is a linking verb. It describes a state of being rather than an action. Therefore, the second sentence does not contain a direct object. (In the second sentence, *frightened* is a different kind of a complement — a *predicate adjective*. It gives information about Edward, the subject of the sentence. You will learn more about predicate adjectives in Lesson Five.)

PRACTICE A

Number your paper from 1 to 10. Copy the direct object or objects from each sentence.

Example: Keep a good tongue in your head.   — Shakespeare
            tongue

1. I accept this award with an abiding faith in America.
                          — Martin Luther King, Jr.
2. A jest breaks no bones.   — Samuel Johnson
3. Life has no meaning except in terms of responsibility.
                          — Reinhold Neibuhr
4. The soul selects her own society. — Emily Dickinson
5. You gain strength, courage, and confidence by every experience.   — Eleanor Roosevelt
6. No one can build his security upon the nobleness of another person.   — Willa Cather
7. Hitch your wagon to a star.   — Ralph Waldo Emerson

8. Three may keep a secret, if two of them are dead.
— Benjamin Franklin

9. Towering genius disdains a beaten path.
— Abraham Lincoln

10. Time wounds all heels. — Dorothy Parker

PRACTICE B

Complete the sentences below by adding direct objects. Add any other words that are needed to make the sentence sound good to you.

Example: Carlo sold _____ to a friend.
Carlo sold his stereo to a friend.

1. I prepared _____ for tonight's dinner.
2. Should we take _____ to the park?
3. My father collects _____ .
4. Charlotte had never seen _____ before today.
5. Jack made _____ from a lump of clay.
6. We spotted _____ and _____ during our walk in the woods.
7. The workers repaired _____ .
8. Linda's dog chased _____ away from the house.
9. Jan left _____ at school.
10. The dance committee will decorate _____ with paper flowers.

PRACTICE C

Below are ten words or groups of words. Use each one as the direct object in a sentence. Underline each direct object.

Example: flowers, candy
We gave flowers and candy to our mother for her birthday.

1. stamps
2. pen, paper
3. elephants
4. campfire
5. snow, ice
6. sister, me
7. friends
8. them
9. televisions, radios, records
10. nothing

123

Lesson Three

Indirect Objects

How many words or groups of words can you think of that would make sense in the blank space below?

The coach gave _____ free passes to the game.

Here are some possibilities:

The coach gave the **teachers** free passes to the game.
The coach gave **us** free passes to the game.
The coach gave **Jane** and **Arthur** free passes to the game.

The words in boldface type are either nouns or pronouns. They come between the verbs and direct objects in their sentences. These nouns and pronouns are called *indirect objects.*

● **An underlined indirect object is a noun or a pronoun that answers the question *to what? to whom? for what?* or *for whom?* after a transitive verb. An indirect object comes between the verb and the direct object in a sentence.**

Here are some sentences containing indirect objects:

Lydia gave her **room** a fresh coat of paint. (*Gave to what? Room* is the indirect object.)

I sent my **aunt** a postcard from Vermont. (*Sent to whom? Aunt* is the indirect object.)

Dad bought the **car** radial tires. (*Bought for what? Car* is the indirect object.)

Chuck wrote his **girl friend** a poem. (*Wrote for whom? Girl friend* is the indirect object.)

These four sentences also contain direct objects. They are *coat, postcard, tires,* and *poem.*

Look at the two sentences below. Which one has an indirect object?

I told her my good news.
I told my good news to her.

In both sentences, *news* is the direct object because it answers the question *what* after the transitive verb *told.* In the first sentence, *her* is the indirect object. But in the second sentence, *her* is not an indirect object; it is the object of the preposition *to*. The object of a preposition is never an indirect object.

Like direct objects, indirect objects may be compound. Here are some sentences with compound indirect objects:

I told **Arthur** and **Michael** my good news.
Give the **windows,** the **mirrors,** and the **appliances** a thorough cleaning.

Indirect objects may be modified by adjectives, articles or possessive pronouns.

Martha told her little **sister** a story.

The indirect object is the noun *sister*. The possessive pronoun *her* and the adjective *little* modify the indirect object.

PRACTICE A

Copy the sentences below on your paper. In each sentence, circle the indirect object or objects. Underline the direct object or objects. Do not underline or circle any modifying words or conjunctions.

Example: May offered her friend some fruit.

   May offered her (friend) some fruit.

1. Robby sent his family a postcard from Los Angeles.
2. Is Matt giving his teacher another excuse for being late?
3. Tina bought herself new sneakers and socks.
4. An old car may give its owner headaches.
5. My aunt sent my mother and father an anniversary present.
6. Al tossed me the ball.
7. Marie showed the class the photo.
8. They brought the child a gift.
9. Jim is sending Heather flowers for her birthday.
10. Lee gave Harry and Brian the homework assignment.

PRACTICE B

Complete the following sentences by adding one or more indirect objects. Add any other words needed to make the sentence sound good to you. Write the completed sentences on your paper.

Example: I lent _____ my notebook.
           I lent Tim my notebook.

1. Ginny brought _____ a housewarming gift.
2. Have you given _____ their dinner yet?
3. John will send _____ a telegram.
4. Tony gave _____ some of his allowance.
5. The gas station attendant offered _____ a map.
6. Fran lent _____ her record collection.
7. My sister tossed _____ the beach ball.
8. The little boy sang _____ a song before he went to sleep.
9. Will you please give _____ the necessary information?
10. Hilda handed _____ the salad.

PRACTICE C

Write ten sentences using the nouns or pronouns below as indirect objects. Underline the indirect object in each sentence.

Example: them
           We gave <u>them</u> the money for the tickets.

1. dog
2. Sandy and Liz
3. man
4. us
5. me
6. team
7. them
8. baby
9. Mom and Dad
10. you

Lesson Four

Predicate Nominatives

Look at the sentence below:

Sherlock Holmes was a famous detective.

The subject of this sentence is *Sherlock Holmes*. The verb is *was*. And the word *detective* is the complement. It is a *subject complement*.

126

- **A <u>subject complement</u> is a noun, a pronoun, or an adjective that follows a linking verb and refers to, describes, or explains the subject.**

In the sentence on the previous page, the complement is a noun: *detective.* It follows the linking verb *was* and refers to the subject, *Sherlock Holmes.*

Here are some more examples of sentences containing subject complements. In each sentence, the subject is in italics, and the subject complement is in boldface type:

The Tyler *jewels* were **missing.**
The *thief* was **unknown.**

(The subject complements are the adjectives *missing* and *unknown.*)

The only *clue* was the half-eaten **carrot** in the hall.
"Clearly," Holmes said, "the *criminals* are a **gang** of outlaw rabbits."

(The subject complements are the nouns *carrot* and *gang.*)

The world's greatest *detective* was **he.** (The subject complement is the pronoun *he.*)

In each sentence above, the subject complement completes the meaning of the sentence by giving information about the subject.

Subject complements that are nouns or pronouns are called *predicate nominatives.*

- **A <u>predicate nominative</u> is a noun or a pronoun that follows a linking verb and refers to, describes, or explains the subject.**

The words in boldface type below are predicate nominatives:

My best friend has always been **Janet.** (The noun *Janet* follows the linking verb phrase *has been* and refers to the subject *friend. Janet* is a predicate nominative.)

Gino is the best **musician** in the band. (The noun *musician* follows the linking verb *is* and refers to the subject *Gino. Musician* is a predicate nominative.)

The soloist in the choir will be **she.** (The pronoun *she* follows the linking verb phrase *will be* and refers to the subject *soloist. She* is a predicate nominative.)

127

Like other complements, predicate nominatives may be compound. Here are examples of compound predicate nominatives:

Gino is the best **musician** and **singer** in the band.
The soloists in the choir will be **Luciano, Leontyne,** and **Beverly.**

Predicate nominatives may be modified by adjectives, articles, or possessive pronouns. The modifying words are not considered part of the predicate nominative.

You are my **sunshine.**
Terry's car is a small blue **convertible.**

The possessive pronoun *my,* the article *a,* and the adjectives *small* and *blue* modify the predicate nominatives.

PRACTICE A

Number your paper from 1 to 10. Copy the predicate nominative from each sentence. Do not copy any modifying words.

Example: Elizabeth Blackwell was the first woman doctor in America.
doctor

1. Elizabeth II is the queen of England.
2. Margaret Thatcher is the first female prime minister of Great Britain.
3. Marie Curie was the first person to win two Nobel prizes.
4. George Sand was the name used by the writer Amandine Dudevant.
5. She became a popular novelist.
6. Properzia di Rossi was the first well-known female sculptor in Italy.
7. Marie Tussaud was a renowned artist.
8. The famous and the infamous were the subjects of her wax models.
9. Today Madame Tussaud's Wax Museum is a favorite tourist attraction in London.
10. Ruth Handler was the creator of the Barbie doll.

PRACTICE B

Copy the sentences below on your paper. Fill in each blank by adding a predicate nominative. Add any other words that are needed to make the sentence sound good to you. Write the completed sentences on your paper.

Example: My favorite sport is _____ .
           My favorite sport is baseball.

1. One place that I really want to visit is _____ .
2. My cousin is _____ .
3. The store on the corner is _____ .
4. The best movie that I ever saw was _____ .
5. Leslie's favorite meal is _____ .
6. One day Henry will become _____ .
7. Jackie's favorite singer is _____ .
8. The most expensive item that I ever bought was _____ .
9. The best time of the year is _____ .
10. One thing that still costs less than a dollar is _____ .

PRACTICE C

Number your paper from 1 to 10. Use each of the nouns below as a predicate nominative in a sentence of your own.

Example: captain
           Paul will be the captain of the team next year.

1. London
2. champion
3. spinach
4. song
5. cities
6. winter
7. cartoons
8. musician
9. planet
10. astronauts

Lesson Five

Predicate Adjectives

In Lesson Four, you read about Sherlock Holmes and the Tyler jewel robbery. Did the great detective ever solve the mystery? Was a gang of outlaw rabbits really to blame? In this lesson, you will find out. Look at the sentence below.

The case of the Tyler jewel robbery was closed.

The subject of this sentence is *case*. The verb is the linking verb *was*. And the adjective *closed* is the subject complement. It is a *predicate adjective*.

- A <u>predicate adjective</u> is an adjective that follows a linking verb and modifies the subject.

In the sentence above, the adjective *closed* follows the linking verb *was* and modifies the subject *case*.

Here are more examples of sentences containing predicate adjectives.

Sherlock Holmes had been **correct.** (*Correct* follows the linking verb phrase *had been* and modifies the subject *Sherlock Holmes*.)

A gang of outlaw rabbits was **responsible.** (*Responsible* follows the linking verb *was* and modifies the subject *gang*.)

They had become **greedy** after hearing of Mrs. Tyler's twenty-carat diamond. (*Greedy* follows the linking verb phrase *had become* and modifies the subject *they*.)

However, the rabbits had been **confused.** (*Confused* follows the linking verb phrase *had been* and modifies the subject *rabbits*.)

Unfortunately for the rabbits, "carats" and "carrots" are **different.** (*Different* follows the linking verb *are* and modifies the compound subject *"carats" and "carrots."*)

Like other complements, predicate adjectives can be compound.

Holmes seemed **proud** and **pleased.**
Mrs. Tyler was **grateful** and **overjoyed.**
The rabbits looked **annoyed** and **embarrassed.**

PRACTICE A

Number your paper from 1 to 10. Copy the predicate adjective or adjectives from each sentence. Do not copy any conjunctions.

Example: That car is old and rusty.
           old, rusty

1. My room is blue and white.
2. Gerry has become quite thin.
3. The baby is sleepy.
4. The movie was sad.
5. Our neighbors always seem noisy late at night.
6. Doreen is happy about the news.
7. Smog is dangerous for people with heart conditions.
8. Jenny's dress is colorful.
9. Your story sounds interesting.
10. The new boy in our class seems shy.

PRACTICE B

Fill in the blanks below by adding predicate adjectives. Write the completed sentences on your paper.

Example: The abandoned house seemed _____ to the children.
           The abandoned house seemed scary to the children.

1. The old dog was _____ .
2. I became _____ before the job interview.
3. The trip to the mountain was _____ .
4. The lake looks _____ tonight.
5. Strawberries taste _____ .
6. This record sounds _____ .
7. Monica sometimes appears _____ .
8. Julio will be _____ when he hears about this.
9. The tour guide was _____ .
10. The actors in the play were _____ .

PRACTICE C

On the next page is a list of twenty adjectives. Choose ten, and use each as a predicate adjective in a sentence of your own.

Example: tired
           I am usually tired after gym.

131

eager	warm
important	lazy
difficult	late
beautiful	delicious
exciting	happy
funny	bored
colorful	cool
sour	embarrassed
heavy	energetic
dull	stormy

Lesson Six

Object Complements

In Lesson Four you learned that the subject of a sentence can have a complement — a noun, pronoun, or adjective in the predicate that completes the meaning of the subject.

A direct object can have a complement, too.

● **An <u>object complement</u> is a noun, pronoun, or adjective that comes after the direct object and completes the meaning of the object.**

The object complement identifies or describes the direct object. Since object complements occur with direct objects, they are always in sentences with action verbs rather than linking verbs.

Here are some examples:

They call the dog **Hector.**
(The noun *Hector* identifies the direct object *dog.*)

My mother made the curtains too **long.** (The adjective *long* describes the direct object *curtains.*)

I consider Mike **one** of my best friends. (The pronoun *one* identifies the direct object *Mike.*)

The team elected him **captain.** (The noun *captain* identifies the direct object *him.*)

Notice the following about object complements:

1. The object complement may have modifiers of its own:

I consider Mike **one** of my best friends. (The prepositional phrase *of my best friends* modifies the object complement *one*.)

My mother made the curtains too **long**. (The adverb *too* modifies the object complement *long*.)

2. An object complement affects the meaning of the sentence. Sometimes it changes the meaning.

They call the dog.
They call the dog **Hector**.

The second sentence means something different from the first sentence.

Sometimes the object complement just adds information.

Mother painted the kitchen.
Mother painted the kitchen **yellow**.

The second sentence tells you more than the first.

Sometimes the object complement completes the meaning of a group of words that would not make sense without it.

I consider Mike
I consider Mike **one** of my best friends.

The first group of words does not express a complete thought. The second does.

3. Only certain verbs can have objects with complements. The most common verbs that can have objects with complements are *find, make, name, call, consider, elect,* and *appoint.* Notice the verbs in these examples:

We **found** the party very dull.
Her gift **made** me very happy.
We **call** my grandfather Popi.
I **named** my turtle Ralph.
The mayor **appointed** her police commissioner.

4. You should not confuse an indirect object plus direct object with a direct object plus object complement. An indirect object tells to whom or for whom something is done.

Jeanne taught me **French**. (The indirect object is *me*. The direct object is *French*.)

An object complement completes the meaning of the direct object.

Jeanne calls **French** the **language** of diplomacy. (The direct object is *French*. The object complement is *language*.)

PRACTICE A

Write the object complement from each sentence on your paper.

Example: My family calls our car Supercar.
Supercar

1. The City Council appointed Mrs. Rodriguez chairperson.
2. The team calls Marge "Speedy."
3. The coach considers Pedro one of the fastest runners in the school.
4. The barber cut my hair too short.
5. The senior class elected her treasurer.
6. Eileen finds her sister's advice helpful.
7. Waiting for a phone call makes him jumpy.
8. The biology class named its pet frog Hoppy.
9. Jay painted his van purple.
10. The jury declared Marla the winner of the photo contest.

PRACTICE B

Make two columns on your paper. Label one *Direct Object*. Label the other *Object Complement*. Write the direct objects and object complements from the sentences below in the correct columns. Not every sentence has both a direct object and an object complement. Some sentences may have neither.

Example: In the fourth grade, a group of my friends formed a club.

Direct Object	Object Complement
club	—

1. We named the club The Explorers.
2. For our first trip we went to the local zoo.

3. The zoo keepers had put many different animals in a large wilderness area.
4. After the trip we Explorers wanted our own wilderness area.
5. The group appointed me keeper of the zoo.
6. We collected animals from local ponds and swamps.
7. We called my yard The Great American Swamp.
8. We made plans for an island with a moat around it.
9. Unfortunately, my parents found the idea unacceptable.
10. They declared The Great American Swamp closed before it even opened.

PRACTICE C

For each verb listed below, write two sentences. In the first sentence, do not use an object complement. In the second sentence, use an object complement. Underline each direct object once and each object complement twice.

Example: consider
          I'll consider your idea.
          The teacher considers Elmer the best typist in class.

1. name
2. call
3. elect
4. choose
5. paint

Review Exercises

I. The following sentences lack complements. Number your paper from 1 to 10. Add a complement to each sentence. Write the completed sentences on your paper. (Lesson One)

Example: Michael cooked _____ .
          Michael cooked dinner.

1. Ellen and her father collect _____ .
2. The weather this afternoon appears _____ .
3. After falling into the pool, the cat was _____ .

4. The excited fans enjoyed _____ .
5. Mr. Arrigo carefully repaired _____ .
6. My brother's old radio sounds _____ .
7. The children carelessly broke _____ .
8. The view from the top of the mountain is _____ .
9. The sport I enjoy watching the most is _____ .
10. Jay telephoned _____ .

II. Copy the following sentences on your paper. Underline each direct object. Circle each indirect object. Not every sentence contains both a direct and an indirect object. Do not underline or circle any modifying words or conjunctions. (Lessons Two and Three)

Example: Alex bought us tickets for the rock concert.
           Alex bought (us) tickets for the rock concert.

1. Larry has an appointment with the dentist tomorrow.
2. Roxanne told us a joke.
3. Nancy wrote a letter to her aunt in Canada.
4. Steve makes delicious sandwiches.
5. Mrs. Allen gave the class a quiz.
6. The department store is having a sale this week.
7. Luis fed the baby some custard.
8. Too much sun can dry a person's skin.
9. My brother wants a new motorcycle.
10. Will you feed my fish?

III. In each sentence below, the subject complement is in italics. Number your paper from 1 to 10. For each sentence, write whether the subject complement is a *predicate nominative* or a *predicate adjective*. (Lessons Four and Five)

Examples: Laura and Andy are the best *debaters.*
           predicate nominative

           The twins are not *identical.*
           predicate adjective

1. Dried mushrooms are a basic *ingredient* in many Chinese receipes.
2. Fresh fish is my favorite *dinner.*

3. The tape is *broken,* so I can't hear the song.
4. Ramon will be the *cook* on Thanksgiving Day.
5. Francie seems *happier* today.
6. The eggs taste *good.*
7. Jazz is my favorite *kind* of music.
8. Rosco felt *weak* after standing in the sun all day.
9. I will be a *pilot* someday.
10. My uncle is only two years *older* than I.

IV. Copy the following sentences on your paper. Underline the object complement in each sentence. Do not underline any modifying words. (Lesson Six)

Example: The team considers my dog its mascot.
           The team considers my dog its <u>mascot</u>.

1. They call the announcer Mr. Newsworthy.
2. The Drama Club dyed the costumes yellow.
3. The prom committee elected him chairperson.
4. The children named their puppies Lost and Found.
5. They painted the table and chair green.
6. The dance teacher considers the class talented.
7. Today's beautiful spring weather makes me cheerful.
8. Bob found the science fair fascinating.
9. Mr. Warren calls his boat the *Undaunted.*
10. I consider Ellen the team's best player.

V. Choose one of the topics below. Write at least seven sentences about the topic. In your sentences, include at least one example of each kind of complement: *direct object, indirect object, predicate nominative, predicate adjective,* and *subject complement.* After each sentence, identify the kind of complement that you used. (Lessons One to Six)

Topics:
My Favorite Kind Of Music
A Special Place
My Neighborhood
A Friend
A topic of your own choice

Writing a Composition

Lesson One
Choosing a Topic

Near the end of Phyllis's English class, her teacher made an announcement. "I'd like each of you to write a composition to hand in next Friday. Your composition should be from four to six paragraphs long. Here is the topic I'd like you to write about." Turning to the board, the teacher wrote the word *Sports*.

Some of the students in class smiled when they saw the topic *Sports*. Kathy, who sat next to Phyllis, said happily, "What a great topic! I can write about how I learned to water-ski last summer." Tom, who sat behind Phyllis, said, "I was just reading a magazine article about college football stars. I'm going to write about that."

However, Phyllis was not pleased with the topic. "Why do I have to write about sports?" she wondered. "I'm not very athletic, and I don't really like going to baseball games or football games, either. I don't even watch the Super Bowl on TV. How can I write a whole composition about sports?"

Someday you may have a problem similar to Phyllis's: You may be asked to write a composition about a topic that you feel doesn't interest you. If this happens, don't worry. There are ways of turning a topic that doesn't seem very promising into one that you can write about with interest and enjoyment. Here are a few suggestions.

Try to relate the topic to something that interests you. For many school assignments, you will be asked to write about a *general topic,* such as sports, current events, astronomy, poetry, or the Civil War. The *specific topic* on which you will focus is up to you. You can probably find a specific topic that interests you, even if the general topic does not seem exciting. To find an interesting specific topic, think about your special interests, hobbies, favorite school subjects, and so on.

Here is an example. Phyllis must write a composition about sports. But sports in general are not interesting to her. She is much more interested in some other topics, including modern dance, psychology, and wild animals. However, Phyllis can turn the general topic of sports into an interesting specific topic by relating it to one of her interests. For example, she could relate sports to dance by comparing the training of athletes with that of dancers or by comparing the moves of a basketball player with the movements used in modern dance. She could relate sports to psychology by writing about the psychology of sports competition or about the psychological pressures on professional athletes. She could relate sports to her interest in animals by comparing the record performances of runners, high-jumpers, and swimmers to the abilities of such animals as the cheetah, the kangaroo, and the dolphin. By relating the general topic of sports to a specific topic that interests her, Phyllis can make the assignment interesting for herself.

Learn more about the topic. In many cases, a topic may seem uninteresting to you because you don't know very much about it. Learning more about the general topic will often help you recognize specific topics that interest you. You may develop a new interest in a topic that you had previously considered boring.

One way to learn more about a general topic is to talk with someone who knows a lot about it. Try asking someone how he or she first became interested in the topic, or how you can find out more about it. The answers may suggest something you would like to write about. If you are assigned to write about sports, for example, you could talk with your school's basketball coach, the sports reporter on the school newspaper, or a star performer on a school team.

Another good way to learn about a topic is to visit the library. Look through some newspaper or magazine articles about your general topic (the librarian can help you to find them). You may find a specific topic that captures your interest. Try browsing through the shelves that contain books on your topic. One of these books may spark an interest in a particular topic.

Phyllis decided to go to her school library and look through the shelves devoted to books on sports. She discovered several books on the Olympic Games. The books made her realize that there *was* one aspect of sports that interested her: every four years she watched the Olympic Games on television. She liked many of the events — the races, the gymnastics, the swimming, and diving. She found herself in awe of the athletes' grace and skill, and she noticed that their performances reminded her of modern dance. Phyllis hadn't thought of the Olympics as an aspect of *sports;* she had thought only of football and baseball. But she was pleased with her discovery. So she decided to write a composition about the Olympics.

Limiting the Topic

When you are asked to write a composition, you will usually be assigned a certain length for the composition. If the required length is, for example, four to six paragraphs, you will need to choose a topic that can be covered in a composition of that length. Perhaps you've decided to write about space travel. Many whole books have been written on the subject of space travel. The topic is too broad to be covered in a short composition. But if you limit the topic to the experiences of one astronaut or a description of the first satellite to orbit the earth, you can probably cover the topic in four to six paragraphs.

Phyllis quickly realized that the topic of the Olympic Games could not be fully covered in four to six paragraphs. The Olympic Games was more specific than the general topic of sports, but it needed to be limited further before she could use it for her composition.

In order to narrow down her topic further, Phyllis spent time thinking about it. She jotted down some aspects of the Olympic Games that she was curious about and would like to learn more about. She glanced through one of the books about the Olympic Games that she had found in the library, and she jotted down some of the details mentioned there that interested her. Then she thought back to her experience of watching the Olympic Games on television and jotted down some notes about things that she remembered most clearly.

Here are some of the notes that Phyllis jotted down while thinking about the Olympic Games:

famous gold medal winners
how athletes train for the Olympics
the early history of the Olympics
rules of the Olympics
how Jesse Owens became a hero at the 1936 Olympics

great women Olympic stars
the American gold medal in hockey at the 1980 Olympics
are the Olympic Games too political?
greatest feats at the Olympics
the decathlon — what it is, who has won it

Phyllis looked over her ideas about the Olympics, thinking about a way to limit the topic. One of the notes she had jotted down was "the early history of the Olympics." Phyllis knew that the Olympic Games had originated in ancient Greece and had been revived in modern times. She was curious to know more about how this had happened. So she decided that a historical approach to her topic might be good.

However, a complete history of the Olympics would still be too broad a topic for a composition of four to six paragraphs. She needed to choose *one* aspect of the topic for her composition. For example, she could describe the first Olympics played in modern times, or she could discuss how the ancient games were different from those that are played today. Finally, Phyllis decided to write about how the earliest Olympic Games were started in Greece centuries ago. This was a topic that she could write about in four to six paragraphs.

EXERCISE ONE

The following list contains ten general topics. Choose three that you might like to write about. For each general topic you choose, think of two specific topics that interest you. Write a phrase or sentence describing each specific topic. The specific topics do not have to be topics you know a lot about, only topics that you would like to learn about and write about.

Example: General Topic: Music
Specific Topics:
Playing the Guitar
The Record Industry

General Topics:
1. Movies
2. United States History
3. Education

4. Family Life
5. Safety
6. My Neighborhood
7. Careers
8. Villains
9. Science
10. Hobbies

EXERCISE TWO

Look at the six specific topics you listed for Exercise One. Choose one. Jot down as many specific ideas related to the topic as you can. If you like, you can talk about the topic with other people or look at newspapers, magazines, or books for ideas. The notes you jot down can be phrases or sentences. Write at least ten ideas.

Example: Specific Topic: Playing the Guitar
           Notes:
           how I learned to play the guitar
           who is the best rock 'n' roll guitarist?
           the electric guitar vs. the acoustic guitar
           Chuck Berry's guitar-playing style
           the invention of the electric guitar
           the history of the guitar
           how guitars are built
           buying a used guitar
           how to tune a guitar
           unusual guitars
           styles of guitar playing

EXERCISE THREE

Look over the ideas you wrote for Exercise Two. Can any of them be covered in four to six paragraphs? If so, choose the one you would most like to write about.

If none of your ideas is an interesting limited topic, try to think of one. You may be able to narrow down one of the ideas you wrote for Exercise One. Or you may think of a new idea that could be used for a topic.

144

When you have chosen a topic that you think you can cover in a composition of four to six paragraphs, write a sentence or phrase that describes it as clearly as possible. Save this paper for use later in the unit.

Lesson Two

Developing a Theme

A builder who simply piled bricks on top of one another would probably not end up with an attractive or useful building. A good building begins with a plan. And the first step in planning a building is deciding what you want to build: a cottage, an office building, an auditorium.

A good composition begins with a plan, too. The first step in planning a composition is to develop a *theme statement.*

- **A theme statement is a sentence that summarizes the main point of the composition.**

A composition isn't just a series of sentences and paragraphs strung together, any more than a building is just a pile of bricks. A composition must make some point about the topic. Writing a theme statement will help you to clarify the point that you want to make about the topic.

You learned in Unit Two that every paragraph should have a topic sentence which expresses the main idea of the paragraph. All the other sentences in a paragraph must relate to the topic sentence. A theme statement is like a topic sentence for a composition. All of the facts and ideas that appear in the composition must relate to the theme statement.

Unlike the topic sentence of a paragraph, a theme statement doesn't have to appear in the composition. However, it is always useful to write a theme statement before writing the composition. You can refer to the theme statement as you write to make sure that every fact and idea you mention relates to the theme statement.

To write a theme statement, you must decide what you want to say about your topic. If the topic is one that you are familiar with from personal experience, you may be able to write a theme statement simply by thinking about the topic. For example, if your topic is "How I Learned to Play the Guitar," your theme statement could simply summarize the experience: "Learning to play the guitar took me one summer of intense concentration, hard work, hours of practice, and sore fingers."

If the topic is one you have a strong feeling about, your theme statement should express your feeling. For the topic, "Who Is the Best Rock 'n' Roll Guitarist?" the theme statement might be, "Eric Clapton is the best rock 'n' roll guitarist because his guitar playing is always exciting and unique, yet perfectly suited to the particular song."

If the topic is one you must learn about from reading or by talking to experts, you will probably have to finish your reading or talking before you can write a theme statement.

After reading about the early history of the Olympic Games in several books, Phyllis realized that the ancient Olympics were very different from the Olympics of today. Here is the theme statement she wrote to sum up this idea: "The ancient Greeks created the Olympic Games over 2,500 years ago as a religious celebration of excellence in both mind and body."

When Phyllis writes her composition, she may or may not include this sentence. However, writing the sentence helped Phyllis to focus her thoughts on one specific idea. Keeping this idea in mind as she writes will help Phyllis to write a clear and unified composition.

EXERCISE FOUR

Look back at the topic you wrote for Exercise Three. Write a theme statement that could be used for a composition about the topic. Be sure your theme statement is a complete sentence. You do not have to write a composition, only a theme statement.

Example: Topic: Buying a Used Guitar
Theme Statement:
It's easy to find a bargain in a used guitar if you know what kind of guitar you want, where to look for it, and how to judge the condition of a used guitar.

Lesson Three

Organizing Your Ideas

After you have decided on a topic and written a theme statement, it's time to organize your ideas about the topic so that they can be put together in a clear and interesting composition.

Begin by writing down all the ideas, facts, and details you can think of that might relate to your theme statement. Some of these notes may come from personal experience; others may be facts or ideas you learned from reading about the topic or talking to others. Include everything you think might be good to include in your composition.

Write these notes in the order in which you think of the ideas. Don't worry about grammar or spelling; the notes are only for your use in organizing your composition.

Here are the notes Phyllis wrote for her paper on the early history of the Olympics:

> place and time early games began: Greek valley, 2,500 years
>   ago
> reasons games were started
> the modern games: problems they face
> where the name "Olympics" came from
> opening ceremonies of the ancient games
> reasons the Olympics should be continued
> events included in the early Olympics; the pentathlon
> growth and change of the ancient games
> olive wreaths used as prizes
> how the ancient Olympics ended
> the 1984 Olympics in Los Angeles
> the Greek Olympics after 146 B.C.

When Phyllis looked over her list, she realized that some of the items did not relate to her theme statement: "The ancient Greeks created the Olympic games over 2,500 years ago as a religious celebration of excellence in both mind and body." Phyllis knew that she had to cross out any idea that did not relate to the theme statement. The three points that Phyllis crossed off her list are at the top of the next page.

the modern games: problems they face
reasons the Olympics should be continued
the 1984 Olympics in Los Angeles

EXERCISE FIVE

Look back at the theme statement you wrote for Exercise Four. Jot down five to ten ideas, facts, or details that might be related to the theme statement. These may include ideas from your reading or from personal experience. Check these items against your theme statement. Does each item relate to the theme statement? Cross out any that do not. Add any other ideas that you think of. Save this paper.

Grouping Related Ideas

Once you have listed your ideas, the next step is to organize them into groups. This will help you to group your ideas into paragraphs when your write your composition.

Look again at the notes Phyllis wrote for her composition (page 147). In reviewing them, Phyllis began to see ways in which the points might be grouped. For example, she saw that three items dealt directly with the founding of the Olympics:

place and time early games began: Greek valley, 2,500 years
   ago
reasons the games were started
where the name "Olympics" came from

Since these points related directly to the same topic — the first Olympics — Phyllis felt that they belonged together in the same paragraph.

Phyllis found other points that seemed to belong together. The points that covered opening ceremonies, prizes, and events all helped to describe the ancient games. These points belonged together in another paragraph. Finally, Phyllis saw that she had a third group of items. These items related to changes in the early Olympics. Phyllis decided to put these items together in another paragraph.

Phyllis rewrote her list of notes, grouping the items.

Here are her rewritten notes:

The founding of the Olympics
place and time early games began: Greek valley, 2,500 years
   ago
reasons the games were started
where the name "Olympics" came from

Description of the early games
opening ceremonies of the ancient games
events included in the early Olympics; the pentathlon
olive wreaths used as prizes

Changes in the early Olympics
growth and change of the ancient games
the Greek Olympics after 146 B.C.
how the ancient Olympics ended

When writing a composition, group items from your notes that
belong together. The groups you create will be the bases for the
paragraphs in your composition.

EXERCISE SIX

Look over the list of notes you made for Exercise Five. Do any
of the points on the list seem to belong together? Try to group
your notes into two, three, or four related groups. If some items
seem unrelated to any others, you can either cross them out or
think of new facts, ideas, or details that are related to them. Do
not have any groups that contain only one item.

Copy the items from your list onto another paper, grouping
items that belong together. Save this list.

Ordering Paragraphs

Once you have grouped ideas that belong together to form
paragraphs, you can decide on how to order the paragraphs of
your composition. You can order them in any of a number of
ways. You can arrange them in *chronological order,* beginning
with paragraphs that tell about things that happened first, and
ending with paragraphs that tell about things that happened last.
You can arrange them in *order of importance,* putting your most
important ideas either first or last in the composition. You can

even use *spatial order* if your composition is descriptive. (See Unit Two, Lesson Five, for a review of each of these methods for ordering ideas.)

For some topics, there may be one way of ordering paragraphs that is especially appropriate. Phyllis found that the paragraphs in her composition about the Olympic Games fell naturally into chronological order. She decided that she would tell first about the founding of the Olympic Games; next, about how the games were played; and finally about how they grew, changed, and came to an end.

The choice of a method for ordering your paragraphs is up to you. There may be more than one way to order your paragraphs effectively. You might want to experiment by trying two or three different plans before choosing the one you like best. The important point is that the paragraphs in your composition should be in an order that makes sense to you.

EXERCISE SEVEN

Decide on an order for the paragraph groupings you wrote for Exercise Six. Number the groups on that list in the order you want to use. Be sure that the order makes sense to you.

Lesson Four
Writing an Introduction

There are three basic parts to a composition: the *introduction,* the *body,* and the *conclusion.*

The *introduction* of a composition is usually one paragraph long. It should give the reader an idea of what the main idea of the composition is. (You may wish to include your theme statement in your introduction.) But a good introduction should do more than state the topic. An introduction should capture the reader's attention so that he or she will want to keep reading.

Phyllis wrote three possible introductions for her composition about the Olympic Games. Which do you think does the best job of capturing the reader's attention?

Introduction One

In this composition, I am going to write about the early years of the Olympics. I will tell how and why the Olympics began and what the early games were like. I will also tell how a Roman emperor put a halt to the Olympic Games.

Introduction Two

You are about to read about a very interesting subject. This composition will tell you about the early Olympics, or it will try. It isn't a subject that a lot of people know about. I hope that when you finish, you'll find it as interesting as I did.

Introduction Three

If you've ever thrilled to the colorful, dramatic spectacle of the Olympic Games, you may have wondered how it all began. Who were the first athletes to test their skills and strength in these contests? You may be surprised to learn that the birth of the Olympic Games took place centuries ago in a warm, green Greek valley, far from the global spotlight that shines on the Olympics of today.

You can probably see which of the three paragraphs is the best introduction to Phyllis's composition. Introduction One is dull; it does little more than tell what the composition is going to cover, step by step. This is unnecessary, since the reader is about to read the composition itself. When you read this introduction, you may wonder if reading further will be worth the effort. Will the composition be as dull as the introduction?

Introduction Two has different faults. It tells the reader that the composition will be "interesting." But that is something the reader will soon judge. Introduction Two also has a hesitant, uncertain feeling. The last sentence doesn't say anything; it simply takes up space.

Like the other introductions, Introduction Three lets the reader know that the composition will be about the early Olympics. But it introduces the topic in an entertaining way. Introduction Three tries to suggest what makes the Olympics exciting, and it arouses curiosity by hinting at what the reader will learn by finishing the composition. Introduction Three is the one that Phyllis chose to use.

Here are a few ways to write an introductory paragraph that will grab your reader's attention.

1. *Use vivid, descriptive words.* An opening paragraph that appeals to the senses can help gain the reader's interest. The reference in Phyllis's paragraph to "the colorful, dramatic spectacle of the Olympic Games" is an example. Here is another example of a descriptive introduction: "Many centuries ago, a young athlete stood poised, waiting for the signal to begin the race. In his eyes was the burning Greek sun, under his feet the hardened earth of the Olympic Valley. His muscles tensed, his teeth clenched. The call was given!"

2. *Ask a question.* Asking an interesting question will make the reader want to learn the answer. In Phyllis's introduction, she asks the question, "Who were the first athletes to test their skills and strength in these contests?" This question will be answered in the body of the composition.

3. *Hint at something to come.* If you hint at what the composition will tell without giving details or explaining, your reader will be curious to learn more. The last sentence of Phyllis's introduction uses this technique.

4. *Use a quotation.* If you have done some outside reading about your topic, you may want to quote a few words by an expert on the topic. An interesting, relevant quotation will show your reader that you know the topic well.

5. *Use humor.* If you are writing about a topic that lends itself to a light tone, humor is often a good way to create the right mood. Don't strain the limits of your topic in order to drag in an unrelated joke, but a casual or humorous introduction that is related closely to your topic can be effective.

EXERCISE EIGHT

Write three different introductory paragraphs for a composition on the topic you chose for Exercise Three. Each introduction should be from four to six sentences long. When you finish, reread all three introductions. Does each one reveal the topic and your main idea? Which one will probably best capture the reader's attention? Choose the introduction you like best and work on it until it is as interesting as possible. Save this paper for use later in the unit.

Lesson Five

Writing the Body of the Composition

The *body* of a composition includes all but the introduction and conclusion of the composition. The body covers most of the ideas you want to express about your topic.

In Lesson Three, you saw that related ideas, facts, and details should be grouped together. Each group of ideas will make up one paragraph of the body of the composition. Paragraphs are written by adding details, descriptive words, and explanations to the list of ideas to be included in the paragraph.

Here is the list of ideas Phyllis wrote for one paragraph of her composition:

place and time early games began: Greek valley, 2,500 years ago
reasons the games were started
where the name "Olympics" came from

Here is how Phyllis turned the list into a complete paragraph:

There is no exact record of when the Olympic Games began. Ancient records place the earliest games over 2,500 years ago. Because the Greeks felt that excellence in both spirit and body was important, they developed a celebration of athletic skills as part of a religious festival. Unlike the modern games, which are athletic contests only, the first Olympics were an important rite of Greek civilization. These early games were held in a sacred valley called "Olympia." The event therefore was known as the "Olympic Games," even when the location was changed.

Notice how Phyllis used facts and details from her reading to add interest to the paragraph. If you were writing about a topic drawn from personal experience, you would use facts and details from your own life to develop the paragraph.

Phyllis used the same basic method to write the second and third paragraphs of the body of her composition.

Transitions Between Paragraphs

To help the ideas in the body of your composition flow smoothly from one paragraph to the next, use *transitional words and phrases* to connect the paragraphs.

As you learned in Unit Two, Lesson Six, transitional words and phrases help to link ideas together. They can link ideas from one sentence to the next within a paragraph. They can also link ideas from one paragraph to the next within a composition. When transitional words and phrases are used to link paragraphs, they usually appear in either the first or the last sentence of a paragraph.

Here are some examples of how transitional words and phrases can be used to link paragraphs:

Fossil fuels are energy sources created from the remains of living things. Many of our most common sources of energy are fossil fuels, including coal, oil, and gas. Because the natural processes that create fossil fuels are extremely slow, it takes millions of years for the earth to produce a supply of any of these fuels. Yet a modern industrial society can use that supply in only a few years.

Therefore, fossil fuels are becoming scarce, and their prices are steadily rising. Scientists, engineers, and business people are searching for other sources of the energy needed for the future.

The transitional word *therefore* at the start of the second paragraph in the example above helps to link the two paragraphs together. The word *therefore* shows that the facts described in the first paragraph are *causes* of the situation described in the second paragraph. The transitional word makes the relationship between the two paragraphs easier to understand.

Ask most people who Thomas Edison was, and they will reply, "The inventor of the light bulb." Edison did develop the first practical incandescent lamp, the bulb that brought electric lighting to the whole nation and much of the world. **However,** the light bulb was not the only achievement of Edison, who has been called "the greatest inventor in history."

In addition to the light bulb, Edison invented literally hundreds of other machines. These inventions include the phonograph, the mimeograph copier, several types of electric motors and generators, the alkaline electric battery, and the kinetoscope, a forerunner of the movies.

In this example, the end of the first paragraph and the beginning of the second paragraph are closely linked. The transitional word *however* at the beginning of the last sentence of the first paragraph shows that the composition is about to describe Edison's achievements other than the light bulb. And the transitional phrase *in addition to* at the beginning of the second paragraph helps to show that the paragraph will list some of the other inventions that were hinted at in the first paragraph.

Several kinds of relationships can be shown through transitional words and phrases: *spatial* relationships, *chronological* relationships, *cause and effect* relationships, *differences* or *contrasts,* and *similarities.* Unit Two, Lesson Six, gives examples of the transitional words that can be used to show these kinds of relationships.

EXERCISE NINE

Look at the groups of notes you wrote for Exercises Six and Seven. Ideas and facts that belong together should be listed together there. Use the notes you wrote to write two, three, or four paragraphs to make up the body of your composition. Use transitional words and phrases to help the paragraphs flow more smoothly.

Lesson Six

Writing a Conclusion

A good composition doesn't end abruptly. It needs a conclusion to "wrap up" the topic in a satisfying and interesting way. A good conclusion can take several different forms. It can sum up what has been said in the composition; it can leave the reader with a thought-provoking idea; it can make a point with a striking example or an appropriate quotation. In any case, a strong conclusion helps to bring a composition to a successful finish.

Here are three possible concluding paragraphs for Phyllis's composition about the ancient Olympic Games. Which one do you think is best?

Conclusion One

There's a lot more I could say about the Olympics, but there isn't enough room. I hope you have a better idea about the history of the early Olympic Games after reading this. I think that the story of the ancient Greek Olympics is a very interesting one. I'm sure you agree.

Conclusion Two

Since 1896, the Olympic Games have been held every four years except for periods during the two World Wars. The Olympic Games of the twentieth century are different in many ways from those first played over twenty-five centuries ago. They are international in scope, and the religious element is gone. Yet the Olympic spirit of long ago still lives in the dedication of the athletes to the achievement of excellence in mind and body.

Conclusion Three

The last Olympic Games were held in 1980 in Moscow. The athletes of the United States did not participate as a protest against some of the policies of the USSR, the host nation. The athletes of the world hope that disputes among nations will not disrupt future Olympic Games.

Conclusion One is a poor conclusion. It doesn't sum up what has been said in the composition, and it doesn't offer any interesting facts or ideas. It merely lets the reader know that there is more material that might have been covered. It is a dull ending.

Conclusion Two gives a bit of new information (in the first sentence). It also sums up the main idea of the composition by describing the spirit of the Olympics that has endured from ancient times until today. Paragraph Two is a good conclusion to the composition.

156

Conclusion Three also gives new information. However, it wanders from the main idea of the composition. Because Conclusion Three is about only the modern Olympics, it seems unrelated to the rest of the composition. Therefore, it is not a good conclusion.

Here are some suggestions for writing a good conclusion for a composition.

1. *Summarize the main idea.* You may want to include the theme statement in your conclusion, or you may want to sum up the main idea of the composition in other words. Either way, your conclusion will leave the reader with a clear idea of the point of the composition.

2. *End with a striking detail.* You may want to use an interesting or surprising fact or detail at the end of your composition. Try to choose a detail that is closely related to the main idea.

3. *End with a quotation.* Like the introduction, the conclusion of a composition can be a good place to introduce an appropriate quotation from an expert on the topic.

4. *End with a question.* A question at the end of a composition can cause the reader to think about the topic afterward. Here is an example of how Phyllis could have used a question to conclude her composition: "After studying the history of the ancient Olympics, I wonder: Are today's Olympic Games becoming too commercial? Is the spirit of sportsmanship that helped create the games centuries ago in danger of vanishing forever?"

Remember that a conclusion should not introduce a completely new topic. It may give the reader "food for thought," but it should not wander from the main idea of the composition.

EXERCISE TEN

Write three different concluding paragraphs for the composition you worked on in Exercise Nine. Refer to the theme statement you wrote for Exercise Four. Remember that your conclusion *may* contain the theme statement or *may* sum up the main idea in other words. It should not wander far from the main idea expressed in the theme statement.

When you finish, reread all three conclusions. Which one is most likely to interest the reader? Which one will probably leave the reader with the clearest idea of the main point of the composition? Choose the conclusion you like best. Save this paper for use later in the unit.

Lesson Seven

Revising Your Composition

By now, you have followed Phyllis through the process of writing a composition. You have also written the three main parts of a composition of your own: the introduction, the body, and the conclusion. Is your work finished?

Not quite. You have completed a *first draft* of your composition. A first draft is one important step on the road to a finished composition. A first draft may contain spelling errors, sentence fragments, awkward sentences, grammatical errors, and other weaknesses. After writing your first draft, you must revise the composition to make it as clear, interesting, and correct as possible.

Here is the first draft of a part of Phyllis's composition.

There is hardly no exact record of when the Olympic Games first began, ancient records tell us that they began over 2,500 years ago. That is a long time. The Greeks wanted to honor body and spirit, so they developed a celebration of athletic skills. Which would be religious, too. They were held in a valley called "Olympia." The name stuck. The opening ceremonies began with someone carrying a torch. The torch was carried from Athens, which was the capital city and still is today, to the place where the Greeks would hold these events. This would honor Zeus, the king of the gods. People don't usually believe in the ancient gods today. There was also a pig that was killed to honor the gods. This was a strange custom, if you ask me. They made the athletes swear on the pig's blud that they would not cheat. If anyone was caught cheating, they made him pay money and never particepate in sports again. That sounds like a good idea to me.

The first thing Phyllis noticed when she reread this paragraph was that it was not unified. It contained two main ideas rather than one: the idea of how the Olympic Games were started, and a description of the ancient games themselves. Phyllis decided to divide the paragraph into two paragraphs, making the division at the sentence beginning "The opening ceremonies began. . . ."

Then Phyllis noticed that some sentences seemed to add very little to the composition, while others were unrelated to her topic. Here are some examples:

"That is a long time."
"People don't usually believe in the ancient gods today."
"This was a strange custom, if you ask me."

Phyllis decided to cross out each of these sentences.

Phyllis noticed some grammatical errors in her first draft, too. She noticed that the first sentence was a run-on. She broke it into two sentences. She also found a sentence fragment ("Which would be religious, too") that needed to be corrected.

Phyllis saw that some of the sentences she had written sounded awkward. She rewrote them until they sounded clear and graceful. For instance, she changed the beginning of the first sentence, "There is hardly no exact record . . ." by crossing out the word "hardly." (As you will learn in Unit Fifteen, Lesson Five, the original sentence was awkward because it contained a *double negative*.)

Finally, Phyllis looked for errors in spelling and punctuation. She used a dictionary to check the spelling of words she was unsure about. She changed "particepate" to "participate," and "blud" to "blood."

Phyllis made her changes and corrections with a pencil right on her first draft. When she was finished with her corrections, she copied the revised composition on a clean sheet of paper.

Here is Phyllis's completed composition. Compare the second and third paragraphs to the first draft on page 158. Notice the many changes Phyllis made to improve her work.

The Games of Olympia

If you've ever thrilled to the colorful, dramatic spectacle of the Olympic Games, you may have wondered how they all began. Who were the first athletes to test their skills and strength in these contests? You may be surprised to learn that the birth of the Olympics took place centuries ago in a warm, green Greek valley, far from the global spotlight that shines on the Olympics of today.

There is no exact record of when the Olympic Games first began. Ancient records place the earliest games over 2,500 years ago. Because the Greeks felt that excellence in both spirit and body was important, they developed a celebration of athletic skills as part of a religious festival. Unlike the modern games, which are athletic contests only, the first Olympics were an important rite of Greek civilization.

The early Olympic ceremonies began with a runner who carried a torch from Athens, the capital city, to the place where the events were to be held. The lighted torch honored Zeus, king of the gods. Also on the first day, a live pig was sacrificed to the gods. All the athletes had to swear on the pig's blood that they would not cheat. Anyone caught cheating was fined and never allowed to participate in sports again.

The earliest Olympic event was a 200-yard run, but soon the pentathlon became the most popular event. The pentathlon consisted of five events: running, jumping, discus throwing, javelin throwing, and wrestling. The winner of the pentathlon was considered the finest athlete in Greece. He was given an olive wreath, prizes, and many special privileges in Athens. The pentathlon champion stood for the ideal of perfection in mind and body that was important in the ancient Greek religion.

Soon other countries joined the Greeks in competing for prizes. The games were shifted to huge stadiums, and other contests were added: chariot racing, horseback riding, boxing, and even a competition for trumpeters! When Rome conquered the Greek empire in 146 B.C., the Romans continued the Olympic Games. But under the Romans, the games became more intensely competitive and sometimes bloody. They continued to be held every four years until, in A.D. 394, the Emperor Theodosius banned them permanently, calling them a waste of time and money. It was a ban that was to last until 1896, when the games were revived.

Since 1896, the Olympic Games have been held every four years except for periods during the two World Wars. The Olympic Games of the twentieth century are different in many ways from those first played over twenty-five centuries ago. They are international in scope, and the religious element is gone. Yet the Olympic spirit of long ago still lives in the dedication of the athletes to the achievement of excellence in mind and body.

Before you hand in a finished composition, proofread it *twice*, checking for spelling and punctuation errors that you might have missed. One good way to proofread your work is to read it aloud. Make any last-minute changes that are needed as neatly as you can.

EXERCISE ELEVEN

Gather the papers on which you have written the introduction, body, and conclusion of your composition. They make up your first draft. Revise your work. Check for awkward or confusing sentences, words and sentences that are not related to the topic, punctuation and spelling errors, and anything else that you feel should be changed. Use the checklist below to check your work. When you have finished your revision, copy the composition on a clean piece of paper. Write or type the composition as neatly as possible. Give your composition a title. Be sure to proofread your work carefully.

Checklist

1. Is your introduction interesting? Will it probably make a reader want to read further? Does it let the reader know the topic of the composition?
2. Does the body of the composition include all of the facts, ideas, or details you feel should be included?
3. Do all of the sentences in each paragraph relate to a single idea?
4. Do all of the ideas in the composition relate to the main idea, as stated in the theme statement?
5. Are the paragraphs in an order that makes sense to you?
6. Do the ideas from one paragraph flow smoothly to the next? Have you used transitional words and phrases to link ideas?
7. Does the conclusion summarize the main idea of the composition or leave the reader with something to think about?

Unit Seven
Phrases

7

Phrases

Lesson One

Verb Phrases

Sandy felt proud when her painting won first prize in her town's annual art contest. She enjoyed getting the silver medal from the mayor, and she liked seeing her painting on display in City Hall. But when a reporter from a local television station asked for an interview, Sandy was worried. "You want me to appear on television?" she asked. "I don't think I'll be able to say one entire sentence."

"You don't have to," the reporter answered. "Just look into the camera and say a few words."

"I'll try," Sandy said.

The camera was set up, and the interview began.

"Tell us, Sandy," the reporter said, "where did you learn to paint like that?"

"At home," Sandy answered.

"Why did you take up painting, Sandy?"

"For fun."

"Did you get any special teaching?"

"From my mother."

"Did your mother's teaching help you become a good painter?"

"Might have helped."

"Do you plan to become a professional artist?"

"Could be."

"Thanks, Sandy. Now back to our studio."

After the camera had been turned off, Sandy asked the reporter, "How did I do?"

The reporter laughed and replied, "You did fine, Sandy. I asked you to say *a few words,* and that's just what you did."

Sandy was too nervous to say even one whole sentence. Luckily, she didn't have to. Because Sandy was speaking rather than writing, she was able to use *phrases* to answer the reporter's questions. In writing, phrases should be used only as parts of sentences, never alone.

164

- **A <u>phrase</u> is a group of related words that is used as a single part of speech. A phrase does not contain both a verb and its subject.**

You will learn about several types of phrases in this unit: *verb phrases, prepositional phrases, participial phrases, gerund phrases, infinitive phrases, and appositive phrases.*

Two of Sandy's answers were *verb phrases:*

might have helped
could be

- **A <u>verb phrase</u> consists of a main verb and one or more helping verbs.**

In the first example above, *helped* is the main verb. *Might* and *have* are the helping verbs. In the second example, *be* is the main verb. *Could* is the helping verb. (For a review of verb phrases, see Unit Three, Lesson Three.)

In a verb phrase, the main verb carries the meaning.

There are two kinds of helping verbs. The first kind helps to express the *time* of the action or state of being described in the main verb. Here is a list of the common helping verbs that express time:

is	be	do
am	being	does
are	been	did
was	has	shall
were	had	will

Sharon **was going** to the movies.   (The helping verb *was* helps to show that the action took place in the *past*.)

Sharon **will go** to the movies.   (The helping verb *will* helps to show that the action will take place in the *future*.)

Sharon **will have gone** to the movies three times this month.   (The helping verbs *will have* help to show that the action will have been completed at some time in the future.)

The second kind of helping verb is used to express a *possibility* of something or a *wish* for something that may or may not happen in the future. Helping verbs of this type are usually not used to describe something that has actually happened. Here is a list of common helping verbs used to express possibility or a wish:

can   must
could   should
may   would
might

Each of these helping verbs expresses a different shade of meaning.

Sharon **can go** to the movies.   (Sharon is able to go to the movies if she wants to.)

Sharon **may go** to the movies.   (It is possible that Sharon will go to the movies.)

Sharon **must go** to the movies.   (Sharon will go to the movies whether she wants to or not.)

As you can see, these helping verbs are very useful. They make it easy to express shades of meaning in a single phrase.

The words that make up a verb phrase may be separated by one or more adverbs:

The treasure **was** probably **buried** in the woods nearby.
The treasure **has** never **been found.**

In a question, the words that make up a verb phrase are often separated by the subject:

Will the treasure **be discovered** someday?

PRACTICE A

Copy the following sentences on your paper. Underline the verb phrase in each sentence. Circle the main verb.

Example: I will be waiting by the station.

I <u>will be (waiting)</u> by the station.

1. The President's plane has arrived at the airport.
2. By January, Mark will have been studying music for six months.
3. The city lights are glowing in the distance.

4. Your application must be approved by the office manager.
5. The sunken ship was raised from the sea bottom by a giant crane.
6. By two o'clock, all twelve cars had crossed the finish line.
7. My cousin Celeste should certainly like this gift.
8. The bridge must be painted with a special rustproof paint.
9. Prices for many goods have nearly doubled in the last five years.
10. Is Sarah waiting for Tina in the lobby?

PRACTICE B

Number your paper from 1 to 5. Think of a verb phrase for each blank below. Write the completed sentences on your paper.

Example: The cat _____ on the windowsill.
The cat was sleeping on the windowsill.

1. A new school building _____ next year.
2. Louise _____ her science project.
3. Senator Hartman _____ to New York City for a meeting.
4. The piano _____ by three husky movers.
5. Inez and Flora _____ in Lake Henry.

PRACTICE C

Choose one of the following topics. Write five to seven sentences about the topic. Include at least five verb phrases. Underline each verb phrase.

Topics:
My First Job
Something I Learned
My Favorite Comic Strip Character
A Person I Admire
A topic of your own choice

Lesson Two

Prepositional Phrases

Prepositional Phrases as Adjectives

Suppose that it is July Fourth. You and your friends are enjoying a picnic on the beach. As you unpack the food, Bob says, "Doesn't that breeze **from the ocean** feel great?"

Sharon says, "The warmth **of the sun** makes me want to go swimming."

Ruth says, "Our ride **in the car** made me hungry!"

Each of the phrases in boldface type is an example of a *prepositional phrase.*

- A <u>prepositional phrase</u> is a group of words that begins with a preposition and ends with a noun or a pronoun. The noun or pronoun is called the <u>object of the preposition.</u>

(For a review of prepositions, see Unit Three, Lesson Six.)

Look again at the prepositional phrases above. Each one contains a preposition and an object:

Preposition	Object
from	**ocean**
of	**sun**
in	**car**

Each of the phrases acts as an adjective. Each gives additional information about a noun or pronoun in the sentence.

Doesn't that breeze **from the ocean** feel great? (The prepositional phrase *from the ocean* modifies the noun *breeze.*)

The warmth **of the sun** makes me want to go swimming. (The prepositional phrase *of the sun* modifies the noun *warmth.*)

Our ride **in the car** made me hungry! (The prepositional phrase *in the car* modifies the noun *ride.*)

Because these prepositional phrases act as adjectives, they are called *adjective phrases.*

- An <u>adjective phrase</u> is a prepositional phrase that modifies a noun or a pronoun. Like an adjective, an adjective phrase answers the question *which one? what kind?* or *how many?*

Here are some more examples of adjectives and prepositional phrases acting as adjectives. The arrows point to the noun or pronoun that the adjective or the prepositional phrase modifies.

Adjective: The **straw** basket was filled with sandwiches.

Prepositional Phrase: The basket **of straw** was filled with sand-wiches.

Adjective: Later, we set up a **volleyball** net.

Prepositional Phrase: Later, we set up a net **for volleyball.**

Each pair of sentences has the same meaning. The prepositional phrase expresses the same meaning as the adjective.

A sentence may contain two or more adjective phrases. All the adjective phrases may modify the same noun or pronoun:

The pounding **of the waves on the shore** never stopped.   (In this sentence, both adjective phrases modify the noun *pounding.*)

Two or more adjective phrases in the same sentence may modify different nouns or pronouns:

Some **of the girls** built a sand castle **with a deep moat.**   (*Of the girls* modifies the pronoun *some,* and *with a deep moat* modifies the noun *castle.*)

An adjective phrase may modify a noun or pronoun which is the object of the preposition in another adjective phrase:

A seagull **on the roof of a houseboat** squawked loudly.   (In this sentence, the adjective phrase *on the roof* modifies the noun *seagull.* The adjective phrase *of a houseboat* modifies the noun *roof.*)

PRACTICE A

Number your paper from 1 to 10. Then copy each of the following sentences. Underline the adjective phrase or phrases in each sentence. Draw an arrow to the noun or pronoun that each phrase modifies.

Example: The necklace of rubies was worth one million dollars.

The necklace of rubies was worth one million dollars.

1. The members of the cheering squad attend every game of the season.
2. Trudy visited the president of the company because she wanted information for her project.
3. The house at the end of the road is being sold.
4. The umpire at home plate shouted, "Play ball!"
5. The visitors from Paris enjoyed touring San Francisco.
6. Some students in the library were making posters.
7. Sherrie likes stories about knights in shining armor.
8. Everybody in the audience could hear the speech.
9. The cakes in the window of the bakery shop look delicious.
10. The candidate promised that she would not raise taxes on property.

Prepositional Phrases as Adverbs

The blank in the sentence below can be filled with a single word. How many different words can you think of to fit in the blank?

The candidate spoke ——————— .

Here are some possible answers:

The candidate spoke **angrily.**
The candidate spoke **clearly.**
The candidate spoke **loudly.**
The candidate spoke **quickly.**

All of the words in boldface type are adverbs. They modify the verb *spoke* by telling *how* the candidate spoke. (For a review of adverbs, see Unit Three, Lesson Five.)

The meaning of the sentence could also be completed with a prepositional phrase. How many different phrases can you think of to fit in the blank? Here are some possible answers:

The candidate spoke **at a big rally.**
The candidate spoke **with emotion.**
The candidate spoke **for an hour.**
The candidate spoke **in a loud voice.**

The phrases in boldface type on page 170 act as adverbs. Each modifies the verb *spoke*. Therefore, each of these phrases is an *adverb phrase*.

● An adverb phrase is a prepositional phrase that modifies a verb, an adjective, or an adverb. Like an adverb, an adverb phrase answers the question *how? when? where? how long? why?* or *to what extent?*

Here are some examples of prepositional phrases acting as adverbs. The adverb phrases are in boldface type.

Two owls are nesting **in our barn.** (The adverb phrase *in our barn* modifies the verb phrase *are nesting*. It answers the question *where?*)

She always plays tennis **on Saturday morning.** (The adverb phrase *on Saturday morning* modifies the verb *plays*. It answers the question *when?*)

Ray walks awkwardly **because of a sprained ankle.** (The adverb phrase *because of a sprained ankle* modifies the adverb *awkwardly*. It answers the question *why?*)

When an adverb phrase modifies a verb it may be separated from the verb by other words:

Sheena and Pablo practiced their lines **for five hours.**

For five hours, Sheena and Pablo practiced their lines.

As the last example shows, an adverb phrase can come before the verb it modifies.

PRACTICE B

Copy each of the following sentences. Underline the adverb phrase in each sentence. Draw an arrow to the word or words that the phrase modifies.

Example: We left after the first song.

We left after the first song.

1. After the dance, we went home.
2. Sal played the drums for five minutes.
3. Leslie and Betsy arrived late for class.

171

4. I took my dog to the park.
5. Todd stayed home because of his cold.
6. Colleen is going to Boston.
7. My friend Alicia studied the piano for four years.
8. Before the operation, the doctor checked the patient.
9. I bought rye bread at the bakery.
10. Owls sleep during the daytime.

Lesson Three

Participial Phrases

Maybe you've seen television commercials like this one:

Announcer: "It's the new Super-Veg Kitchen Do-It-All! Hold it this way — it's a fork! Hold it that way — it's a knife! Snap on this piece — it grates cheese! Snap on that piece — it squeezes lemons! Buy the new Super-Veg and throw away every kitchen gadget you own!"   (The sound of crashing metal comes from the set.)

According to the commercial, the Super-Veg can do several jobs in your kitchen. Some kinds of words could be advertised in the same way. Like the Super-Veg, these words are handy if you know how to use them. And although they can't peel onions or slice perfect french fries, they can do several different jobs in your sentences.

In the next three lessons, you'll learn about three kinds of words that can do more than one job in a sentence. Each kind of word is formed from a verb. But each can be used in ways that a verb cannot. These three kinds of words are *participles, gerunds,* and *infinitives.*

Participles as Adjectives

As you learned in Unit Three, every verb has four forms, known as the principal parts of the verb. The principal parts of a verb are the base form (infinitive), the present participle, the past, and the past participle. (Turn to Unit Three, Lesson Three, for a review of principal parts.)

The present participle of a verb is formed by adding the ending -*ing* to the base form of the verb. The present participle can be used as the main verb in a verb phrase:

The dog was **barking** at the cat.

However, the present participle of a verb can also be used as an adjective:

The **barking** dog chased the cat. (The word *barking* is used as an adjective to modify the noun *dog*.)

Here are more examples of the two ways a present participle can be used:

As a verb: Penny is **talking** to Cortez.
As an adjective: Cortez is a **talking** parrot.

As a verb: Ken was **working** on his car.
As an adjective: The car was not in **working** order.

The past participle of a verb is usually formed by adding the ending -*ed* or -*d* to the base form. Like the present participle, the past participle can be used as part of a verb phrase or as an adjective. Here are some examples:

As a verb: The wind has **scattered** papers on the ground.
As an adjective: Angel and Tina picked up the **scattered** papers.

As a verb: The pioneers had **covered** their wagons with canvas.
As an adjective: They traveled west in their **covered** wagons.

Like most adjectives, a participle usually comes before the noun it modifies:

The **playing** and **shouting** children didn't hear the school bell.

However, a participle may also follow the noun it modifies:

The children, **playing** and **shouting,** didn't hear the school bell.

PRACTICE A

Each of the following sentences has at least one participle used as an adjective. Copy the sentences on your paper. Underline each participle. Circle the word the participle modifies.

173

Example: The farm is in the rolling hills of Pennsylvania.

The farm is in the <u>rolling</u> (hills) of Pennsylvania.

1. The growling lion paced in her cage.
2. Marcia brought six boiled eggs to the picnic.
3. Jeff's fractured leg was put in a cast.
4. Bending and stretching, Ingrid warmed up for the race.
5. Charlie was awakened by the sound of a wailing siren.

Participial Phrases as Adjectives

Since a participle is formed from a verb, it can have a complement, just as a verb can. And since a participle is used as an adjective, it can be modified in the same ways an adjective can: by an adverb or by a prepositional phrase. Whenever a participle has a complement or is modified, it is part of a *participial phrase*.

● **A <u>participial phrase</u> consists of a participle together with its complements and modifiers.**

Participial phrases act as adjectives in a sentence; they are used to modify nouns or pronouns. Here are some examples:

Carrying the kitten, the fire fighter climbed down the ladder.

The participle *carrying* has the complement *kitten. Kitten* is the direct object of *carrying. Carrying the kitten* is a participial phrase. The whole phrase works as an adjective, modifying the noun *fire fighter*.

Smiling broadly, he handed the kitten to Wally.

The participle *smiling* is modified by the adverb *broadly. Broadly* tells *how* he smiled. The participial phrase *smiling broadly* works as an adjective, modifying the pronoun *he.*

Two sentences can sometimes be combined by changing one of the sentences into a participial phrase. The participial phrase must modify a noun or a pronoun in the other sentence.

Two Sentences: I was delighted with the present. I thanked my parents for it.

Combined Sentence: **Delighted with the present,** I thanked my parents for it.

Two Sentences: Karen leaned from the window. Karen watched the parade.

Combined Sentence: Karen, **leaning from the window,** watched the parade.

PRACTICE B

Each of the following sentences contains a participial phrase. Copy the sentences on your paper. Underline each participial phrase. Circle the word it modifies.

Example: Mom saw Leeni climbing the tree.

Mom saw (Leeni) climbing the tree.

1. The loudly cheering crowd greeted the team.
2. Shifting the car into low gear, the driver turned the corner.
3. Lorraine's birthday cards, mailed to her old address, arrived late.
4. The cat sitting on the porch belongs to my neighbor.
5. Shaded from the sun, the garden is cool and pleasant.

PRACTICE C

Below are five pairs of sentences. Combine each pair by turning the first sentence in the pair into a participial phrase. Write the completed sentences on your paper.

Example: Jane believes in her talent. Jane was the first person to try out for the play.
Believing in her talent, Jane was the first person to try out for the play.

1. Larry hopes to get a raise. Larry works as hard as he can.
2. The team proved that they were ready for the playoffs. The team won the game easily.
3. Maria cried as she peeled the onions. Maria could hardly see.
4. The tomato plants were chilled by the cold rain. The tomato plants were slow to develop.
5. Bert was daydreaming about the party. Bert didn't hear Mrs. Mitchell when she called on him.

Lesson Four

Gerund Phrases

You've learned that a verb form ending in *-ing* can be used as part of a verb phrase and as an adjective. There is still another way that an *-ing* verb form can be used: as a noun. When it is used as a noun, a verb form ending in *-ing* is called a *gerund*.

● A <u>gerund</u> is a verb form ending in *-ing* that is used as a noun.

Like nouns, gerunds can be used as subjects, direct objects, indirect objects, predicate nominatives, and objects of prepositions. Here are examples of gerunds used in each of these ways:

Subject: **Farming** is hard work.
Direct Object: I enjoy **skating.**
Indirect Object: Marian gave **studying** her full attention.
Predicate Nominative: The hardest skill in baseball is **batting.**
Object of Preposition: She swam two miles without **stopping.**

Because a gerund is a verb form, it can have complements, including direct objects, indirect objects, and subject complements. It can also be modified by an adverb. Because a gerund is used as a noun, it can be modified by adjectives, possessive pronouns, and adjective phrases. When a gerund has one or more complements or modifiers, it is part of a *gerund phrase*.

● A <u>gerund phrase</u> consists of a gerund together with its complements and modifiers.

Gerund phrases can be used in all of the same ways that nouns can be used. Here are examples of gerund phrases used in these ways:

Subject: **Slow jogging** is not too hard.

The gerund *jogging* is modified by the adjective *slow*. The gerund phrase *slow jogging* is the subject of the verb *is*.

Direct Object: I like **biking in the park.**

The gerund *biking* is modified by the prepositional phrase *in the park*. The gerund phrase *biking in the park* is the direct object of the verb *like*.

Indirect Object: The judges awarded **my skating** the highest score.

The gerund *skating* is modified by the possessive pronoun *my*. The gerund phrase *my skating* is the indirect object of the verb *awarded*.

Subject Complement: Tom's favorite household chore is **baking bread**.

The gerund *baking* has a direct object, *bread*. The gerund phrase *baking bread* is a predicate nominative after the linking verb *is*.

Object of Preposition: Paula was exhausted after **cooking dinner for thirty people tonight**.

The gerund phrase *cooking dinner for thirty people tonight* is the object of the preposition *after*. The gerund *cooking* has a direct object, *dinner*, and is modified by the prepositional phrase *for thirty people* and the adverb *tonight*.

PRACTICE A

The following sentences contain gerund phrases. Copy the sentences on your paper. Underline each gerund phrase. Circle each gerund.

Example: Fred likes driving his old truck.

   Fred likes (driving) his old truck.

1. Judy got the part because of her singing at the audition.
2. Drinking cold liquids quickly can give you a stomachache.
3. My uncle's favorite hobby is whittling wooden dolls.
4. Before eating your lunch, please wash your hands.
5. Walking my three dogs at the same time is difficult.
6. Typing all day made Randy's fingers sore.
7. Driving a car too fast down Mountain Road is dangerous.
8. The loud banging on the wall of my room awakened me this morning.
9. Someday, I will succeed in climbing to the top of Mount Hood.
10. Paul has worked hard on planning his garden.

Use ten of the following words as gerunds in sentences of your own.

Example: playing
           Playing tennis on a hot day makes me thirsty.

telling	dancing	laughing
speaking	running	flying
singing	driving	bowling
playing	jogging	reading
pretending	dreaming	living

Lesson Five

Infinitive Phrases

In the last two lessons, you learned about two verb forms that can be used as other parts of speech. In this lesson, you will learn about a third: the *infinitive*.

● The infinitive is the base form of a verb.

An infinitive usually follows the word *to*. It can be used as a noun, an adjective, or an adverb.

When it is used as a noun, an infinitive may be the subject, the direct object, or the predicate nominative in a sentence.

Subject: **To vote** is a basic right.
Direct Object: She wants **to stay.**
Predicate Nominative: My goal in life is **to paint.**

An infinitive can also be used as an adjective or adverb:

Adjective: We had little time **to talk.**

The infinitive *to talk* modifies the noun *time*. It tells *what kind of time* — time to talk.

Adverb: Infinitives are easy **to spot.**

The infinitive *to spot* modifies the adjective *easy*.

Do not confuse an infinitive with a prepositional phrase begin-

178

ning with *to*. Remember that a prepositional phrase ends with a noun or a pronoun. An infinitive consists of the word *to* followed by the base form of a verb.

Prepositional Phrases: **to the market, to me, to the game**
Infinitives: **to listen, to go, to wear**

An infinitive can have one or more complements, including a direct object, an indirect object, or a subject complement. It can also be modified by an adverb or an adverb phrase. When an infinitive has a complement or a modifier, it is part of an *infinitive phrase*.

● **An infinitive phrase consists of an infinitive together with its complements and modifiers.**

An infinitive phrase, like an infinitive alone, can be used as a noun, an adjective, or an adverb.

To spend all of your money on gumdrops is foolish.

The infinitive phrase *to spend all of your money on gumdrops* is used as a noun and is the subject of the verb *is*. The infinitive *to spend* has a direct object, *all,* which is modified by the prepositional phrase *of your money*. The prepositional phrase *on gumdrops* modifies the infinitive.

The Scarlet Letter is the next book **to be read for English class.**

The infinitive phrase *to be read for English class* is used as an adjective; it modifies the noun *book*. The infinitive *to be read* is modified by the prepositional phrase *for English class*.

I was invited **to visit her soon.**

The infinitive phrase *to visit her soon* is used as an adverb; it modifies the verb *was invited*. The infinitive *to visit* has a direct object, *her,* and is modified by the adverb *soon*.

PRACTICE A

The following sentences contain infinitive phrases. Copy the sentences on your paper. Underline the infinitive phrases.

Example: We love to go to the beach.
            We love to go to the beach.

1. Rome is a wonderful city to visit in the spring.
2. I'm trying to fix my car.
3. To pass the French exam will be easy for Ella.
4. Will you be able to recognize Uncle Carl?
5. Bicycling is the best way to get to the fairgrounds.
6. Jenny learned to play the guitar.
7. My cousin Sheila is planning to travel through Central America this summer.
8. Fritz wants to climb the highest mountain in the state.
9. I hope to get a seat near the jugglers.
10. Joan worked hard to finish her sculpture for the exhibition.

PRACTICE B

Use five of the following infinitives in a sentence of your own.

Example: to dress
The actors had only ten minutes to dress in their costumes.

to suggest	to help	to jump
to bring	to stay	to forget
to visit	to try	to write
to call	to dance	to send
to worry	to tie	to wish

Lesson Six

Appositive Phrases

Imagine that one day you receive a postcard from a friend. On the front is a picture of palm trees and a beach. On the back is the following message:

The weather is beautiful here! I wish I could stay longer than a week. Tell my sister I bought her a present.

Carlos

You have a problem. Carlos has two sisters. Which one should you tell about the present? If Carlos had used an *appositive,* you wouldn't have a problem:

Tell my sister **Loretta** I bought her a present.
Tell my sister **Marlena** I bought her a present.

● An <u>appositive</u> is a word — with or without modifiers — that follows a noun or pronoun and identifies or explains it.

Here are examples of appositives:

The planet **Jupiter** is fifth from the sun.   (The appositive *Jupiter* identifies the noun *planet.*)

Living in Florida, Gerti seldom gets to enjoy her favorite sport, **skiing.**   (The appositive *skiing* identifies what Gerti's favorite *sport* is.)

The singer **John Denver** appeared in the movie.   (The appositive *John Denver* identifies the *singer.*)

Sometimes an appositive is modified by other words. An *appositive phrase* is an appositive together with its modifiers. Here are some examples of appositive phrases:

Jupiter, **the largest planet in our solar system,** is the fifth planet from the sun.   (The appositive phrase, *the largest planet in our solar system,* identifies *Jupiter.*)

In 1978, Ai won the Lamont Prize, **an annual award for an American poet's second book of poetry.**   (The appositive phrase *an annual award for an American poet's second book of poetry* identifies *the Lamont Prize.*)

Appositive phrases will often help you combine two short sentences into one:

Two Sentences: Marci showed the class her slides from Pompeii. Pompeii was the Roman city destroyed by a volcanic eruption in A.D. 79.

Combined Sentences: Marci showed the class her slides from Pompeii, **the Roman city destroyed by a volcanic eruption in A.D. 79.**

Essential and Nonessential Appositives

An appositive may be either *essential* or *nonessential.*

181

● An <u>essential</u> appositive answers the question *which one?* about the noun or pronoun it follows. It is needed to identify the noun or pronoun. An appositive that does not answer the question *which one?* is <u>nonessential</u>.

Compare these two sentences:

The singer **John Denver** appeared in the movie.
The largest planet, **Jupiter,** is fifth from the sun.

In the first sentence, *John Denver* is an essential appositive. It answers the question *which singer?* If the appositive were left out of the sentence, you could not tell which singer appeared in the movie.

In the second sentence, *Jupiter* is a nonessential appositive. It is not needed to identify the noun *planet,* because the planet has already been identified as the *largest planet.* If the appositive were left out of the sentence, you could still tell which planet is fifth from the sun.

A nonessential appositive should be separated from the rest of the sentence by commas. (If it is at the end of the sentence, only one comma is needed.) An essential appositive should not be separated by commas.

Essential: The poem **"Kubla Khan"** was written by Coleridge.
Nonessential: "Kubla Khan," **my favorite poem,** was written by Coleridge.

Essential: The baseball star **Joe DiMaggio** appeared at the dinner.
Nonessential: Joe DiMaggio, **sometimes called "the Yankee Clipper,"** appeared at the dinner.

Note: The terms *restrictive* and *nonrestrictive* are sometimes used in place of the terms *essential* and *nonessential.* In this book, only the terms *essential* and *nonessential* will be used.

PRACTICE A

Each of the following sentences contains an appositive or an appositive phrase. Copy the sentences on your paper. Then underline the appositive or appositive phrase in each sentence.

Example: The bouquet, twelve yellow roses, lasted a week.
   The bouquet, <u>twelve yellow roses</u>, lasted a week.

1. Thomas Jefferson, third President of the United States, founded the University of Virginia.
2. We visited Bath, a town famous for its hot water springs.
3. Our neighbor Mr. McAllister collects antique cars.
4. Some New Yorkers and many tourists celebrate New Year's Eve by going to Times Square, the heart of the theater district.
5. The drama club performed a scene from *Henry VI,* one of Shakespeare's earliest plays.
6. Many beautiful works of art in Florence, an Italian city, were damaged in a flood.
7. My uncle Roger served in the navy during the Vietnam War.
8. So many fans jammed the stadium to hear Clash, the British rock group, that the police were called to keep order.
9. My favorite month of the year, June, passes much too quickly.
10. The future king of England, Prince Charles, studied in Wales and Australia.

PRACTICE B

The following exercise contains five pairs of sentences. Change the second sentence in each pair into an appositive phrase, and combine it with the first sentence in the pair. Write the five new sentences on your paper.

Example: Henry Hudson discovered a river that was later called the Hudson.
Henry Hudson was a famous English explorer.
Henry Hudson, a famous English explorer, discovered a river that was later called the Hudson.

1. My sister is an excellent chess player.
My sister is Diana.
2. *Guernica* was painted to protest a bombing raid during the Spanish Civil War.
Guernica is Picasso's most famous painting.
3. Walt Disney was the creator of Mickey Mouse.
Walt Disney was a pioneer cartoonist.
4. Our soccer coach was once a professional soccer player.
Our soccer coach is Mr. Benevento.
5. William Worthington gave a talk at our school.
William Worthington is a well-known novelist.

Review Exercises

I. Below are ten verb phrases. Use each one in a sentence. Write the completed sentences on your paper. (Lesson One)

Example: has grown
The tree in our yard has grown three feet this year.

1. am learning
2. will paint
3. can eat
4. are pretending
5. is fixing

6. should follow
7. are sailing
8. has been planted
9. will be frozen
10. may need

II. Each of the following sentences contains one or more prepositional phrases. Number your paper from 1 to 10. Next to each number, write the prepositional phrase or phrases from that sentence. Underline each preposition. (Lesson Two)

Example: I read about Mary's wedding in the newspaper.
<u>about</u> Mary's wedding, <u>in</u> the newspaper

1. Juanita jumped into the water wearing all her clothes.
2. Mimi went to the carnival with her brother.
3. After my sixteenth birthday, my mother will allow me to drive the family car on weekends.
4. Rick showed us the photos from his trip to Minnesota.
5. Dianne put her packages above her seat in the overhead compartment of the bus.
6. Jeanne thanked Robby for the photographs of her dog.
7. During the summer, Henry always eats ice cream on the porch at night.
8. The dogs barked at the stranger in the yard.
9. Mike told us about his family.
10. Alfredo took us to the concert in the park.

III. On the following page are ten pairs of simple sentences. Combine each pair into one sentence by changing the first sentence of the pair into a participial phrase. Write the completed sentences on your paper. (Lesson Three)

Example: Mario was distracted by the noise. Mario dropped the fly ball.

Distracted by the noise, Mario dropped the fly ball.

1. We were carrying five bags of groceries. We climbed the stairs.
2. The seeds were scattered by the wind. The seeds sprouted everywhere.
3. The words on the scroll were faded by time. The words on the scroll could hardly be read.
4. Jeff was gazing out to sea. Jeff saw three sailboats.
5. The city of Washington was created by Congress in 1790. The city of Washington is named after our first President.
6. The children were fascinated by the dinosaur exhibit. The children did not want to leave the museum.
7. The watchdog was awakened by the noise outside. The watchdog began barking loudly.
8. Tina was gathering shells on the beach. Tina spotted something shiny in the sand.
9. The fans were hoping to meet their favorite football star. The fans waited outside the clubhouse door.
10. The senator was surprised by the reporter's question. The senator did not know what to say.

IV. Each of the following sentences has a blank space. Complete the sentences by putting a gerund or a gerund phrase into each blank space. Write the completed sentences on your paper. (Lesson Four)

Example: _____ is a good way to lose weight.
Eating fewer sweets is a good way to lose weight.

1. _____ is my favorite outdoor activity.
2. There will be _____ at the party.
3. Pamela won a medal for her _____ .
4. _____ calls for skill and practice.
5. Jason was tired from _____ all day.
6. _____ can be dangerous.
7. Carolyn is taking lessons in _____ .
8. _____ is a popular fad.
9. My family enjoys _____ on the weekend.
10. I am good at _____ .

185

V. Each of the following quotations contains at least one infinitive or infinitive phrase. Copy the quotations on your paper. Underline each infinitive or infinitive phrase. (Lesson Five)

Example: To err is human, to forgive, divine. — Alexander Pope
To err is human, to forgive, divine.

1. Injustice is relatively easy to bear; what stings is justice.
— H. L. Mencken
2. The truth is found when men are free to pursue it.
— Franklin D. Roosevelt
3. That fellow seems to me to possess but one idea, and that is a wrong one. — Samuel Johnson
4. To travel hopefully is a better thing than to arrive.
— Robert Louis Stevenson
5. To fear love is to fear life, and those who fear life are already three parts dead. — Bertrand Russell

VI. Combine each pair of sentences into one sentence by changing the second sentence in the pair into an adjective phrase or an appositive phrase. (Lessons Two and Six)

Examples: The house is ninety years old. The house is down the street.
The house down the street is ninety years old.

Hal will soon compete for a state medal in music. Hal is our school's best drummer.
Hal, our school's best drummer, will soon compete for a state medal in music.

1. The piano has been tuned. The piano is on the third floor.
2. A box fell off the truck. It was a box of grapes.
3. Mr. Piozzi is getting married next week. Mr. Piozzi is my dance teacher.
4. The tag tells how much the bookcase costs. The tag is on the bookcase.
5. Soccer is now becoming popular in the U.S. Soccer is the most popular game in the world.
6. Our principal is from Venezuela. Our principal is Mrs. Ramirez.

7. Sherlock Holmes never really existed. Sherlock Holmes was the world's greatest detective.
8. My cousin is a good basketball player. My cousin is from Texas.
9. Chaucer wrote *The Canterbury Tales.* Chaucer was the greatest English poet before Shakespeare.
10. The tunnels contain wires and pipes. The tunnels are under the shopping center.

VII. Choose one of the topics below. Write a paragraph of five to seven sentences about it. In your paragraph, include and underline each type of phrase listed below. (Lessons One to Six)

1. one verb phrase
2. one prepositional phrase
3. one participial phrase
4. one gerund phrase
5. one infinitive phrase
6. one appositive phrase

Topics:
An Unusual Hobby
The Most Beautiful Street in Town
A Job I Learned to Like
An Invention That Changed My Life
A topic of your own choice

Writing a Comparison

It's Saturday afternoon, and you're watching "National Grandstand" on television. It's time for the part of the show called "Pick-a-Hit," when the host, Dirk Cluck, chooses two teenagers from the audience to decide which of two new songs deserves to be a hit.

The two judges, Justine and Bob, listen carefully to the first record, "Bacon Fat," while the rest of the audience dances wildly on the studio floor. Then Dirk Cluck asks Justine and Bob to listen to the second new song, "Step on My Feet."

When it's over, Dirk Cluck asks Justine and Bob, "Well, kids, which song do *you* think deserves to be America's next Top Forty hit?"

"I like 'Bacon Fat' better than 'Step on My Feet,' " says Bob. " 'Bacon Fat' has interesting words, unlike 'Step on My Feet.' It has a slower beat than 'Step on My Feet,' and it's shorter. For those reasons, I like 'Bacon Fat' better than 'Step on My Feet.' 'Bacon Fat' deserves to be a hit."

Justine disagrees. "I like a song that has no words, only music, like 'Step on My Feet.' I like a fast beat, like the beat of 'Step on My Feet,' and I like it when a song seems to go on forever. That's why I prefer 'Step on My Feet.' I think every teenager will want to buy the record."

Dirk Cluck flashes a big smile. "Fine, Justine! Wonderful, Bob! Thank you very much. For being our two judges, we'd like you to have this fabulous gift — a case of twelve dozen assorted shoelaces in many designer colors! Wear them in good health! And now it's time for a commercial!"

During the commercial, you wonder how you would have voted if you had been Justine or Bob. You think about the various features that make the two songs similar and different. Justine and Bob mentioned some of them, but you can think of several others:

"Bacon Fat"	"Step on My Feet"
good to dance to	good to dance to
a catchy tune	a catchy tune
interesting words	no words
slow beat	fast beat
short	long
quiet drums	loud drums
organ solo	saxophone solo

This list shows that in some ways the two songs are similar. Both are good to dance to and have catchy tunes. But in other ways the two songs are different. By thinking about the differences, you can decide which song you like better, and why, just as Justine and Bob did.

When you look closely at the features that make two things similar and different, you are making a *comparison*. You make comparisons all the time, sometimes without knowing it. You might compare two record albums when deciding which one you want to buy. You might compare one movie with another when deciding which one you'd enjoy seeing. In choosing a way to travel across town, you might compare taking the bus to riding your bike. You would probably make these comparisons quickly.

There are other situations when you need to *write* a comparison. In school, for example, you may be asked a question on a test that calls for a comparison: "Compare the character of Tom Sawyer to that of Huckleberry Finn," or "Compare the natural resources of Nevada to those of Michigan."

Someday you may need to write a comparison on the job. For instance, your boss may ask you to test two computers and write a comparison to help the company decide which computer to buy. A written comparison takes more time and thought than one that you make only in your mind.

In this unit, you will learn how to make comparisons. You will practice finding the similarities and differences between two things. And you will learn how to express these similarities and differences in a written comparison. These skills will help you in writing comparisons for school, on the job, and in other situations. They will also help you in making careful decisions whenever two choices must be compared. Making comparisons is a thinking skill as well as a writing skill.

Lesson One

Similarities and Differences

Finding Similarities

In *Alice's Adventures in Wonderland* by Lewis Carroll, the Mad Hatter offers a riddle to Alice: "Why is a raven like a writing desk?" When Alice gives up, the Mad Hatter admits, "I haven't the slightest idea." Lewis Carroll intended the Mad Hatter's riddle to have no answer. But throughout the years, readers of *Alice* have suggested answers. Here are a few of them:

1. Both a raven and a writing desk produce a few notes that are very flat. (A raven makes musical notes that are flat when it sings. A desk can be used in writing notes — short letters — which, of course, are flat.)
2. Both should be made to shut up.
3. Edgar Allan Poe wrote on both. (Poe wrote a famous poem about a raven, and he wrote on a desk.)

Can you think of any other answers to the Mad Hatter's riddle?

Finding similarities between things has humorous uses, like solving riddles. It can also be a helpful way to think about serious matters. In her book *A Distant Mirror,* the historian Barbara Tuchman pointed out many similarities between two very different times: the fourteenth century and the twentieth century. Both were times of terrible wars fought over conflicting beliefs. Both were times of social unrest, riots, economic problems, and revolutions. Both were times when people tried — often without success — to find ways of settling differences among nations peacefully. Those who read *A Distant Mirror* might discover clues to the problems of today in the problems of an earlier time.

Looking for similarities between two things can help you to understand each of the two things better than you did before. Sometimes the similarities are obvious. For example, a duck and a goose are similar in several ways that are easy to find.

1. Both have feathers.
2. Both fly.
3. Both can be eaten.
4. Both have webbed feet.

But sometimes, finding the similarities between two things takes a little imagination. For example, in what ways is a duck similar to a marshmallow? You may say, at first, "There are no similarities between a duck and a marshmallow." But think again.

1. Both can be roasted.
2. Both are sold in supermarkets.
3. Both are soft.
4. Both are edible.

Finding the similarities between two things that seem very different — like a duck and a marshmallow or a raven and a writing desk — may take time. But if you think carefully about each of the two things, you will probably be able to find some similarities.

EXERCISE ONE

Choose three of the five pairs of objects listed below. On your paper, list five similarities between the objects in each pair you chose.

1. a cow and a sheep
2. a quarter and a one-dollar bill
3. a record player and a radio
4. an egg and a glass of milk
5. a shirt and a coat

Finding Differences

No matter how similar two things are, there are almost always some differences between them. "What about identical twins?" you might ask. But even identical twins have different habits, different ways of walking and talking, and different kinds of facial expressions. Two things that seem identical are almost always slightly different, but you must look closely to find their differences.

For example, the differences between two shoes in a pair may be very subtle. Maybe one shoe has a scuff mark that the other doesn't. Maybe the soles and heels have worn differently on the two shoes. Maybe the laces of one shoe are frayed, while the laces of the other are not. Maybe there are other differences, too. The closer you look, the more differences you will find.

Choose three of the five pairs of objects listed below. Look closely at specific examples of each pair of objects you chose. On your paper, list five differences between the objects in each pair you chose.

1. two hands
2. two sneakers
3. two pairs of blue jeans
4. two copies of this book
5. two streetlamps

EXERCISE THREE

Study the two pictures on page 205. Write a list of ten similarities you can find between the two pictures. Write another list of ten differences.

You might compare your lists with the lists of other members of your class. Did your classmates find some similarities and differences you overlooked?

Lesson Two

Organizing a Comparison

Remember Bob and Justine (page 190), who compared two songs on the TV show "National Grandstand"? They listened to "Bacon Fat" and "Step on My Feet" and made comparisons between the two songs. They gave their reactions quickly and casually, "off the tops of their heads."

Imagine a different situation, which calls for a written comparison. Terence Tune is starting a job at a local radio station. His job is to listen to the new records released each week and decide which ones are likely to become hits. At the end of the week, he will give a written report to his boss, Program Director Gloria Gold. Gloria needs to know which songs Terence thinks will become hits, as well as the reasons for his choices. Based on Terence's report, Gloria will decide which songs to play on the air.

For his first week on the job, Terence has two new records to consider: "Blisters on My Fingers," by the Weird Ones, and "Ooh Wacka Doo Wacka Woo," by Toni T. and the Tonettes. He must decide which song is more likely to become a hit and write a report for Gloria, comparing the two records.

Suppose you were Terence. How would you begin? You'd probably start by listening to both records several times. As you listen, you might jot down your thoughts and reactions, just as they occurred to you. That is what Terence did. His notes looked like this:

"Ooh Wacka Doo Wacka Woo" — slow beat, romantic lead singing by Toni T.
"Blisters on My Fingers" — fast, loud, exciting, a real rocker
two great guitar solos in "Blisters on My Fingers"
both songs have catchy tunes, easy to remember
nice guitar and organ playing in "Ooh Wacka Doo Wacka Woo," but drumming is so-so
no words in "Blisters on My Fingers"—teenagers usually don't like songs without words
both songs have a good dance beat

Terence added several more thoughts to his notes as he listened to the records for the last time. He decided that "Ooh Wacka Doo Wacka Woo" was more likely to become a hit, especially since Toni T.'s singing was so romantic. But when he sat down to write his report for Gloria, he realized that one more step was needed. His notes were written in no particular order. They jumped back and forth from one song to the other, and from one idea to the next, with no organization. If Terence simply copied his notes in writing his report, Gloria would probably find it confusing to read. He realized that, before writing his comparison, he needed to organize his ideas.

When making a comparison, you must begin as Terence did: by thinking about and studying the two things to be compared. Before writing your comparison, however, it's important to organize the similarities and differences you have found into a logical order. Organizing your ideas will make the finished comparison easier to read and understand.

There are two good ways of organizing a comparison:

1. First tell all the similarities between the two things. Then tell all the differences.
2. First describe one of the two things you want to compare. Then describe the other, pointing out the similarities and differences.

Which method of organizing a comparison is better? Both ways can be good. You can choose whichever method you prefer when writing your own comparison.

If Terence Tune decides to organize his report the first way, he will first write about the similarities between the two songs. Then he will write about the differences. Here is how his report might read:

There are two new songs this week: "Blisters on My Fingers," by the Weird Ones, and "Ooh Wacka Doo Wacka Woo," by Toni T. and the Tonettes. Both songs have several of the qualities needed for a Top Forty hit. Both songs have catchy tunes that are easy to remember; listeners will probably start humming the songs after hearing them. Both songs have a good dance beat, so people will probably play them at parties and dances. And both songs have been recorded skillfully, with a clean, crisp sound.

However, the two songs are different in a number of ways. "Blisters on My Fingers" is fast and loud, with a real rock 'n' roll feeling. "Ooh Wacka Doo Wacka Woo," on the other hand, is slow and soft, with romantic lead singing by Toni T. Toni's many fans are sure to enjoy her singing on this new record, which is the best she has ever done. There is no singing at all in "Blisters on My Fingers," which may hurt its popularity, since most teenagers prefer songs with words.

The quality of the backup musicians is slightly higher in "Blisters on My Fingers." Erik Redde, the lead guitarist, plays two great guitar solos, and Aaron Zildjian, the drummer, gives his usual exciting performance. In "Ooh Wacka Doo Wacka Woo," the guitar and organ are played well, but the drumming is only fair. Those who like dynamic instrumental performances will not be impressed by "Ooh Wacka Doo Wacka Woo."

It wasn't easy for me to decide which of these two songs is more likely to become a hit. Each song has strengths and weaknesses. Overall, however, I think that "Ooh Wacka Doo Wacka Woo" is more likely to be the big winner. Toni T.'s great voice and stylish delivery lift "Ooh Wacka Doo Wacka Woo" above the ordinary. They make the song something special that teenagers will want to hear again and again.

In this comparison, Terence tells the similarities between the two songs in the first paragraph. He then tells the differences in the second and third paragraphs. The fourth paragraph is the conclusion. It sums up Terence's comparison of the two songs, and it presents his opinion as to which song will probably become a hit.

Note: If you want, you can reverse this method of organization when you write a comparison. You can tell the differences first, and then tell the similarities. This usually works better when you feel that the similarities are more important than the differences. If you feel that the differences are more important than the similarities, tell the similarities first.

If Terence chooses to organize his comparison the second way, he will tell all about one song first. He will then tell about the other, pointing out the similarities and differences. Here is how the report might read:

This week's first new song is "Blisters on My Fingers," by the Weird Ones. "Blisters on My Fingers" is a good song. It has a catchy tune that listeners will find hard to forget, as well as a good, strong beat for dancing. It is fast and loud, with a real rock 'n' roll feeling. "Blisters on My Fingers" is a straight instrumental, with no singing.

The best feature of "Blisters on My Fingers" is the instrumental performance. Erik Redde plays a great lead guitar, including two exciting guitar solos. Drummer Aaron Zildjian keeps a solid beat. The clean, crisp recording quality helps bring out the excellent quality of the playing.

The second new song for this week is "Ooh Wacka Doo Wacka Woo," by Toni T. and the Tonettes. Like "Blisters on My Fingers," it has a memorable tune and a beat that makes it good for dancing. However, unlike "Blisters on My Fingers," it is a soft, slow tune rather than a rock 'n' roll number, and it has singing.

Toni T.'s singing on "Ooh Wacka Doo Wacka Woo" is stylish, sophisticated, and romantic. This is her best singing performance to date, and Toni T.'s many fans are sure to enjoy the record.

197

The instrumental performances on "Ooh Wacka Doo Wacka Woo" are not as good as those on "Blisters on My Fingers." Although the guitar and organ are played well, the drumming is only fair. Those who like dynamic instrumental performances will not be impressed by "Ooh Wacka Doo Wacka Woo." The recording quality, however, is very good.

I predict that the singing of Toni T. will make "Ooh Wacka Doo Wacka Woo" into the next Top Forty hit. Although "Blisters on My Fingers" is also a good song, those who enjoy Toni T.'s romantic singing are likely to make "Ooh Wacka Doo Wacka Woo" into a bigger hit.

When you organize a comparison in this way, it's important to discuss the details of the two things being compared in the same order. In Terence's comparison, he discusses the features of "Blisters on My Fingers" in the following order:

1. catchy tune
2. good beat for dancing
3. fast and loud
4. no singing
5. excellent instrumental performances
6. good recording quality

He then discusses the features of "Ooh Wacka Doo Wacka Woo" in the same order:

1. catchy tune
2. good beat for dancing
3. soft and slow
4. romantic singing
5. fair instrumental performances
6. good recording quality

Discussing the details of the two things being compared in the same order makes the comparison easy to understand.

Here is a summary of the two ways to organize a comparison:

1. All the similarities between the two things, followed by all the differences, *or* all the differences followed by all the similarities
2. All the details about one thing, followed by all the details about the other

Both methods of organization can work equally well. It is up to you to decide which method you want to use.

EXERCISE FOUR

Below is a list of notes to be used in writing a comparison. The notes are in no particular order. Read the notes. Then copy the notes on your paper in an order that makes sense to you, using one of the two ways of organizing a comparison. Do not write the comparison; just put the notes in an order you could use in writing the comparison.

Notes for a comparison of two restaurants:
Beef 'n' Bun serves only hamburgers.
A meal at Beef 'n' Bun costs about three dollars.
Captain Jack's is decorated to look like the inside of a sailing ship.
Service at Captain Jack's is usually fast.
The food at Beef 'n' Bun is usually fresh.
The food at Captain Jack's is usually fresh.
A meal at Captain Jack's costs about five dollars.
Service at Beef 'n' Bun is very slow.
Beef 'n' Bun is always crowded at lunchtime.
Captain Jack's is very clean.
Beef 'n' Bun is very clean.
Beef 'n' Bun is decorated to look like a cattle ranch in Texas.
Captain Jack's serves only seafood.
Captain Jack's is always crowded at lunchtime.

Lesson Three

Writing and Revising

In Lesson Two you saw how Terence Tune needed to use his skill in writing comparisons in his job at the radio station. You will probably never have a job that requires you to pick the next Top Forty hit song. But you will certainly have many opportunities to make comparisons, whether at school, at work, or in your free time. Notice the importance of comparisons in the following situations:

Mike and Lucy are outside the Twin Cinemas. They are trying to decide whether to see *It Came From Planet X* or *The Thing That Ate Des Moines.* Mike and Lucy compare what they know about each of the two movies: the stars, the stories, and what their friends said about them.

Pedro has agreed to lend his car to his friend Anthony. But Pedro's car has a standard transmission, while Anthony has only driven cars with automatic transmissions. Pedro is showing Anthony the similarities and differences between automatic and standard transmissions, so that Anthony will be able to drive Pedro's car.

The last composition that Amy wrote for her English class contained several errors in grammar. Her previous composition had none. To help Amy understand and correct her mistakes, her English teacher puts the two compositions side by side and points out the differences between them.

Coach Robbins is teaching the players on the girls' softball team two ways to slide into second base: the *hook slide* and the *bent-leg slide.* Coach Robbins compares the two slides to show how each one is used in a different base-running situation.

As you can see from the four situations described above, comparisons can be helpful in making decisions, in learning skills, and in communicating ideas. The four situations illustrate the four most common purposes for which comparisons can be used.

1. *A comparison can be used in making decisions.* This is the most common purpose for a comparison. When Mike and Lucy try to decide which movie to see, they are making a comparison for this purpose. Newspapers and magazines often contain articles that compare two or more products — two shampoos, for instance, or two compact cars — to help consumers decide which one to buy. Terence Tune's comparison of two songs is another example of a comparison with this purpose.

2. *A comparison can help explain something unfamiliar by comparing it to something familiar.* When Pedro explains the standard transmission to Anthony by comparing it with the automatic transmission, Pedro is using a comparison for this purpose. The English Parliament could be explained to an American by com-

paring it to the United States Congress. A scientist could explain to a child how a rocket works by comparing a rocket to a toy balloon.

3. *A comparison can be used to illustrate a fact or idea.* Amy's English teacher compares Amy's two compositions as a way of illustrating some of the rules of grammar. A writer who wanted to support the opinion that people of today are better informed than those of the past could compare TV news shows and newsmagazines of today with newspapers of previous centuries.

4. *A comparison can be used to help examine the two things being compared.* Examining two things side by side can be a good way to learn more about each of them. Coach Robbins compares the two types of slides used in softball in order to show the players the special purpose for which each slide is used. An art teacher who is teaching students to paint both with oil paints and with water colors will point out the differences in the techniques to be used with each kind of paint.

When you write a comparison, you may have the purpose for the comparison in mind from the start. For example, you might be asked in a history test to write an answer to this question: "Who was a greater general in the Civil War: Robert E. Lee or Ulysses S. Grant? Explain your answer." This question calls for a decision about which of two things is better — the first purpose listed above.

In other cases, you might make notes on the similarities and differences between the two things before deciding on the purpose of your comparison. Your notes may even suggest an idea for the purpose of the comparison. For example, an English test might contain this question: "Compare any two characters from Stephen Crane's novel *The Red Badge of Courage.*" This question allows you to select your own purpose for the comparison. After choosing two characters to compare and thinking about them, you might decide that the comparison illustrates some fact or idea about Stephen Crane's novel — the third purpose listed above. Or you might decide that the purpose of your comparison will be to show clearly the personalities of the two characters being compared — the fourth purpose listed above.

The Theme Statement

The purpose of your comparison should be expressed in the form of a *theme statement*. (You may want to review Unit Six, which describes the use of a theme statement in organizing a composition.) Here are possible theme statements that could be used in writing comparisons for the four situations described on page 200:

I'd rather see *It Came From Planet X* than *The Thing That Ate Des Moines* because it sounds scarier, more suspenseful, and more realistic.

Driving a car with a standard transmission is similar to driving a car with an automatic transmission, but there is one important difference: you must decide when to shift gears yourself, rather than have the car shift automatically.

A comparison of your last two compositions shows that you need to review the rules for avoiding sentence fragments and run-on sentences.

When running the bases, a player should decide whether to use the hook slide or the bent-leg slide, depending on the location of the fielder and the ball at the time of the play.

The theme statement may or may not appear in your comparison. In any case, you should make sure that the theme of your comparison is clear. One way is to explain the theme in a short paragraph of two or three sentences. This paragraph can appear at the beginning of the comparison, as an introductory paragraph, or at the end, as a summary. The choice is up to you. When writing a comparison, you might want to try both ways, and choose the way you prefer before writing a final draft.

As you learned in Unit Six, the details included in a composition should relate to and support the theme of the composition. Therefore, after choosing a theme for a comparison, you should look back at your list of similarities and differences. Ask yourself whether the details included in the list relate to and support your chosen theme. If any of them do not, cross them out. You may also think of additional similarities or differences that relate to and support your chosen theme. Add them to your list.

EXERCISE FIVE

Below are ten pairs of items that could be compared. Choose two pairs. On your paper, list at least five similarities and five differences between the items in the pairs you chose. List as many similarities and differences as you can.

Save the list. You will use it later in this unit.

Example: two sports (You name the sports.)
hockey and basketball
Similarity:
Both are played on a rectangular field.
Difference:
Hockey is played on ice; basketball is played on a wooden floor.

1. two sports (You name the sports.)
2. two singers or musicians you like (Name them.)
3. two books you have enjoyed (Name the books.)
4. two kinds of pets (Name the kinds of animals.)
5. two forms of transportation (Name them.)
6. two famous people from history (Name the people.)
7. two of your favorite movies (Name the movies.)
8. two hobbies (Name the hobbies.)
9. two jobs (Name the jobs.)
10. two magazines you like to read (Name them.)

EXERCISE SIX

Choose one of the two pairs of items you used for Exercise Five. You will use the pair you choose as the basis of a written comparison.

Look over the list of similarities and differences you wrote for Exercise Five. Do they suggest a possible purpose for your comparison? For example, one item may be better than the other in some way, or the similarities and differences between the two items may suggest an idea or fact that the comparison illustrates. Decide on a purpose for the comparison, and write it in the form of a theme statement.

Read the list of similarities and differences again, thinking about the theme statement you have written. Do any of them fail to relate to or support the theme? If so, cross them out. You may think of additional similarities or differences that relate to the theme. If so, add them.

Choose a way of organizing the comparison. You can use either of the methods of organization summarized on page 198. Number the similarities and differences in your list in the order in which you will write about them in your comparison.

Write the comparison. It should be from four to six paragraphs long. One paragraph should state the theme of the comparison. This paragraph can come first or last in the comparison.

When you are finished, read over your work. Evaluate it with the help of the Checklist below.

Checklist

1. Does the comparison include both similarities and differences?
2. Is the comparison organized clearly according to one of the methods discussed in Lesson Two?
3. Is the theme of the comparison stated clearly in a paragraph?
4. Does the comparison include details to make the similarities and differences clear?
5. Do the details included in the comparison relate to the theme of the comparison?

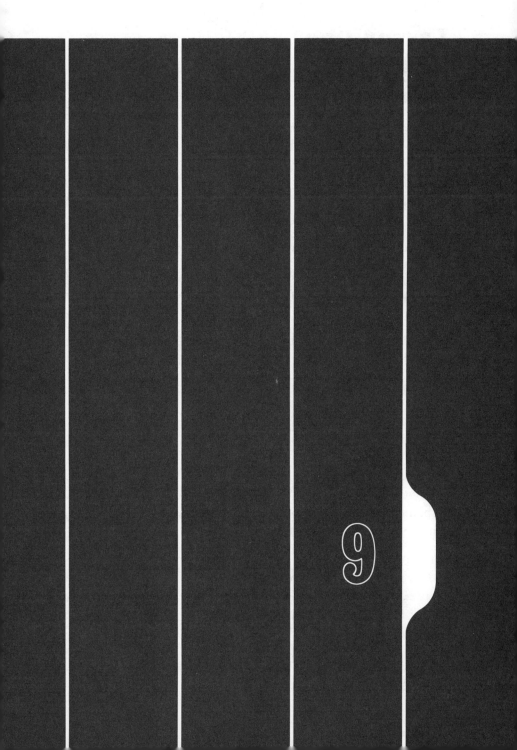

9

Clauses

Lesson One

Independent and Subordinate Clauses

Sentences can be compared to houses. Some are small and simple, like a cottage with only one room:

The crowd cheered.

Just as a builder can add rooms to a house, a writer can add phrases to a simple sentence:

The crowd **of spectators** cheered **with excitement.**

A sentence can be made even larger and more complex, like a building with many rooms:

As the mayor proudly added the last brick to the new City Hall, the crowd of spectators **who had gathered for the ceremony** cheered with excitement.

The groups of words in boldface type in the sentence above are *clauses.*

- A <u>clause</u> is a group of related words that contains a verb and its subject.

Remember that a phrase, unlike a clause, does not contain a verb and its subject. Compare these examples of phrases and clauses:

Phrase: **to the new City Hall**   (This is a prepositional phrase. It does not contain a verb and its subject.)

Clause: **as the mayor proudly added the last brick to the new City Hall**   (This is a clause. It has both a verb, *added,* and its subject, *mayor.*)

Phrase: **had gathered**   (This is a verb phrase. It does not contain a subject.)

Clause: **who had gathered**   (This is a clause. It contains both a verb phrase, *had gathered,* and its subject, the pronoun *who.*)

There are two kinds of clauses: *independent clauses* and *subordinate clauses.*

Independent Clauses

● **An independent clause expresses a complete thought. It can stand by itself as a sentence.**

When an independent clause stands by itself, it is called a *simple sentence.* (See Unit One, Lesson Six, for a review of simple sentences.)

The party began at eight o'clock.   (The subject of the sentence is *party;* the verb is *began.*)

A sentence may contain two or more independent clauses joined by a conjunction. When it does, the sentence is called a *compound sentence.* (See Unit One, Lesson Six, for a review of compound sentences.)

The party began at eight, but **some of the guests arrived after nine.**   (The compound sentence consists of two independent clauses joined by the conjunction *but.*)

Subordinate Clauses

Look at the following groups of words:

**before the music starts
if you want to come
which I enjoy eating**

Each of these groups of words contains a subject and a verb. However, none expresses a complete thought. None can stand by itself as a sentence. Therefore, they are *subordinate clauses.*

● **A subordinate (or dependent) clause does not express a complete thought. It cannot stand by itself as a sentence.**

Subordinate clauses begin with such words as the following: *after, as, because, before, if, since, that, unless, until, when, which,* and *who.*

A subordinate clause must be joined to an independent clause:

Before the music starts, the band members must tune their instruments.
You must buy a ticket today **if you want to come.**
Pancakes with syrup is a breakfast **which I enjoy eating.**

Look again at this sentence:

As the mayor proudly added the last brick to the new City Hall, the crowd of spectators **who had gathered for the ceremony** cheered with excitement.

This sentence contains an independent clause, in regular type, with two subordinate clauses, in boldface type. As you can see, a sentence may contain more than one subordinate clause. However, *a sentence must always contain at least one independent clause.*

PRACTICE A

Some of the following clauses are independent clauses. Some are subordinate clauses. Number your paper from 1 to 10. If the clause is an independent clause, write *I* next to the number. If the clause is a subordinate clause, write *S*.

Examples: we danced
            I

            before the song started
            S

1. the train pulled into the station
2. if the Senate accepts the treaty
3. as the rope broke
4. several chairs were missing
5. which she has studied carefully
6. may I borrow your pen
7. the boat was eighteen feet long
8. since they depend on us for help
9. this clock is slightly fast
10. because the last flight has already departed

PRACTICE B

Each of the following sentences contains an independent clause and a subordinate clause. Copy the sentences on your paper. Underline the subordinate clause in each sentence.

Example: As soon as you left, the dog began to whimper.
           As soon as you left, the dog began to whimper.

1. I invited her because she is my closest friend.
2. Everyone was silent until someone began to giggle.
3. Before Diana and Liz arrived, Bill was sitting alone in the library.
4. You will feel cool if you sit still.
5. The person who answered the telephone yesterday is my aunt.
6. Aaron will be staying with us while his parents are on vacation.
7. Lisa jogged until she couldn't go any further.
8. You may present your argument when it is your turn to speak.
9. I'd like to sing you a song that I wrote.
10. When the fog lifted, we saw the icebergs looming ahead of the ship.

PRACTICE C

Choose one of the topics below. Write five to seven sentences about the topic. Include the following:

1. one sentence consisting of an independent clause that stands alone
2. two sentences that include subordinate clauses
3. one sentence consisting of two independent clauses

Topics:
My Favorite Kind of Music
A Holiday Custom of My Family
An American Resource
My Life Ten Years From Now
A topic of your own choice

Lesson Two

Subordinate Clauses as Adjectives

Look at the three sentences below:

The **town** council has voted to build a new gym.
The council **of the town** has voted to build a new gym.
The council **that governs the town** has voted to build a new gym.

In all three sentences, the words in boldface type modify the noun *council*. In the first sentence, the noun *council* is modified by the adjective *town*. In the second sentence, the noun *council* is modfied by the adjective phrase *of the town*. In the third sentence, the noun *council* is modified by the subordinate clause *that governs the town*.

- An adjective clause is a subordinate clause that modifies a noun or a pronoun. Like an adjective or an adjective phrase, an adjective clause answers the question *which one? what kind?* or *how many?*

In the following examples, the adjective clauses are in boldface type. The arrows point to the nouns that the adjective clauses modify.

The runner **who finishes first in this race** will compete in the Olympics. (The clause tells *which runner* will compete in the Olympics.)

A car **that has air conditioning** can overheat in heavy traffic. (The clause tells *what kind of car* can overheat.)

As you can see in these examples, an adjective clause follows the word that it modifies.

An adjective clause often begins with one of the five relative pronouns: *who, whom, whose, that,* or *which. Who, whom,* and *whose* are used to refer to people; *which* is used to refer to things; *that* may be used to refer to either people or things. Each of these words relates the clause to the noun or pronoun it modifies.

The relative pronouns *who, that,* and *which* are often the subjects of the clauses they begin. In the examples above, the pronoun *who* is the subject of the verb *finishes,* and the pronoun *that* is the subject of the verb *has.* However, in the following examples, the relative pronouns are not the subjects of the verbs:

The sport **that I enjoy most** is touch football. (The subject of the verb *enjoy* is *I.*)

My favorite dish, **which my mother prepares every Sunday,** is spaghetti and meatballs. (The subject of the verb *prepares* is *mother.*)

Essential and Nonessential Clauses

An adjective clause may be either *essential* or *nonessential.*

● **An essential clause is one that identifies the noun or pronoun it modifies. A nonessential clause gives information about the noun or pronoun it modifies, but it is not needed to identify the noun or pronoun it modifies.**

Compare these two examples:

The police officer **who saved the drowning child** received a medal.
Sharon Liddell, **who has been a police officer for eight years,** has received ten medals.

In the first sentence, *who saved the drowning child* is an essential clause. It is needed to identify the police officer. If it were left out of the sentence, you would not know which police officer received the medal. An essential clause answers the question *which one?* about the noun or pronoun it modifies.

In the second sentence, *who has been a police officer for eight years* is a nonessential clause. It is not needed to identify *Sharon Liddell,* since she has already been identified by name.

A nonessential clause should be separated from the rest of the sentence by commas. (If the clause is at the end of the sentence, only one comma is needed.) An essential clause should not be separated from the rest of the sentence by commas.

Note: The terms *restrictive* and *nonrestrictive* are sometimes used in place of *essential* and *nonessential.* In this book, only the terms *essential* and *nonessential* will be used.

Combining Sentences With Adjective Clauses

You can often combine two sentences by changing one sentence into an adjective clause and adding it to a related sentence.

Two Sentences: The farmhouse was a shambles. It hadn't been lived in for years.

Sentence With an Adjective Clause: The farmhouse, **which hadn't been lived in for years,** was a shambles.

PRACTICE A

Each of the following sentences contains an adjective clause. Copy each sentence on your paper. Underline the adjective clause. Draw an arrow to the word the adjective clause modifies.

Example: The record that I bought cost six dollars.

The record that I bought cost six dollars.

1. The horse, which hadn't been ridden lately, proved difficult for me to handle.
2. Val, whose brother is in my music class, lives in an old house.
3. The sweater that my grandmother knitted keeps me very warm.
4. Donald told us the story that we had been waiting to hear.
5. My lab partner, who likes to play jokes, often annoys me.
6. A career that will guarantee success is a hard one to find.
7. The roses that bloom by the fence are the largest in town.
8. The student-government president, who was elected in May, resigned in October.
9. My cousin, who is from Italy, is studying French at a school in Switzerland.
10. A song that I dislike is number one across the country.

PRACTICE B

Think of an adjective clause to complete each of the following sentences. Write the completed sentences on your paper. Be sure to use commas if the clause you add is nonessential.

Example: The cat _____ was six weeks old.
The cat that we got from the animal shelter was six weeks old.

1. The noise ＿＿＿＿＿ made it impossible to concentrate.
2. Tom phoned Rita ＿＿＿＿＿ .
3. The novel ＿＿＿＿＿ was too interesting to put down.
4. Friends of mine ＿＿＿＿＿ visited a town ＿＿＿＿＿ .
5. The dress ＿＿＿＿＿ cost two months' allowance.

PRACTICE C

Change the second sentence in each of the following pairs of sentences to an adjective clause beginning with a relative pronoun. Then add the clause to the remaining independent clause. You may need to add or take away some words. Write the new sentences on your paper.

Example: Margaret hopes to study at Yale. She wants to be an archaeologist.
Margaret, who wants to be an archaeologist, hopes to study at Yale.

1. We trimmed the ivy. It was beginning to grow over the windows.
2. The Greeks built a temple in honor of Athena. Athena was the Greek goddess of wisdom.
3. The farthest planet from the sun is Pluto. It takes 248 years to circle the sun.
4. Frederick Douglass was born a slave in Maryland. He became an antislavery leader.
5. Jack bought a cat. He named it Tabby.

Lesson Three

Subordinate Clauses as Adverbs

As you learned in Lesson Two, using an adjective clause is a good way to add information to a sentence. Here is another good way: an *adverb clause*. Look at the following sentences:

Sara called me **yesterday.**
Sara called me **before school.**
Sara called me **before she left for school.**

In each sentence, the word or words in boldface type are used as adverbs to modify the verb *called*. They answer the question *when?* In the first sentence, the verb *called* is modified by the adverb *yesterday*. In the second sentence, *called* is modified by the adverb phrase *before school*. In the third sentence, *called* is modified by *before she left for school,* an *adverb clause.*

● **An <u>adverb clause</u> is a subordinate clause that modifies a verb, an adjective, or an adverb. Like an adverb or an adverb phrase, an adverb clause answers the questions *when? where? how? why? to what extent?* or *how long?***

Like adjective clauses, adverb clauses are always *subordinate clauses*. They do not stand alone as sentences.

In the following examples, the adverb clauses are in boldface type. The arrows point to the words which the adverb clauses modify.

Indiana Jones cringes **whenever he sees a snake.** (The adverb clause tells *when* Indiana Jones cringes.)

Carl displayed his painting **where everyone can see it.** (The adverb clause tells *where* the painting was displayed.)

After the weather clears, we will have the barbecue. (The adverb clause tells *when* we will have the barbecue.)

As you can see in the last example, an adverb clause can come at the beginning of a sentence, before the word that it modifies. An adverb clause that begins a sentence is followed by a comma.

An adverb clause begins with a *subordinating conjunction*. Here is a list of some common subordinating conjunctions:

after	before	unless
although	if	until
as	in order that	when
as if	since	whenever
as long as	so that	where
as soon as	than	wherever
because	though	while

Combining Sentences With Adverb Clauses

You can often combine two sentences into one by changing one of the sentences into an adverb clause and joining the clause to another related sentence.

Two Sentences: We could not see the stage. A tall man blocked our view.

Sentence With an Adverb Clause: We could not see the stage **because a tall man blocked our view.**

PRACTICE A

Each of the following sentences contains an adverb clause. Copy each sentence on your paper. Underline each adverb clause. Circle the word that the clause modifies.

Example: He cried because he was sad.

He (cried) because he was sad.

1. Wherever I visit, I buy a souvenir.
2. Although Miguel was disappointed, he shook hands with the winner.
3. The actor was nervous until he said his first line.
4. Please call me when you get back.
5. Because Linda fell off the horse, her hip is sore.
6. Selma became excited when we began to plan the class trip.
7. Art worked all summer so that he could save money for college.
8. Play the song after I turn on the tape recorder.
9. Whenever I hear that song, I think about Leslie.
10. While Jessica waited for the bus, she read the school newspaper.

PRACTICE B

Complete each of the following sentences by adding an adverb clause. Write the ten completed sentences on your paper.

Example: Fran called me _____ .
Fran called me after she got the job.

1. The librarian helped me find the article _____ .
2. _____ , she won't be forgotten.

217

3. Mitch will probably arrive _____ .
4. Please remain seated _____ .
5. _____ , Kate chopped onions.
6. Will Brian go to the dance _____ ?
7. I found the notebook _____ .
8. _____ , I bought the record.
9. Len dressed in his work clothes _____ .
10. We will go to the skating rink _____ .

PRACTICE C

Change the second sentence in each of the following pairs of sentences into an adverb clause beginning with a subordinating conjunction. Then join the clause to the first sentence in the pair. You may need to add or take away some words. You may put the clause at the beginning or at the end of the sentence. Write the ten new sentences on your paper.

Example: The reporter interviewed the senator. She wrote a report for her newspaper.
The reporter interviewed the senator before she wrote a report for her newspaper.

1. I washed and ironed my white shirt. I had spilled ketchup all over it.
2. The marchers turned the corner. The police officer stopped the traffic.
3. Jeremy will go to the movies. Everyone has finished dinner.
4. The flowers bloomed all summer. We fertilized them last fall.
5. Jorge has made many friends. He has been here only a few months.

Lesson Four

Noun Clauses

Can you tell the difference between these two sentences?

Your algebra teacher did a good job.
Whoever taught you algebra did a good job.

Both sentences express the same idea. However, the subject of the first sentence is a noun with two modifiers:

your algebra **teacher**

The subject of the second sentence is a *noun clause*:

whoever taught you **algebra**

● **A noun clause is a subordinate clause used as a noun.**

As you have seen, nouns can be used in several ways in a sentence. A noun can be a subject, direct object, indirect object, object of a preposition, subject complement (predicate nominative), or object complement. Here are examples of both nouns and noun clauses used in all of these ways. Notice that each boldface noun has one or more modifiers, which are italicized. The noun clause expresses the same idea as the noun and its modifiers.

Subject

> *His* **statement** made no sense.
> **What he said** made no sense.

Direct Object

> Jack told me *a* **story** *about finding a thousand-dollar bill.*
> Jack told me **that he had found a thousand-dollar bill.**

Indirect Object

> The store gave *dissatisfied* **customers** a refund.
> The store gave **whoever was dissatisfied** a refund.

Object of a Preposition

> This ticket is for *the* **person** *who arrives first.*
> This ticket is for **whoever arrives first.**

Subject Complement (Predicate Nominative)

> That lake is *a popular vacation* **spot.**
> That lake is **where hundreds of people go for their vacation.**

Object Complement

> The child calls the dog *any* **name** *that he happens to think of.*
> The child calls the dog **whatever comes to mind.**

Here are some words that often introduce noun clauses:

how	which
that	whichever
what	who
whatever	whoever
when	whom
where	whomever
whether	why

You may have noticed that some of these words can also be used to introduce adjective clauses or adverb clauses. In the sentences below, the same word introduces three different kinds of subordinate clauses.

I wonder **where they are.**   (noun clause, object of verb *wonder*)

That place **where we left them** was spooky.   (adjective clause, modifies noun *place*)

Soon we will be **where they are.**   (adverb clause, modifies verb *will be*)

So you see, you cannot identify an adjective, adverb, or noun clause just by looking at its introductory word. You must figure out how the clause is used in the sentence.

PRACTICE A

On your paper write the noun clause from each sentence below.

Example: Luis knows that he must make a decision soon.
           that he must make a decision soon

1. Luis does not know how he will spend his summer.
2. The question is whether he will work or take a vacation.
3. Whatever he does will be rewarding.
4. I understand why he is confused.
5. He thinks that he should earn some spending money.
6. Then he wonders when he will have time to spend it.
7. He can make his summer whatever he wants it to be.
8. Whoever hires Luis will get a good worker.
9. He always does whatever needs to be done.
10. He has thought about where he might go on vacation.

PRACTICE B

Use each clause below as a noun clause in a sentence. Write the complete sentence on your paper.

Example: why I am so happy
         I will explain why I am so happy.

1. how she fixed the car
2. whoever is interested in tennis
3. that his plane will be on time
4. what Cyrus said
5. when the Inca Indian empire was at its height

Lesson Five

Four Sentence Structures

In this unit, you have learned that there are two kinds of clauses: independent clauses and subordinate clauses. These two kinds of clauses can be used to build different kinds of sentences. You have already learned about two kinds of sentences: *simple sentences* and *compound sentences*.

● **A simple sentence consists of one independent clause.**

Dan will bring his guitar to the party.

A simple sentence may contain a compound subject, a compound verb, or both a compound subject and a compound verb:

Dan and **Sue** will perform at the party.
They **play** several instruments and **sing** beautifully.
Their **singing** and their **playing please** their friends and **add** life to any party.

● **A compound sentence consists of two or more independent clauses.**

Dan will bring his guitar to the party, and Sue will bring her flute.

(You may want to review simple sentences and compound sentences in Unit One, Lesson Six.)

Independent and subordinate clauses can be combined to build two more kinds of sentences: *complex sentences* and *compound-complex sentences.*

- A <u>complex sentence</u> consists of one independent clause and one or more subordinate clauses.

  If Dan comes to the party, he will bring his guitar. (This sentence contains one subordinate clause in boldface type and one independent clause.)

  When Dan and Sue get tired, Peter, **who is an amateur magician,** will saw his sister in half. (This sentence contains two subordinate clauses in boldface type and one independent clause.)

- A <u>compound-complex sentence</u> consists of two or more independent clauses and one or more subordinate clauses.

  If they come to the party, Dan will bring his guitar, and Sue will bring her flute. (The sentence contains one subordinate clause in boldface type and two independent clauses.)

Use all four types of sentences in your writing. Your writing will be more interesting and enjoyable to read if you vary the sentence structure. Look at the following paragraph:

Some people in the neighborhood used the vacant lot. They used it as a dump. They left their unwanted furniture there. Children also used the lot. They used it as a playground. The children had no other place to play. Some parents were concerned about their children's safety. The parents formed a committee. They worked every weekend. They carted away the trash. The city donated trees and playground equipment. The parents created a safe place for their children to play.

If you read this paragraph aloud, you can hear how monotonous it sounds. All the sentences are simple sentences. The passage can be improved by changing the structure of some of the sentences. Here is the same paragraph, revised to include different types of sentences:

Some people in the neighborhood used the vacant lot as a dump where they left their unwanted furniture, and children used the lot as a playground because they had no other place to play. Some parents who were concerned about their children's safety formed a committee to cart away the trash. The parents worked every weekend. The city donated trees and playground equipment, and the parents created a safe place for their children to play.

When you write, keep track of the sentence structures you use. Try to vary the length and structure of your sentences.

PRACTICE A

Below are ten sentences. Number your paper from 1 to 10. Next to each number, write whether the sentence is *simple, compound, complex,* or *compound-complex.*

Example: Give me a ride to Podunk Heights, and I will catch the connecting train.
compound

1. If my mother gets home early, she'll help me with my costume.
2. The skipper returned to the harbor after he had almost lost his boat in the storm.
3. The janitor usually cleans the cafeteria after lunch, but today is his day off.
4. Although she doesn't like to cook, Mary promised to help with dinner, and her brother will buy the dessert.
5. Chicken is low in calories and is relatively inexpensive.
6. My brother Jeff decided to grow a beard so that he would look older.
7. After the dog's leg healed, she could climb the stairs.
8. The ballfield turns to mud whenever it rains.
9. Sir Francis Drake was an explorer and a pirate, and the Queen of England rewarded him for capturing Spanish gold.
10. Mickey Mouse watches have become valuable, but my mother lost her Mickey Mouse watch years ago.

PRACTICE B

Each of the following groups of sentences contains two or three simple sentences. Combine the sentences in each group into one sentence. You may need to add, remove, or change some words. Include all the thoughts expressed by the original sentences.

223

Example: The thunderstorm began. We were in a open field. We might have been hit by lightning.
    When the thunderstorm began, we were in an open field where we might have been hit by lightning.

1. The plane took off. We watched the movie. It kept us amused during most of the flight.
2. The rain stopped. The children crawled out of their tents.
3. Alison has a sprained ankle. She doesn't want to miss basketball practice.
4. I was exhausted. I stayed awake. I had promised to wait up for my brother.
5. The roof on our rented cottage began to leak. We moved to a motel. We were more comfortable there.

PRACTICE C

Write a paragraph of five to seven sentences about one of the following topics. In your paragraph, include the following:

1. one simple sentence
2. one compound sentence
3. one complex sentence
4. one compound-complex sentence

Topics:
A Historic Event in My Lifetime
My Favorite Neighbors
How to Care for a Pet
Travel in the Year 2000
A topic of your own choice

Review Exercises

I. Each of the following sentences contains one independent clause and one subordinate clause. Copy the sentences on your paper. Put one line under each independent clause and two lines under each subordinate clause. (Lesson One)

Example: My brother was angry when he dropped the ball.
    My brother was angry when he dropped the ball.

1. Although Frank was discouraged about the loss of his job, he got a new one the next day.
2. There is a traffic jam on Main Street that has delayed traffic for more than an hour.
3. While her sister Judy is at college, Raellen will use Judy's bedroom.
4. Rosa wants a job at the riding stable so that she can improve her riding.
5. Calvin cut his finger when he was doing yard work.
6. Will you eat popcorn if it isn't buttered?
7. The lifeguard did a lot of reading because it was too cold for swimmers to go into the water.
8. The part of the teenage daughter was given to an actress who is thirty years old.
9. Trish cleaned out her locker when she could not find the library books.
10. Taxes will be cut this year if the governor's plans are carried out.

II. Use each of the following clauses in a sentence. Write the completed sentences on your paper. (Lesson Two)

Example: who hands out the tickets
The woman who hands out the tickets is standing by the door.

1. who won the race
2. which I bought yesterday
3. whom the voters have chosen
4. that my sister enjoys
5. whose dog has been digging in my yard
6. who can answer this question
7. which is too small for me
8. whom I admire
9. that I bought last week
10. whose car is parked outside

III. Change the first sentence in each of the following pairs of sentences into an adverb clause. Then join the clause to the second sentence. You may have to add, remove, or change some words.

You may put the clause at the beginning or at the end of the sentence. Write the completed sentences on your paper. (Lesson Three)

Example: Ron injured his knee. He couldn't play in today's football game.
Because Ron injured his knee, he couldn't play in today's football game.

1. The flashlight didn't work. We had to sit in the tent without light.
2. Nancy writes to me first. I will write her a letter.
3. Barbara is a talented pianist. She enjoys playing drums more.
4. The dog barked for its supper. Pete fed it.
5. Tim practiced two hours a day. He made the football squad.
6. Roxanne hopes to start her own business someday. Roxanne is studying business management in college.
7. I am studying. I often turn on the radio.
8. Ted began painting the room. Ted stirred the paint thoroughly.
9. The music stopped playing. I was able to fall asleep.
10. The spring thaw comes late this year. The growing season will be short.

IV. Copy each noun clause from the sentences below.   (Lesson Four)

Example: The test will show what you know.
what you know

1. Everybody believes that children should go to school.
2. The point is that we should have turned left back there.
3. I didn't see who delivered the package.
4. She worries about what people will say.
5. Let's ask her where the museum is.
6. My favorite dish is whatever you're serving tonight.
7. Luke can explain how a digital watch works.
8. You can go to the library for whatever you need.
9. Whoever likes clams should go to the clambake.
10. What you don't know won't hurt you.

V. Number your paper from 1 to 10. Next to the number of each sentence, write what type of sentence it is: *simple, compound, complex,* or *compound-complex.* (Lesson Five)

Example: Glass has been used to decorate buildings since the Syrians developed glassblowing in the first century B.C.
complex

1. The Romans were the first to make glass windows, which they used in their baths.
2. Stained glass windows were first used in 1095 in a church at Augsburg, Germany.
3. Stained glass windows became common in churches in the twelfth century after architects learned new ways to support the walls.
4. Large windows became possible, and architects began using windows with panels of colored glass.
5. The glass was painted with enamel and heated to fuse the colors to the glass.
6. Color was also added while the glass mixture was melting.
7. Artists designed windows which showed biblical scenes.
8. Sunlight on the glass created beautiful colored patterns.
9. Stained glass windows were used in most churches until some religious leaders began to discourage their use.
10. Many churches still have stained glass windows, but there are not many people who can repair and replace them.

VI. Choose one of the topics below. Write a paragraph of five to seven sentences about it. In your paragraph, try to include each type of sentence listed below. (Lessons One to Five)

1. one simple sentence
2. one compound sentence
3. one complex sentence
4. one compound-complex sentence

Topics:
A Restaurant I Enjoy
A Mistake From Which I Learned Something
Today's Craziest Fad
Is There a Right to Privacy?
A topic of your own choice

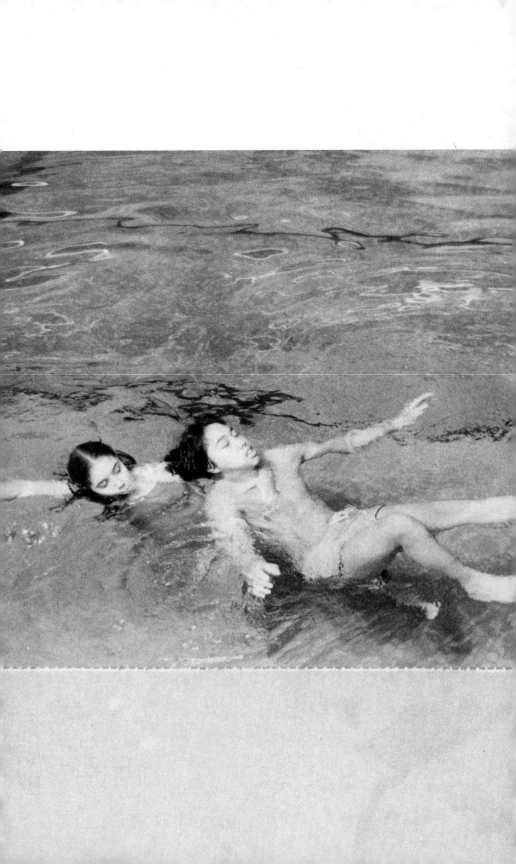

Writing Answers to Essay Questions

Writing Answers to Essay Questions

Something strange is happening in Mr. Harrison's class at Waverly High. As Mr. Harrison speaks, the students begin to feel very peculiar. Martin's palms start to sweat. Cold chills run up and down Arlene's spine. Gary's mouth suddenly feels as dry as dust, and Linda's heart beats faster than usual. What is the matter with these students? Have they caught the flu? Has a poisonous spider just crawled in through the classroom window? Is Mr. Harrison telling an especially frightening ghost story?

No, none of these things has happened. The students are responding to something Mr. Harrison has said: "There will be a test next week. Be prepared for one or two essay questions."

Many students feel nervous about answering essay questions. Some students don't know how to study for them. Some find the questions difficult to understand. Others aren't sure how to organize an answer.

However, an essay test doesn't have to be cause for panic. There are methods you can learn that will help you write an essay answer quickly and well. In this unit, you will learn about these keys to success on essay tests.

Lesson One

Understanding Test Questions

After doing odd jobs in her neighborhood one weekend, Arlene found that she had earned enough money to buy herself a pair of fancy jeans. She picked out a pair that fit perfectly. But when Arlene washed them, something unexpected happened. After the jeans were dry, Arlene found that she could barely squeeze herself into them. What was worse, the jeans stopped two inches above her ankles. Arlene checked the washing instructions on the label of the jeans, and then she discovered where she had gone wrong. The label said, "Wash in cold water only." Arlene had used hot

230

water, and the jeans had shrunk. Because she had not bothered to read the directions on the label, Arlene had to give the jeans to her little sister.

Many students have the same problem when answering essay questions. They sometimes fail to read the test instructions or the questions carefully before answering the questions. As a result, they lose test points by not doing exactly what they are supposed to do.

The proverb "Look before you leap" is good advice when taking an essay test. *Planning ahead* before you begin answering questions is a good way to make sure you use your time and energy wisely. Here are some techniques that will help you approach essay tests effectively.

1. *Read the test instructions carefully.* As Arlene found, skipping the instructions can lead to costly mistakes. Before you look at the questions, make sure you know how many questions you have to answer and how your answers should be written. Are you supposed to choose two questions out of four to answer, or must you answer all the questions? Should you write your answer only on one side of the paper, or on every other line? How much time do you have? Be sure you know the answers to these questions before you tackle the questions.

2. *Before you start work, read through the entire test.* This will show you the number and kind of questions. If the test offers a choice of questions, reading ahead will help you choose the questions you are best able to answer. If you fail to read all the questions first, you may miss a question near the end of the test that you are especially well prepared to answer.

3. *Notice how many points each question is worth.* If some questions are worth more points than others, plan to divide your time appropriately. A 25-point question should be given more time than one worth only 10 points.

4. *Budget your time.* Before you go to work, estimate how much time each question will take. When you've spent all the time you should on a question, go on to the next one. This will keep you from getting caught at the end of the test after having spent all your time on only one question. No matter how well you may have answered that question, it won't make up for the points you'll lose on the questions you didn't do. When you are taking a test, minutes are precious; spend them wisely!

Key Words in Essay Questions

Essay questions usually include *key words* that tell you what kind of answer your teacher is looking for. In this lesson, you will learn the most common key words and the kind of answer that each one requires.

Note: Test questions are not always written as questions. For example, on a science test, "Describe the antelope" would be called a question, even though it does not end in a question mark.

Here is a list of key words used in test questions. Learn to recognize them when they appear on tests.

1. List

"List the major characteristics of the alligator."

When an essay question asks you to *list,* you need only to write down items that answer the question. You might list the items in order of importance, but unless a specific order is asked for, there is no right or wrong way. An essay answer for a *list* question does not call for a detailed or lengthy discussion, and it is usually not necessary to write in complete sentences.

Here is the beginning of a possible answer for the sample question above:

Characteristics of the alligator:
1. a member of the reptile family
2. has a rounded snout, a scaly body, and a long tail
3. lives in warm, wet areas, such as swamps and rivers
4. lays 20 to 50 eggs in the mud or sand at one time

2. Describe

"Describe the living habits and physical features of the penguin."

As you learned in Unit Four, a description is a detailed picture of something. An essay question that asks you to describe something calls for more details than a list. Write your answer in complete sentences and paragraphs.

Here is a possible beginning for a description of the penguin:

"The penguin is a black and white bird living in the Southern Hemisphere, especially in regions that are near cold ocean currents. Penguins range in height from 19 inches to over three feet. These birds are unable to run or fly, but they are good swimmers and excellent divers for fish . . ."

3. Define

"Define *democracy* as it was practiced in ancient Greece."

To *define* a word means to give its meaning. Essay questions often ask for definitions of important words related to the subject you are studying. The word you are asked to define is often a general or broad one, like *democracy, fiction,* or *natural selection.* Your answer will be most effective if it refers to one or two specific examples that make the meaning of the general term clear.

Here is a possible beginning for an answer to the sample question above:

"The term *democracy* comes from a Greek word that means 'rule of the people.' Democracy is a political system in which the people share in guiding the activities of the government. In ancient Greece, the laws were made by an assembly composed of all the citizens. This system, known as 'direct democracy,' was possible because the cities of Greece were small in population . . ."

4. Identify

"Identify Kit Carson."

To *identify* someone or something is to tell briefly who or what the person or thing was or is. Most *identify* questions can be answered in a few sentences. Your answer should give only the most important facts about the person or thing.

Here is a sample answer for the *identify* question above:

"Kit Carson was an American frontiersman, scout, and soldier in the Old West. He was born in Kentucky in 1809 and became famous as a hunter and guide for the Frémont expeditions to California in the 1840's. He fought against the Navahos during the 1860's and in 1865 became a brigadier general. He died in 1868."

5. Discuss

"Discuss the major characteristics of the alligator."

To *discuss* means to talk about. In a written discussion, you would expand on basic information. For example, on page 232, the sample question asked you to "List the major characteristics of the alligator." Here, the question asks you to *discuss* the characteristics of the alligator. This means that you should add details to the items on your list. Your answer should be written in complete sentences and paragraphs.

Here is how a possible answer for this sample question might begin:

"Alligators are large reptiles that belong to the crocodile family. They differ from crocodiles in their snouts, which are shorter and more rounded than the snouts of crocodiles.

"Alligators are found in the United States along the Atlantic coast from North Carolina to Florida and in the Gulf states. They live in wet regions, such as swamps and rivers. . . ."

6. Explain

"Explain the concept of color."

To *explain* means to make clear and understandable. Here is a possible beginning for an answer to the question above:

"The colors we see depend on the kinds of light absorbed or reflected by objects. Sunlight is made up of many colors. When light falls on a red object, the object absorbs all the colors of the spectrum except red. The red is then reflected to the eye . . ."

In an essay question, "explain" can also mean "give the reasons for." For example: "Explain the stock market crash of 1929."

7. Compare or Compare and Contrast

"Compare and contrast the sleeping habits of cats and dogs."

To *compare* means to state the similarities and differences between two things. To *contrast* means to state the differences only. Teachers often use the words *compare and contrast* in test questions to make sure that you include both similarities and differences in your answer.

As you learned in Unit Eight, there are two ways to organize your answer to a *compare and contrast* question. One way is to write about the similarities and differences in two separate paragraphs. When answering the sample question above, you might tell all the ways that the sleeping habits of dogs and cats are similar in the first paragraph. In the second paragraph, you would tell all the ways their sleeping habits are different.

Another way to organize information for a *compare and contrast* question is to discuss the two things being compared in two separate paragraphs. For the same question, you would devote one paragraph to the sleeping habits of dogs and one paragraph to the sleeping habits of cats.

8. Summarize

"Summarize the plot of Charles Dickens's novel *Great Expectations*."

To *summarize* something is to state its main points briefly and concisely. A summary of a factual book or article would include the main ideas of the whole work. A summary of a short story, play, novel, or movie would give only the main events of the story. Don't include specific details in a summary unless they are of crucial importance to the plot.

Here is a possible beginning for an answer to the question above:

"*Great Expectations* tells the story of Pip, who lives with his sister and brother-in-law in a blacksmith shop. Pip's life is changed when he meets an escaped convict in a graveyard . . ."

In Unit Sixteen, Lesson Three, you will read more suggestions about writing a plot summary.

Before you begin to write the answer for an essay question, read the question two or three times. Look for any key words the question may contain — *compare, summarize, describe, identify,* and so on. Make sure you understand the question.

EXERCISE ONE

Answer any three of the following questions. Read each question carefully. Find the key word or words. Then write a paragraph of six to ten sentences to answer each question you choose. (If you choose Question 1, you do not have to write in sentences or paragraphs.) When you finish, reread the questions and your answers. Make sure your answer contains the kind of information called for in the question.

1. List at least eight places in your hometown or county that you feel every visitor should see.
2. Describe a well-known building, statue, or historic landmark you have visited.
3. Define your idea of the word *generosity*.
4. Name a person from history you'd like to meet, and identify him or her.
5. Discuss the reasons why you would like a certain job for the summer (name the job).
6. Explain how to feed a particular pet (name the type of pet).
7. Compare and contrast the styles of two popular singers (name the singers).
8. Summarize a magazine article you have recently read (give the name of the article and the magazine in which it appeared).

Lesson Two

Planning Your Answer

When you are sure that you've understood the test question, take a minute or two to plan your answer before you start to write. First, jot down the points you want to cover. Then, number them in an order that is clear and logical. This outline will help you when you write your answer.

Look at this sample question that might appear on a history test:

"Summarize the career of Eleanor Roosevelt."

As you learned in Lesson One, when you are asked to "summarize" something, you have to give the main points about it briefly and concisely. Before writing your summary of the career of Eleanor Roosevelt, you could make a list of the items you want to cover, like this:

—born 1884
—died 1962
—in 1905 married FDR, who became 32nd President
—served as UN delegate after husband's death

—chaired UN commission that wrote the Universal Declaration of Human Rights
—author of six books and a newspaper column
—most active First Lady in history, working for minority rights, political reforms
—had five children
—during 1920's was a leader of women's activities in Democratic Party

Notice that this list is not written in complete sentences. Abbreviations are used, such as *FDR* for Franklin Delano Roosevelt, and *UN* for United Nations. This list is only for your use in planning your answer; it doesn't have to be clear to anyone except you.

After you have made the list, look it over. If there are any points that are unnecessary to answer the question, cross them out. For example, you may decide that it isn't important for a summary of Eleanor Roosevelt's career to include the number of children she had. Cross out the item about her children on the list.

Then organize the items on the list in a logical order. For a biographical summary, the best order is chronological. So you would number the items on your list like this:

1. born 1884
8. died 1962
2. in 1905, married FDR, who became 32nd President
5. served as UN delegate after husband's death
6. chaired UN commission that wrote the Universal Declaration of Human Rights
7. author of six books and a newspaper column
4. most active First Lady in history, working for minority rights, political reforms
3. during 1920's was a leader of women's activities in Democratic Party

Now you are ready to write your answer, using this numbered list as an outline. For a different kind of essay answer, you might want to organize your facts according to order of importance or some other order. Choose a method of organization that makes sense to you.

Keep your list simple and brief. You should spend only three or four minutes planning an essay answer, or even less time for a very short answer. This will leave you enough time to write your answer.

EXERCISE TWO

Below is an essay question that might be asked on a test. After the question is a list of facts that might be used in an answer. The facts are not listed in a logical order, and some of the facts may be unnecessary to answer the question. Decide which facts to include in an answer, and copy them on your paper in an order that is logical to you. You do not have to write a complete essay answer.

Question:
Explain the major causes of the American Revolution.

Facts:
—George Washington led American armies in Revolution
—2nd most important cause: unfair taxes imposed by England
—4th most important cause: use of force against American colonists by English
—U.S. Constitution written 10 yrs. after the Revolution
—most important cause: no American representation in English gov't.
—slogan "no taxation without representation" stirred American feelings
—unfair taxes included Stamp Act, Intolerable Acts
—3rd most important cause: English control of American trade

Lesson Three

Writing the Essay Answer

If you have planned your essay answer carefully, as suggested in Lesson Two, writing it should not be hard. Follow the simple outline you have prepared, and write as clearly as you can. Don't try to use fancy words or complicated sentences. Instead, concentrate on presenting the facts accurately and clearly. Your teacher will be more impressed by a simple, well-organized answer than by one that is wordy or overly complicated in style.

Writing an Effective Opening Sentence

A good opening sentence for an essay answer lets your teacher know that you have understood the question. It gets right to the point by indicating the kind of information you will present in your answer.

One good way to write an opening sentence is to rephrase the question. For example, if the question is "Discuss the major causes of the Civil War," you might begin like this:

"There were five major causes of the Civil War."

The sentence above shows that you have understood the question. It also reminds you of what the point of your answer should be. Here are more examples of good opening sentences. Each one tells you clearly what the question asks and what kind of information the rest of the answer will contain.

"There are four important qualities that make *The Adventures of Huckleberry Finn* one of Mark Twain's most memorable works."
"The systems of government in Great Britain and in the United States have both differences and similarities."
"Sudan is the largest country in Africa, nearly four times bigger than the state of Texas."

Here are two examples of weak opening sentences:

"There are probably five or six reasons that the Civil War happened."
"I'm not sure how to answer this question, but I'll try to do the best I can."

In the first sentence above, the writer sounds unsure about how many reasons will be included. If you have planned your answer properly, you should know how many main points you will make. In the second sentence above, the writer seems to lack confidence in his or her ability to answer the question. The sentence also fails to get directly to the point.

Sticking to the Point

In an essay answer, it's important to stick to the point of the question. For example, if you are asked to summarize the achievements of the United States space program, don't include your own personal views on the space shuttle program or on the possibility of life on other planets. You will waste valuable time by writing sentences that stray from the subject.

If you have studied hard for the test, you may have gathered a great deal of information, and you may be tempted to use as much of that information as you can. Perhaps you feel you can impress the teacher in this way. But a good essay answer should include only facts that answer the question being asked.

For example, you may have studied the poems of Robert Frost for an English test and know them very well. On the day of the test, you find that the test question reads, "Discuss the theme of Robert Frost's poem 'Mending Wall.' " Because you're prepared to discuss several of Frost's other poems, you might be tempted to show how much you know by including information about them in your answer. But since the question did not ask for details about other poems, it's a mistake to include them. You will not get credit for facts that do not answer the question, no matter how interesting or impressive they may be.

EXERCISE THREE

The following list contains five essay questions. Write only the opening sentence for an answer to each question.

Example: Identify George Washington.
George Washington was a hero of the American Revolution and the first President of the United States.

1. Discuss four reasons why you would or would not like to live in a particular foreign country. (You name the country.)
2. Explain how to prepare and serve your favorite food.
3. Identify a famous artist, writer, or musician of your choice.
4. Define the term *courage*.
5. Compare and contrast your favorite sport with a sport you do not like.

EXERCISE FOUR

Choose any two of the following essay questions to answer. First make a list of the ideas you want to include in your answer. Cross out any items that are not important to your answer. Then organize the items in a logical order. Make sure that your opening sentence is clear and refers to the question. Be sure that your answer sticks to the point of the question. Each answer you write should be from eight to ten sentences long.

1. Describe one important geographical feature, such as a lake, mountain, forest, or island, that is located near your home.
2. Explain how to repair a particular household item. (You name the item.)
3. Compare and contrast two movies that you have enjoyed.
4. Discuss the reasons you would like to have a million dollars.
5. Name and identify a famous person that you would like to meet.
6. Summarize the plot of a television program that you have recently seen.

Hints for Studying for an Essay Test

The following tips will help you prepare for an essay test:

1. *Begin to study a few days in advance.* Don't try to "cram" at the last minute. The pressure of having to learn a lot of material in a short time can make you nervous and unable to study effectively.

2. *Go over your class notes and textbook.* Spend extra time studying the topics that you think are most important. They are probably the same topics that your teacher has stressed in class discussions.

3. *Make up some possible essay questions that might be asked.* Outline your answers to these questions. You will have more confidence on the day of the test if you've already had some practice in writing about the topic.

Unit Eleven

Correct Agreement

11

Correct Agreement

Lesson One

Agreement Between Subject and Verb

What would happen if one donkey tried to pull two carts? What if two bus drivers tried to drive one bus, or one surfer tried to ride two surfboards?

The legs of the donkey would soon give out. The bus would probably run off the road while the two drivers fought for the wheel. And the surfer would probably end up treading water instead of riding the waves.

Two carts need two donkeys; one bus needs one driver; and one surfer can handle only one surfboard at a time. If the numbers don't match in this way, there is certain to be trouble.

In the same way, the subject and verb of a sentence must also "match" or agree.

Singular or Plural

To tell whether a subject and its verb agree, you need to know the difference between *singular* and *plural* words.

● **Singular words** refer to one person, place, thing, or idea.

● **Plural words** refer to more than one person, place, thing, or idea.

Nouns, pronouns, and verbs can be either singular or plural in number. A singular noun can usually be turned into a plural noun by adding *s* or *es:*

Singular	Plural
boy	boys
bone	bones
beach	beaches

Many plural nouns are formed in other ways. You will learn more about the formation of plural nouns in Unit Nineteen.

244

Pronouns, too, can be either singular or plural. (For a review of the singular and plural forms of pronouns, see Unit One, Lesson Two.) Here are a few examples:

Singular	Plural
I	we
she	they
this	these
each	many

Verbs can also have singular and plural forms. Many verbs that end in *s* or *es* are singular. Here are some examples of singular and plural verbs:

Singular	Plural
(he) **writes**	(they) **write**
(she) **reads**	(they) **read**
(it) **does**	(they) **do**

Not all verbs that end in *s* or *es* are singular. You will learn more about the formation of plural verbs in Unit Thirteen.

The singular and plural forms of the verb *be* may be hard to recognize. Here they are:

Present Tense

Singular	*Plural*
I **am**	we **are**
you **are**	you **are**
he, she, it **is**	they **are**

Past Tense

Singular	*Plural*
I **was**	we **were**
you **were**	you **were**
he, she, it **was**	they **were**

PRACTICE A

Number your paper from 1 to 15. Copy each of the following words. After the word, write whether it is a *noun, pronoun,* or *verb.* Then write *S* if the word is singular and *P* if the word is plural.

245

Examples: peaches
peaches   noun   P

becomes
becomes   verb   S

1. friend	**6.** was	**11.** those
2. am	**7.** boat	**12.** takes
3. she	**8.** foxes	**13.** it
4. does	**9.** glass	**14.** each
5. they	**10.** this	**15.** is

Subjects and Verbs

Read the following sentences. Do they sound strange to you?

The old donkey pull the cart along a dusty road.
Ms. Bevacqua drive the school bus three days a week.
The two best surfers is Ken and Sharon.
They surfs almost every day.

The sentences above sound strange because the subjects and verbs do not agree in number.

● **A singular subject needs a singular verb.**

● **A plural subject needs a plural verb.**

In the first two sentences above, the subjects are singular. The verbs should be singular, too.

The old **donkey pulls** the cart along a dusty road.
Ms. Bevacqua drives the school bus three days a week.

The singular subjects, *donkey* and *Ms. Bevacqua,* need the singular verbs, *pulls* and *drives.*

In the third and fourth sentences above, the subjects are plural. The verbs should be plural, too.

The two best **surfers are** Ken and Sharon.
They surf almost every day.

The plural subjects, *surfers* and *they,* need the plural verbs, *are* and *surf.*

Here are other examples of subjects and verbs that agree in number:

Singular: Each **basket contains** six dozen apples.
Plural: The **baskets contain** nearly one thousand apples altogether.

Singular: **Pat writes** to her aunt every week.
Plural: The **sisters write** in their diaries every day.

PRACTICE B

Number your paper from 1 to 10. Of the two verbs given in parentheses, choose the one that agrees with the subject of the sentence. Write the correct verb on your paper.

Example: The foreign dictionaries (is, are) on the top shelf.
are

1. The sunlight (is, are) strong today.
2. They (plans, plan) to attend the party.
3. One little mistake (does, do) not matter.
4. Several seagulls (was, were) high overhead.
5. Lois (visits, visit) her grandmother once a month.
6. The children (has, have) a tree house.
7. Dana (makes, make) dinner for his family every Friday.
8. She (thinks, think) the movie was exciting.
9. The buses (is, are) crowded at rush hour.
10. Sometimes fashions (changes, change) too quickly.

Phrases Between Subjects and Verbs

It is easy to find the subject of a sentence when the subject comes directly before the verb. But not all sentences are written that way. Sometimes other words come between the subject and the verb. When this happens, the subject can be hard to find. Is this sentence correct?

The boys with the blue surfboard is the Henderson twins.

What is the subject of this sentence? *Surfboard* is not the subject; it is the object of the preposition *with*. (For a review of prepositional phrases, see Unit Seven, Lesson Two.) The object of a prepositional phrase can never be the subject of a sentence.

When you are looking for the subject of a sentence, mentally remove any words that are in prepositional phrases. Now you can find the subject of the sentence.

The **boys** is the Henderson twins.

The sentence is not correct. Because *boys* is a plural subject, the verb must be plural, too:

The boys with the blue surfboard **are** the Henderson twins.

Here is the rule to remember:

● **A verb must agree in number with its subject, no matter what words come between the subject and the verb.**

Here are other examples of sentences with prepositional phrases between the subjects and verbs:

The **house** near the stables **is** for sale. (singular subject and verb)

The **mountains** between Carver City and the Salem River **are** the oldest in this part of the state. (plural subject and verb)

PRACTICE C

The following sentences contain errors in agreement. Number your paper from 1 to 5. Then rewrite each sentence correctly on your paper. Change the verb to make it agree with its subject.

Example: The piano, along with her music books, were sold at the auction.
The piano, along with her music books, was sold at the auction.

1. Several pieces of an ancient statue was found in the cave.
2. A screwdriver, in addition to a pair of pliers, are needed to assemble the table.
3. The stamps in her collection is worth over ten thousand dollars.
4. The glare from the spotlights were almost blinding.
5. Ahmed's story about knights and dragons were very entertaining.

Subjects That Follow Verbs

When the subject of a sentence comes after the verb, check the sentence carefully to make sure that the subject and the verb agree in number. Here are some kinds of sentences in which the subject often follows the verb:

1. In a question, the subject usually follows the verb.

   Are they the best surfers in town?   (plural subject and verb)
   When **is** the surfing **contest?**   (singular subject and verb)

2. When a sentence begins with *there* or *here,* the subject usually follows the verb.

   There **are** forty **surfers** in the surfing contest.   (plural subject and verb)
   Here **is** a **kiss** for good luck!   (singular subject and verb)

   Remember this rule:

- **When a subject comes after the verb in a sentence, the subject and verb must still agree in number.**

PRACTICE D

Of the two verbs given in parentheses, choose the one that agrees with the subject. Write the sentence correctly on your paper.

Example: There (is, are) two large oak trees near our house.
   There are two large oak trees near our house.

1. When (is, are) your cousin going to visit?
2. There (was, were) ten signatures at the bottom of the letter.
3. How much (is, are) this tape recorder worth?
4. There (is, are) twenty-four letters in the ancient Greek alphabet.
5. Here (is, are) the book of short stories that you must read.

Lesson Two

Indefinite Pronouns

Louella Peepers writes a gossip column for a big-city newspaper. Today she has a problem. She has a good bit of gossip about two movie stars. She knows her readers will like it. But she also knows that the two movie stars hate gossip columns. If they see their names in Louella's column, they'll be furious. Louella may never be allowed to interview them again.

Louella decides to write the story anyway. She brings her column to Maxine, the editor of her newspaper. It begins:

Today's hot item: Jessica Sandstorm, the beautiful red-headed movie star, was seen dancing last night with tall, tanned, blue-eyed leading man Lance Worthy. The best friends of Jessica and Lance are wondering if wedding bells will soon be ringing!

"Good story," Maxine says, "but you know how Sandstorm and Worthy feel about gossip columns. You'd better take out their names and make the story indefinite. Your readers will have fun guessing who the stars are, anyway."

Here is how Louella rewrote her column:

Today's hot item: A certain beautiful red-headed **someone** was seen dancing last night with a tall, tanned, blue-eyed **somebody**. **Everybody** is wondering if wedding bells will soon be ringing!

It is now impossible to tell who the story is about—unless Louella's readers are good at guessing. Louella has made the story indefinite by using *indefinite pronouns.*

As you learned in Unit Three, Lesson Two, an indefinite pronoun does not refer to a specific person, place, thing, or idea. When the subject of a sentence is an indefinite pronoun, subject-verb agreement may take some thought. Some indefinite pronouns are singular; others are plural; still others can be either singular or plural.

● **An indefinite pronoun used as the subject of a sentence must have a verb that agrees with it in number.**

The following indefinite pronouns are singular and need singular verbs:

another	everybody	no one
anybody	everyone	one
anyone	much	other
each	neither	somebody
either	nobody	someone

Here are some examples of singular indefinite pronouns used as subjects. Each has a singular verb.

Everybody reads Louella Peepers's column.

250

No one writes a better gossip column.
Each of her columns **is** filled with trivia.

The following indefinite pronouns are plural and need plural verbs:

both
few
many
others
several

Here are some examples of plural indefinite pronouns used as subjects. Each has a plural verb.

Few believe all the gossip in Louella's column.
Many think that the gossip is often false.
Others are sure the gossip is true.

Some indefinite pronouns may be either singular or plural, depending on their meaning in the sentence. They are the following pronouns:

all   most
any   none
more   some

It is easy to tell whether one of these indefinite pronouns is being used as a singular pronoun or as a plural pronoun. Simply look for a prepositional phrase following the indefinite pronoun. If the object of the preposition is singular, the indefinite pronoun is singular. If the object of the preposition is plural, the indefinite pronoun is plural. Here are some examples:

All of Louella's column **is** fun to read.

The subject is the indefinite pronoun *all.* The object of the preposition, *column,* is singular. Therefore, the pronoun *all* is singular, and it needs the singular verb *is.*

All of my friends **are** fans of Louella Peepers.

The object of the preposition, *friends,* is plural. Therefore, the indefinite pronoun *all* is plural, and it needs the plural verb *are.*

Of the two verbs given in parentheses, choose the one that agrees with the subject. Write the sentence correctly on your paper.

Example: One of the stories (was, were) about mountain climbing.
           One of the stories was about mountain climbing.

1. Some of the runners (has, have) crossed the finish line.
2. Either of those sweaters (is, are) a bargain.
3. Most of the movie (takes, take) place in India.
4. All of the seats for the concert (is, are) reserved.
5. Everyone (is, are) having a good time at the party.
6. Many of the team members (is, are) hoping to win the state championship.
7. Nobody (has, have) a car like Pete's.
8. Both of my shoes (was, were) ruined by the rain.
9. None of the snow on the hills (has, have) melted yet.
10. Someone with two packages to deliver (is, are) at the door.

PRACTICE B

Below is a list of ten indefinite pronouns. Use each pronoun as the subject of a sentence. Make sure that the verb in each sentence agrees with the subject.

Example: everybody
           Everybody enjoys a day at the beach.

1. all
2. someone
3. many
4. most
5. each
6. one
7. some
8. several
9. anyone
10. nobody

Lesson Three

Compound Subjects

Here are three wise sayings:

A fool and his money are soon parted.

— Unknown author

Good health and good sense are two of life's greatest blessings.

— Publilius Syrus

Arts and sciences are formed and perfected by degrees.

— Michel de Montaigne

These sayings have two things in common. Each expresses an interesting opinion. And each has a *compound subject.*

As you learned in Unit One, Lesson Five, a compound subject is two or more subjects that share the same verb and are joined by a connecting word, or *conjunction.* In each of the four sayings above, the conjunction *and* was used to join the two subjects. And in each saying, the plural verb *are* was used.

● **A compound subject in which the parts are joined by the conjunction *and* needs a plural verb.**

Here are more examples of sentences with compound subjects and plural verbs:

Sara and Bob cook delicious hamburgers.
Their **friends and family enjoy** their cooking.
Sara's **cakes and pies are** good, too.

There are two exceptions to this rule.

1. When a compound subject names two or more things that are really *one item,* the subject needs a singular verb.

The **skull and crossbones was** a symbol used on pirates' flags. (The compound subject, *skull and crossbones,* names one symbol. Therefore, it agrees with the singular verb *was.*)

Ham and eggs is my favorite breakfast. (The compound subject, *ham and eggs,* names one dish. Therefore, it agrees with the singular verb *is.*)

2. When the word *each* or *every* comes before a compound subject, the subject needs a singular verb.

Each picnic table and bench is made of redwood.
Every dog and cat was checked by the doctor.

Not all compound subjects are joined by the conjunction *and.* They are sometimes joined by other conjunctions, such as *or* or *nor.*

● A compound subject that is made up of two singular subjects connected by *or* or *nor* needs a singular verb.

A nail or a screw is needed to fix this toy.
Neither **the President nor the Vice-President was** pleased with the vote.

● A compound subject that is made up of two plural subjects connected by *or* or *nor* needs a plural verb.

Moles or gophers have dug several holes in my garden.
Neither **the fans nor the players were** satisfied with the condition of the field.

● When a compound subject is made up of a singular subject and a plural subject connected by *or* or *nor,* the verb agrees with the subject that is closer to the verb.

Either the **twins** or **Mark has** time to drive you home. (The singular noun *Mark* is closer to the verb. Therefore, the singular verb *has* is correct.)

Either **Mark** or the **twins have** time to drive you home. (The plural noun *twins* is closer to the verb. Therefore, the plural verb *have* is correct.)

PRACTICE A

Of the two verbs in parentheses, choose the one that agrees with the subject. Write the sentence correctly on your paper.

Example: Every book and magazine (was, were) sold.
Every book and magazine was sold.

1. The windows and the door (was, were) nailed shut.
2. Each student and teacher (has, have) given something to the scholarship fund.
3. Oil and vinegar (is, are) a tasty dressing for a salad.
4. Either rabbits or a groundhog (has, have) been eating the vegetables in the garden.
5. Anne or June (is, are) bringing the records for the party.
6. A bus and a truck (was, were) stalled in traffic.
7. Neither the mayor nor the council members (has, have) a plan for fighting crime.
8. Either oil or gas (is, are) leaking from the car's engine.
9. Paul and Artie (sings, sing) at their mother's birthday party every year.
10. Each song and dance (was, were) performed by a different group of students.

PRACTICE B

Below is a list of ten phrases that could be used as compound subjects. Use each one as the subject of a sentence. Use either *is* or *are* as the verb. Make sure the subject and verb in each sentence agree.

Example: Tom and Jerry
Tom and Jerry are two of my favorite cartoon characters.

1. ham and eggs
2. either Steve or his parents
3. three cars or a bus
4. baseball and football
5. neither Amy nor Karen
6. lions and tigers
7. Batman and Robin
8. police officers or a private detective
9. a violin and three kazoos
10. rain or snow

Lesson Four

Other Problems in Agreement

Collective Nouns

You've probably heard of a *flock* of sheep, a *herd* of cows, and even a *school* of fish. But have you ever heard of a *gam* of whales, a *knot* of toads, or a *sleuth* of bears? Do you know anyone who has a *clowder* of cats? These are all real words used to describe groups of animals.

Words that refer to groups of animals, people, or things are called *collective nouns*. Other examples of collective nouns are the words *committee, family, jury, team, orchestra,* and *club*. A collective noun is singular in form, but its meaning may be either singular or plural. So a verb that has a collective noun as its subject may be either singular or plural, depending on how the noun is used.

- A collective noun is singular when it refers to the group as a whole.

- A collective noun is plural when it refers to the separate members of the group.

Look at some examples:

Singular: The **jury has been meeting** all afternoon.

In this sentence, the collective noun *jury* is singular because it refers to the group as a whole. *Meeting* is something all the members of the jury do together. Therefore, *jury* agrees with the singular verb phrase *has been meeting*.

Plural: The **jury have gone** to their rooms for the night.

In this sentence, *jury* is plural because it refers to the separate members of the group. The members of the jury go to their rooms separately, not together. Therefore, *jury* agrees with the plural verb phrase *have gone*.

Here are some other examples of collective nouns with singular and plural meanings:

Singular: The **team is** ready to play.
Plural: The **team have** taken their positions on the field.

256

Singular: The **flock was** owned by a wealthy farmer.
Plural: The **flock were** scattered all over the hillside.

Singular: The **class has** a new teacher.
Plural: The **class have** finished their term papers.

PRACTICE A

The subject of each of the following sentences is a collective noun. Read each sentence carefully, and decide whether the subject has a singular or a plural meaning. Number your paper from 1 to 5. Of the two verbs in parentheses, choose the one that agrees with the subject. Write the correct verb on your paper.

Example: A pride of lions (is, are) a majestic sight.
is

1. The ship's crew (has, have) put on their dress uniforms.
2. The class (has, have) decided to give a dance this spring.
3. The orchestra (was, were) finding it hard to learn their parts.
4. This committee (is, are) having an all-night meeting.
5. My family (is, are) all planning separate vacations this summer.

Words That State Amounts

Like collective nouns, words that state amounts can cause confusion in subject-verb agreement.

- **A subject that states an amount usually has a singular meaning and needs a singular verb.**

Look at these examples:

Singular: **Three minutes** in the dentist's chair **seems** like an hour to me.

In this sentence, the subject *three minutes* refers to one period of time. Therefore, it agrees with the singular verb *seems*.

Singular: **A thousand dollars is** too much to pay for that old car.

The subject *a thousand dollars* refers to one amount of money. Therefore, it agrees with the singular verb *is*.

- When a subject that states an amount refers to a number of separate people or things, its meaning is plural and it needs a plural verb.

Plural: **Three quarters** of the students **are** absent.

The subject *three quarters* refers to a number of separate people. Therefore, it is plural, and agrees with the plural verb *are*.

PRACTICE B

Number your paper from 1 to 5. Choose the verb in parentheses that agrees with the subject and write it on your paper.

Example: Half of the cherries (is, are) still green.
              are

1. Four years (was, were) a long time to spend in that jungle.
2. Three fifths of the cattle on this farm (is, are) dairy cows.
3. Two feet of string (is, are) all I need to tie this package.
4. Many days of practice (has, have) helped the team's defense.
5. Half of the roses (has, have) wilted.

Doesn't and Don't

The contractions *doesn't* and *don't* may cause confusion about agreement. To use these contractions correctly, remember that *doesn't* means *does not* and *don't* means *do not*.

Also remember the rule:

- The verb *do* should be used with all plural subjects, and with the singular pronouns *I* and *you*. The verb *does* should be used with all other singular subjects.

Look at these examples:

Incorrect: **John don't** want to go.
Correct: **John doesn't** want to go.   (singular subject)

Incorrect: The **players doesn't** want their coach to call time out.
Correct: The **players don't** want their coach to call time out.   (plural subject)

If you are not sure whether *don't* or *doesn't* is correct, drop *n't* and say the sentence aloud. If the verb is wrong, you will probably hear the mistake.

Incorrect: **John do** want to go.
              The **players does** want their coach to call time out.

Because these sentences sound wrong, you can tell that the contraction *don't* in the first sentence should be changed to *doesn't*. The contraction *doesn't* in the second sentence should be changed to *don't*.

PRACTICE C

Complete each of the following sentences by adding *don't* or *doesn't*. Number your paper from 1 to 5 and write the correct contraction after the number.

Example: The telephone _____ seem to be working.
            doesn't

1. She _____ remember my name.
2. Our dogs _____ like to go out in the rain.
3. That plant _____ seem to be healthy.
4. I _____ need that kind of advice.
5. This watch _____ have any broken parts.

PRACTICE D

Number your paper from 1 to 10. Of the two verbs in parentheses, choose the one that agrees with the subject of the sentence. Write the correct verb on your paper.

Example: Jesse (doesn't, don't) like cold weather.
            doesn't

1. Large chunks of ice (was, were) blocking the mountain pass.
2. Just beyond the bay (is, are) a dangerous reef.
3. One of the guests (is, are) bringing dessert.
4. There (is, are) several eggs in this nest.
5. Most of the house (has, have) fallen in ruins.
6. That train (doesn't, don't) run on time.
7. Strawberries and cream (is, are) my favorite dessert.
8. Here (is, are) the books you asked me to bring you.
9. A pencil and a piece of paper (was, were) on each student's desk.
10. Our school orchestra (is, are) the best in the state.

Lesson Five

Agreement Between Pronouns and Antecedents

Tommy and Tina are kindergarten pupils. Today is a special day for them. Their teacher, Mr. Collins, has taken their class to visit the city zoo.

They stop first at the lion cage. They see a huge lion, with a thick yellow mane, lying in the warm sun. "Mr. Collins," Tommy says, "is that lion a *he* or a *she*?"

Mr. Collins notices the lion's mane and replies, "That lion is a *he*, Tommy."

The class moves on to the cage where the deer are kept. Tina points to one of the animals. "Mr. Collins," she says, "is that deer a *he* or a *she*?"

Mr. Collins sees that the deer Tina is pointing to has no antlers. "That deer is a *she*, Tina," he replies.

The next stop is the reptile house. The class admires a large green snake lying in coils on the floor of a glass tank. "Mr. Collins," Tommy and Tina call out together, "is that snake a *he* or a *she*?"

Mr. Collins looks closely at the snake. He thinks hard. He scratches his head. Finally, he replies, "That snake is definitely, positively—an *it*."

Tommy and Tina have not yet studied English grammar. But they already understand one important rule about using pronouns correctly:

● **A pronoun must agree with its antecedent in gender.**

The *antecedent* of a pronoun is the noun the pronoun refers to. The word *gender* refers to the masculine and feminine forms of words. The pronouns *he, him,* and *his* are used to refer to masculine antecedents.

Mr. Collins enjoys taking **his** students to the zoo.
He is a clever teacher.

The pronouns *she, her,* and *hers* are used to refer to feminine antecedents.

260

Tina is enjoying **her** day at the zoo.
She loves to look at the animals.

The pronouns *it* and *its* are *neuter* in gender. They are used to refer to antecedents that are neither masculine or feminine.

Schoolchildren visit the zoo every day. **It** is a favorite place for class trips.
Its employees are trained to answer the questions children ask.

The pronouns *they, them,* and *their* are used to refer to antecedents of any gender.

Two boys have forgotten to bring **their** lunches.
Some of the girls will share **their** lunches with **them.**
They are thoughtful girls, aren't **they**?

There is a second rule about agreement between pronouns and antecedents:

● **A pronoun must agree with its antecedent in number.**

As you learned in Lesson One of this unit, the word *number* refers to the singular and plural forms of words.

A singular pronoun is used to refer to a singular antecedent. The following pronouns are singular: *I, me, my, mine, he, him, his, she, her, hers, it,* and *its.*

A plural pronoun is used to refer to a plural antecedent. The following pronouns are plural: *we, us, our, ours, they, them, their,* and *theirs.*

The pronouns *you, your,* and *yours* can be either singular or plural.

Here are some examples of pronouns that agree with their antecedents in number. In each of the following sentences, the pronoun and its antecedent are both in boldface type.

A zookeeper gave the **lioness her** dinner.
The **lion** got **his** dinner a few minutes later.
The zoo **employees** keep **their** distance when feeding the lions.
That **job** is dangerous, isn't **it**?

The following rules will help you make sure that the pronouns you use agree with their antecedents in number.

1. Use a singular pronoun to refer to a singular indefinite pronoun.

261

Incorrect: **Each** of those trees has lost **their** leaves.
Correct: **Each** of those trees has lost **its** leaves.

The singular pronoun *its* agrees with the singular indefinite pronoun *each*.

Incorrect: The lifeguard showed **one** of the girls how to improve **their** backstroke.
Correct: The lifeguard showed **one** of the girls how to improve **her** backstroke.

The singular pronoun *her* agrees with the singular indefinite pronoun *one*.

Incorrect: **Somebody** on the team forgot **their** uniform.

In this sentence, the pronoun *somebody* is singular. However, the pronoun *their* is plural. This kind of error can be corrected in one of several ways, depending on the meaning you want. If all of the team members are male, you could write:

Somebody on the team forgot **his** uniform.

If all of the team members are female, you could write:

Somebody on the team forgot **her** uniform.

If some of the players are male and some are female, the best solution is to write *his or her*:

Somebody on the team forgot **his or her** uniform.

2. Use a plural pronoun to refer to a plural indefinite pronoun.
As you learned in Lesson Two of this unit, plural indefinite pronouns include such words as *both, few, many,* and *several.*

Both of the catchers on the team brought **their** equipment.
Many of the players brought gloves with **them.**

3. Use a plural pronoun to refer to two or more nouns joined by *and*.

Alfredo and Brian didn't finish **their** meals.
The Griffins and the Kamms brought **their** records to the party.

4. Use a singular pronoun to refer to two or more singular nouns connected by *or* or *nor*.

262

Either Alfredo or Brian didn't finish **his** meal. (The singular pronoun *his* refers to Alfredo *or* Brian, not to both.)

Either Betty or Esther brought **her** records to the party. (The singular pronoun *her* refers to Betty *or* Esther, not to both.)

5. **If a singular antecedent is connected to a plural antecedent by *or* or *nor*, the pronoun agrees in number with the antecedent that follows *or* or *nor*.**

Either Betty or the Kamms brought **their** records to the party.
Either the Griffins or Esther brought **her** records to the party.

PRACTICE A

Number your paper from 1 to 10. Of the two pronouns in parentheses, choose the one that agrees with its antecedent in the sentence. Write the correct pronoun on your paper.

Example: Each girl brought (her, their) own lunch along on the field trip.
her

1. I found neither the book nor the magazine in (its, their) place in the library.
2. Many of the windows in the old house had no glass in (its, their) frames.
3. Neither of the boys was wearing (his, their) hat.
4. Every lion in the circus act performed one of (their, its) tricks.
5. Either Flora or the Garcia sisters will lend me (her, their) notes.
6. Tom and Stan helped (his, their) mother paint the ceiling.
7. One of the women lost (her, their) briefcase.
8. Both of the dancers wore blue ribbons in (her, their) hair.
9. Everyone on the boys' swim team should bring (their, his) towel to the meet.
10. Ralph, Mike, and Gino easily found (his, their) way back to the campsite.

PRACTICE B

Think of an appropriate pronoun to complete each of the following sentences. Write the completed sentences on your paper.

Example: If anyone wants to try out for the girls' softball team,
_____ should come to the tryout today.
If anyone wants to try out for the girls' softball team,
she should come to the tryout today.

1. Neither Bruno nor Ken has decided which jacket _____
will buy.
2. Few in the audience were prepared for the surprise _____
received.
3. Ellen and Kim wore _____ sandals at the beach.
4. Everyone should have _____ history textbook in class
tomorrow.
5. Either Phil or the Hansens will bring _____ car to
the game.
6. Each tool must be replaced in _____ own place on
the rack.
7. Many of the spectators had brought _____ umbrellas
with them.
8. Both the mayor and the governor were applauded after
_____ speeches.
9. Either of the girls will lend you _____ pencil.
10. Did Marsha or Peggy finish _____ essay first?

Review Exercises

I. For each sentence below, choose the verb in parentheses that
agrees with the subject. Write the correct verb on your paper.
(Lesson One)

Example: My cousin Sara (lives, live) on a dairy farm that is
forty miles from my home.
lives

1. All my life, I (has, have) lived in the city.
2. Sara, along with other friends of mine, (says, say) that city
life is too hectic.
3. They (prefers, prefer) the quiet of the country.
4. But life among the rolling hills and peaceful plains (is, are)
not restful for me.

5. When I visit the farm, the silence of the countryside (seems, seem) eerie.
6. There (is, are) no noises at night to help me sleep.
7. Through my window (comes, come) no sounds of traffic, music, and talking.
8. There (is, are) no light from streetlamps or store windows.
9. The darkness of the farms and the woods (seems, seem) scary.
10. How (does, do) people living in the country ever get a good night's rest?

II. Each sentence below has an indefinite pronoun as its subject. For each sentence, choose the verb in parentheses that agrees with the subject. Write the correct verb on your paper. (Lesson Two)

Example: When television was invented, many (was, were) sure that radio would be hurt.
          were

1. According to some people, most of the radio stations (was, were) doomed.
2. Each of these beliefs (was, were) false.
3. TV did not kill radio; today, both (is, are) popular.
4. Anyone who enjoys music (finds, find) more to choose from on radio.
5. None of the TV networks (broadcasts, broadcast) daily concerts.
6. Yet many of the popular radio stations (does, do).
7. All of the major sports (is, are) broadcast on the radio.
8. Most of the minor ones (is, are), too.
9. Some of radio's importance (is, are) gone today.
10. But nobody now (predicts, predict) that radio will disappear.

III. Combine each pair of sentences below into one sentence with a compound subject. Use the word in parentheses to join the two subjects. Make sure the verb agrees with its subject. Write the new sentences on your paper. (Lesson Three)

Example: Mark is giving a party. Arlene is giving a party.   (and)
          Mark and Arlene are giving a party.

1. A robin has built a nest in this tree. A blue jay has built a nest in this tree.   (or)

265

2. The bicycle in the yard is rusty. The wagon in the yard is rusty.   (and)
3. Martha was painting the shed. Lou was painting the shed.   (and)
4. Fred is making the dinner. His sisters are making the dinner.   (or)
5. A plane from Toronto is landing. A plane from Seattle is landing.   (or)
6. Steve's hat was covered with snow. His coat was covered with snow.   (and)
7. The starter of my car is broken. The transmission of my car is broken.   (or)
8. Anna deserves the music award. Cathy deserves the music award.   (or)
9. The lions are hungry. The tiger is hungry.   (and)
10. The salad is delicious. The sandwich is delicious.   (and)

IV. For each sentence below, choose the correct word from the two in parentheses. Write the correct words on your paper. (Lesson Four)

Example: The committee (is, are) supposed to meet on Thursday.
is

1. Six hundred dollars (isn't, aren't) too much for this antique clock.
2. As the lights came on, the audience (was, were) putting on their coats.
3. (Doesn't, Don't) the train stop at this station any more?
4. Two thirds of the seniors (is, are) planning to attend college.
5. The class (has, have) completed its spring project.
6. Allan and Kim (doesn't, don't) want to go biking with us.
7. The physics of space flight (is, are) a complex topic.
8. Twenty-six miles (is, are) the length of a marathon.
9. (Do, Does) the jury want to deliberate longer?
10. The band (is, are) playing my favorite song.

V. In five of the following ten sentences, the pronouns are used correctly. Number your paper from 1 to 10. For each correct sentence, write C on your paper. Rewrite the incorrect sentences.

Make sure that pronouns agree with their antecedents. (Lesson Five)

Example: Everyone on the girls' softball team received their own trophy.
Everyone on the girls' softball team received her own trophy.

1. Each tennis player was allowed to choose their partner.
2. Arlene and Rick offered their solution to the problem.
3. The teacher helped one of the students with their composition.
4. I found a hat and scarf in a thrift shop, and I bought it for fifty cents.
5. Every lamp and table in the yard sale had their own price tag.
6. All of the players will try their best to be on time for the game.
7. Either Bianca or Jessica left her keys in the door.
8. Everyone received his or her invitation a month before the wedding.
9. Most of the bowlers had bought his own bowling shoes.
10. Some of the dogs had ribbons in their hair.

VI. Choose one of the topics listed below. Write a paragraph of eight to twelve sentences about the topic. Make sure that all the verbs agree with their subjects and that all the pronouns agree with their antecedents. (Lessons One to Five)

Topics:
What My Clothes Say About Me
The Funniest Animal I Know
What Makes a Champion
A Pleasant Surprise
A topic of your own choice

Writing Persuasion

Lesson One

Choosing What to Say

Today is Mel's birthday, and his friends are having a party for him. They all chipped in to buy Mel a present. He can't wait to open it, but he hesitates. After all, he doesn't want to look too eager.

Finally, Mel takes the lid off the box. In front of him is the ugliest sweater he has ever seen! What should he do? He knows he has to say something, but he is speechless. His mind is a blank.

Rita screams, "How do you like it?"

Chuck demands, "So what do you think?"

Mel's mind, which only seconds ago was blank, now fills with thoughts:

"What a color! It looks like a mustard jar exploded. Are they color blind?"

"I wouldn't wear this to a dogfight."

"Could this be a joke?"

Suddenly, reality rushes back. Mel has to say something to persuade his friends that he likes the present. Or he could pretend to pass out!

As Mel stares at the gift, his mind begins to work:

"It'll keep me warm on dark winter nights—*very* dark winter nights."

"It looks like real wool, at least."

"They *must* have looked all over town for this thing. They shouldn't have done it. Why on earth did they?"

But before Mel speaks, his mind chooses from among these thoughts and rearranges them. What he says comes out like this:

"It's pure wool. I'll be warm all winter. This will be great for football season. You really shouldn't have gone to so much trouble. You must have been in every store in town to find a sweater like this!"

Chuck and Rita beam. Mel's friends smile and take turns

looking at the latest addition to his wardrobe. Everyone is happy, even Mel. He has said the right thing.

Do you know someone who always seems to say the right thing? That person is skilled at *choosing* what to say from among the many thoughts he or she has.

Look back at the different thoughts that raced through Mel's mind when he saw the sweater. If Mel had said those thoughts out loud, he might not have had many friends afterwards. He would certainly have hurt his friends' feelings. But he sorted through his thoughts, rejected some, and changed others. What he actually did say was just right. He convinced his friends that he was grateful for their present.

It's even easier to choose among your thoughts when you write them down on paper. You don't have to think "on your feet."

When you are first presented with a topic to write about, you may feel that your mind is blank, that you have nothing to say or write about the topic. But if you take a moment to let your mind think of something, anything at all, about the topic, you'll find that your ideas will start to flow. When you have jotted your ideas on paper, you can see them, add to them, move them around, and change them. You can take your time searching for just the right words.

Persuasion

You may never have to persuade someone that you are grateful for a present. But you'll often find yourself wanting to persuade people about other things. You may want to persuade someone to agree with your opinion about something or to act in a certain way. In order to be successful, you must know how to choose your words and arrange your ideas.

In this unit, you will study the important steps in planning a piece of persuasive writing:

1. Choose facts and ideas that are likely to persuade.
2. Consider the experience and concerns of the people you hope to persuade.
3. Organize your presentation clearly and effectively.

The most important point to keep in mind is this: You have plenty of thoughts and ideas already in your mind. Give yourself the time to let them come out.

EXERCISE ONE

Imagine that your friends have given you a birthday present. It's not exactly what you had hoped for. It is a lamp — a very unusual lamp. It is in the shape of a large duck. When it's turned on, the duck glows, from its orange beak to its webbed yellow feet. Imagine all of the thoughts that might go through your mind upon receiving this gift.

Jot down on a sheet of paper at least ten separate thoughts. A thought might be expressed in a single word, in a few words, or in a sentence.

When you finish, you might share your ideas with others in the class. If so, listen carefully to what others say.

Choose ten ideas that you wrote or heard. Write each idea as a sentence that you could use to persuade your friends that you really appreciate the gift, even if you don't like it.

Lesson Two

Facts and Opinions

When you thought of what you could say to your friends about the duck lamp, you probably had some ideas that were based on *opinions* and some that were based on *facts*. For example, you might have felt that the duck lamp was *silly*. That is your opinion. Other people might feel that the lamp is *clever* or *practical*. Those are their opinions.

Another of your thoughts might have been based on fact; for example: *This will be the only lamp in my room that is not broken.* A *fact* is something that can be proved. Facts may be proved in a number of different ways — through research in books, magazines, or newpapers, or by observation. In this case, you could prove that all the other lamps in your room are broken by observation — that is, by looking at them.

Unlike facts, opinions cannot be proved true or false. Opinions are neither right nor wrong — they are people's feelings about things. When you want to persuade someone to see things your way, it's often best to use a combination of facts and opinions. Opinions alone may be interesting, but they are more likely to be persuasive when combined with facts that support them. For example, if you want to convince your friends that you like a duck lamp, you might say, "It will really be handy." But that would not be as effective as saying, "It will be the only lamp in my room that works."

Suppose it's your opinion that your school is beautiful. If you wanted to persuade a friend who had never seen the school, what kinds of facts could you use to support your opinion? Maybe facts like these would persuade your friend:

"The school was designed by the state's most famous architect."

"The front of the school is decorated with a mosaic made of multicolored ceramic tiles."

"The school received the top prize in a national contest for fine architectural design."

When supported by facts, an opinion can become persuasive.

EXERCISE TWO

Below are ten statements that could be made about a school. Number your paper from 1 to 10. Read each statement and decide whether it is a fact or an opinion. Write *fact* after the number of each sentence that states a fact and *opinion* after the number of each sentence that states an opinion.

Examples: Our school has the largest enrollment of any school in the county.
fact

Our school is the best in the county.
opinion

1. Our school library has fewer books than the average school library in our state.
2. Our school library has so few books that there is no point trying to find what you need.
3. More students should take art classes.
4. Our school has the hardest-working teachers in the state.
5. Our school sports programs are losing money.
6. Football games at our school are dull because no one cheers.

273

7. More people would go to football games at our school if the team weren't so bad.
8. Eight out of ten students interviewed by the school paper said they'd go to football games if the team were in the regional playoffs.
9. Eighty percent of the seniors in our school go on to college.
10. More students in our school take home economics than any other subject except English.

EXERCISE THREE

Write five facts and five opinions about your school. For this exercise, your facts don't have to be true. After each fact, give an example of how that fact could be proved true or false.

Example: Fact:
Our school has the largest gymnasium of any high school in the state.   *This fact could be proved by measuring the size of each high school gymnasium in the state.*
Opinion:
Our school is ugly.

Lesson Three

Audience

Miguel was a fire fighter in the town of Las Palmas. One day, Miguel got a call from Sarah, who worked on fire prevention for the Las Palmas Fire Department. "Miguel," Sarah said, "I have a problem. I'm supposed to give two talks on fire prevention at the Riverview School today. One talk will be for the first graders in Mr. Parker's class. The other talk will be for the members of the Parents' Association. The trouble is that I've just come down with a terrible cold. Do you think you can fill in for me?"

Miguel replied, "I'd be happy to do it, Sarah. But how will I know what to say?"

"That's easy," Sarah answered. "Just stop off at my office in the firehouse. I left my notes for the talks right on my desk. Pick them up before you go to the school and use them when you give the talks. And thanks for helping out, Miguel."

When Miguel went to Sarah's office, he found the following notes on her desk:

How to Prevent Fires

1. Never play with matches.
2. Put fire alarms in your house or apartment.
3. Make sure your wiring is sound.
4. Don't touch stoves and ovens.
5. Never smoke in bed.
6. Don't touch electrical outlets.
7. Make sure your appliances have strong electrical cords.
8. If you see a fire, tell your parents right away.

As Miguel looked over these notes, he realized that he couldn't use the same notes for both talks. When he spoke to the first graders, he couldn't tell them to put fire alarms in their houses or apartments. That was a job for their parents to do. And when he spoke to the Parents' Association, he couldn't warn the adults not to play with matches. Miguel saw that he would have to decide which ideas from Sarah's notes would be appropriate for each audience.

After a few minutes with a pencil and paper, Miguel had written two sets of notes:

First Graders

1. Never play with matches.
2. Don't touch stoves and ovens.
3. Don't touch electrical outlets.
4. If you see a fire, tell your parents right away.

Parents' Association

1. Put fire alarms in your house or apartment.
2. Make sure your wiring is sound.
3. Never smoke in bed.
4. Make sure your appliances have strong electrical cords.

When Miguel had chosen the right ideas for each audience, he felt ready to give the talks.

It's important to consider your audience when you are writing, too. Here are three examples of situations that call for persuasion. Who is the audience in each of these situations?

1. You want to buy a new stereo system, but you can't afford it. You decide to ask your parents to lend you $600.00, which you will repay out of the weekly salary from your part-time job.

2. You see an ad in a local newspaper asking for a teenager to work at a skating rink as a roller-skating teacher. You are a good roller skater and you decide to apply for the job. You must explain to the manager of the skating rink why you would be good for the job.

3. The local school board is having a public hearing on a proposal to do away with after-school sports at your high school in order to save money. As a student athlete, you want to convince the board members to veto the proposal.

In the first situation, the audience is your parents. In the second, it is the manager of the skating rink. In the third, it is the members of the school board.

In planning what to say or write, you must take into account the *knowledge* and *experience* of your audience. It's important to explain anything that your audience may not know. At the same time, you should avoid explaining ideas that are not related to your topic or that your audience already understands.

For example, if you ask your parents for a loan, you don't need to tell them about your part-time job or about your love for music. They already know about these things. But they may need to know that the stereo you want is a bargain and that the price is going to rise at the end of the month.

When you ask the manager of the skating rink for a job, you don't need to mention your high grades in algebra or your skill at Italian cooking. You do need to mention that you are a good roller skater.

When you speak to the school board about the sports budget, the board members don't need to hear how school budgets are planned. They do need to know how you, a student athlete, are likely to suffer if your school's sports program is cut.

Anticipate Objections

You should also consider the *possible objections* that your audience may raise. Plan ahead so you can answer their objections effectively. In fact, it's best to respond to possible objections even before they are raised. In doing so, you will show your audience that you have thought carefully about the issue.

One possible objection your parents might have when you request a $600.00 loan is that $600.00 is too much to spend on a stereo. Here are some ways you could reply:

"I've checked the catalogs of six makers of stereo systems, and I've found that no other system offers as many features at such a low price."

"A consumer magazine says the stereo system I want to buy is the most reliable and durable one made. Isn't it better to pay a little more and get a system that will last a lot longer?"

When you ask the manager of the skating rink for the job as a skating teacher, he might object, saying, "You've never worked as a teacher before." You might respond this way:

"That's true, but I taught my brother and sister and two of their friends to skate."

And when you speak to the school board about the after-school sports budget, the board members might object by saying that the school does not have enough money for sports. A possible response is this:

"The school can pay for half the cost of after-school sports. The students can raise the rest of the money by having a dance and a picnic."

When you are writing to persuade, try to imagine the objections your audience is likely to raise. Be ready to respond with facts and ideas that are convincing.

EXERCISE FOUR

Each of the following situations could call for the writing of a persuasive letter. Think about who the audience might be for each letter. Then consider what kind of information that audience is likely to need. Look at the two sentences given for each situation. Decide whether the information presented in each sentence is needed by the audience. Write *needed* or *not needed* on your paper next to the letter for each sentence.

Example: You want to persuade the manager of the Luxe Theater to show more movies of interest to teenagers.
a. My friends and I would go to the Luxe Theater more often if you showed more adventure movies.
b. People from the ages of thirteen to nineteen are considered "teenagers."
a. needed
b. not needed

1. You want to persuade the mayor that the city should hire more teenagers to work in the parks during the summer.
   a. Last summer, many students at our school who wanted jobs could not find them.
   b. July and August are usually the warmest months of the summer.

2. You want to persuade your sister to lend you her tape recorder so you can record a rehearsal of your school glee club.
   a. The basic process used in tape recording was invented in 1898 by Valdemar Poulsen.
   b. I've used the tape recorder several times, and I've never damaged it in any way.

3. You want to persuade your class advisor to sponsor a dance to celebrate the end of the fall term.
   a. Dances at our school usually start between 8:00 and 8:30 p.m.
   b. My cousin's band is willing to perform at our dance for half its usual pay.

4. You want to persuade the town council to continue to provide funds for drivers' education in schools.
   a. Many studies have shown that drivers' education reduces the number of accidents caused by teenage drivers.
   b. Unlike in America, drivers in England stay on the left side of the road.

5. You want to persuade the readers of the school newspaper to support the school's athletic teams.
   a. My father was a star on our high school basketball team twenty-two years ago.
   b. The captain of the football team says the team plays better when the fans are cheering them on.

EXERCISE FIVE

Look again at the five situations described in Exercise Four. Choose two of them. For each situation you choose, imagine two objections which an audience might raise. Write each objection. Then write a sentence in which you respond to each objection in a way you think will persuade your audience.

Example: You want to persuade the manager of the Luxe Theater to show more movies of interest to teenagers.
Objection: *There may not be enough teenagers living nearby to fill the theater every night.*
Response: *If a movie is good enough, teenagers will travel far to see it.*
Objection: *Some teenagers go to movie theaters only to make noise and fool around.*
Response: *If a good movie is showing, more responsible teenagers will go to the theater, and they will help to control the few rowdy ones.*

Lesson Four

Beginnings and Endings

Although you may not realize it, it's likely that you receive persuasive messages many times each day. For instance, the commercials on radio and TV are designed to persuade you to do something — to buy a certain product, to see a certain show, and so on. These messages are written by professionals who have studied the art of persuasion.

Although there are many kinds of commercials, they often follow the same general pattern. Commercials that try to sell you a product usually begin with an interesting or unusual fact or idea that introduces the product.

"At last! An economical car that's fun to drive!"
"Great Moments in History #493: Krunch-O Bars discovers a new use for the peanut."

Then the commercials give facts, opinions, or both, which have been carefully chosen to persuade.

279

"Yes, six out of seven doctors surveyed recommend pleasant-tasting No-Hax cough drops."

"Your dog will love the taste of new Poocho Kernels!"

Finally, commercials usually end with the message the writer wants you to remember.

"Buy some No-Hax today. You'll be glad you did!"

"Order now — at these low prices, they won't last long!"

When you write to persuade, you can use some of the basic tactics of commercial writers. Begin with an interesting fact or idea that introduces the "product" you are trying to "sell." Follow through with well-chosen facts and opinions designed to persuade your audience. And end with a clear and convincing statement of your message.

Beginnings

The beginning of what you write is very important. Unless the beginning is interesting, you may lose your audience, just as a boring commercial may drive you away from the TV.

Here are some tips for writing a good beginning for a piece of persuasive writing:

1. *Introduce the topic clearly.*
After reading your opening sentence, your audience should know what you are writing about.

2. *Present an interesting fact or idea.*
State your most interesting, unusual, or persuasive fact or idea. This will get the attention of your audience and make them want to read more.

3. *State your point of view forcefully.*
When stating what you think, don't be timid. Don't use phrases such as "in my opinion" and "it seems to me" or words such as "maybe" or "perhaps."

Timid: In my opinion, sports programs at our school probably shouldn't be cut.

Forceful: Sports programs at our school should not be cut.

Endings

The makers of commercials hope to leave their message firmly implanted in your mind. Therefore, commercials often end with a direct appeal or command, such as "Buy some No-Hax today!"

When you are writing to persuade, leave your audience with a definite idea of what you want them to do or think, and why.

Here are some tips for writing a strong ending in a piece of persuasive writing:

1. *Sum up your point of view.*

Your reader is likely to remember what comes last. Therefore, the topic sentence may be placed last, where it can bring together all the ideas presented. For example, after giving several reasons why the school budget for sports should not be cut, you could end with this sentence: "For all these reasons, it will be a disaster if the budget for after-school sports is cut."

2. *State your strongest idea.*

Another good way to end is with your most persuasive fact or opinion. By doing this, your ending will be the "clincher," which should convince your audience. For example: "Most important, taking part in after-school sports helps students stay fit and healthy. Our health is more important than saving a few dollars."

3. *Make a direct appeal or ask a question.*

One way to get your audience involved is to "speak" to your readers directly. This can take the form of an appeal or a polite command: "Vote 'No' on the plan to cut funding for high school athletics." Or it can take the form of a question: "Don't our dedicated high school athletes, coaches, and fans deserve your continued support?" It's not necessary to answer the question, because the facts and opinions you've presented should make the answer obvious.

No matter what your topic of persuasion is, your readers will probably remember your beginning and ending. Make them forceful and memorable.

EXERCISE SIX

Suppose that the legislature in your state is considering a bill that would raise the minimum age for obtaining a driver's license from sixteen to eighteen. You want to write a letter to your state senator asking him or her to vote against the bill.

Below are five possible beginnings for your letter. Some would be effective beginnings, and some would not. Number your paper from 1 to 5. Then write *effective* or *not effective* next to the number for each possible beginning.

Example: Raising the minimum age for driving in our state would be unfair to many good teenage drivers.
effective

1. I am writing to ask you to vote "No" on the bill to raise the driving age in our state.
2. It is hard for a teenager to save enough money to buy his or her own car.
3. Highway safety is an important issue in our state, but raising the driving age is not the answer.
4. Although you may disagree, I feel that the bill to raise the driving age is, in my opinion, a bad idea.
5. As a teenage driver, I know that many young people who must drive to school or work will be harmed if the driving age is raised.

EXERCISE SEVEN

Below are five possible endings for the letter described in Exercise Six. Some would be effective endings, and some would not. Number your paper from 1 to 5. Then write *effective* or *not effective* next to the number for each possible ending.

Example: Good drivers who happen to be younger than eighteen should not suffer because of their age.
effective

1. When the bill to raise the driving age comes up for a vote, please vote no.
2. There are probably many other reasons why the driving age should not be raised.
3. I realize that many people think that the driving age should be raised.
4. Why should all teenage drivers be penalized because of the carelessness of a few?
5. Knowing how to drive is a very valuable skill.

EXERCISE EIGHT

Look again at the five situations listed in Exercise Four (Lesson Three, page 278). Choose two of them. For each situation you choose, write a possible beginning and ending.

Example: You want to persuade the manager of the Luxe Theater to show more movies of interest to teenagers.
Beginning: I am a teenage movie fan, and I would like the chance to see more of my favorite movies at your theater.
Ending: My friends and I would go to the Luxe every week if we liked the movies that were playing.

Lesson Five

Writing and Revising

In this unit, you have learned many of the basic skills in persuasive writing. You have learned how to gather facts and opinions to support an idea, how to anticipate and respond to objections, and how to write an effective opening and closing. Now you will put these skills together in writing a complete persuasive letter.

Earlier in the unit, you "received" a birthday gift. In the following exercises, you will help to pick out a gift.

EXERCISE NINE

Imagine that this year your class treasury has more money in it than can possibly be spent. The students have voted to use the extra money to buy a gift for your school.

As head of the Class Gift Committee, you think that the gift should be a useful item. You want to give something that will make your school better.

There's one problem: a number of different people must approve the gift before it can be bought. Here's a list of those people:

the principal and vice-principals of your school
the members of the faculty committee that advises your class

283

the members of the parents' organization
the School Board, made up of local citizens

The Class Gift Committee has voted to allow you to make the final decision on the best gift. However, before the gift choice becomes official, you must persuade the people on the above list that your choice of a gift is the one they should approve.

Prepare to write your persuasive letter as follows:

Think of a possible gift idea that would benefit your school. Here are three gift ideas. You can choose one of these or come up with an idea of your own.

1. reference books for the school library
2. a new scoreboard for the football field
3. a college scholarship fund

Write the gift idea you choose at the top of a page.

Look back at the four groups of people listed on page 283 and the top of this page. You will write only one persuasive letter. Decide which group you want to address in your letter. The people in that group will be your audience.

Next, think of at least five reasons why your gift choice would be a good gift for the school. Write down your reasons as phrases or as complete sentences.

What important facts about your gift idea does your audience probably not know? Write two facts your audience may not know. For this exercise, the facts do not have to be true. Add these facts to the list of reasons you just wrote.

What objections to your gift idea might the audience raise? List two objections. After each objection, write a fact or opinion which you could use to respond to the objection. Add these objections and responses to your list of reasons.

Your notes should now include the following: your gift idea; the audience for your letter; five reasons why your gift idea is a good one; two facts your audience may not know; two objections they may raise; and responses to the objections. Keep these notes for later use.

Example: Gift idea:
           a college scholarship fund
           Audience for my letter:
           the members of the parents' organization

Reasons why this is a good idea:

1. *A college education is essential for success in a career.*

2. *College graduates benefit our community with their skills and knowledge.*

3. *Last year, several good students from our school did not go to college because they could not afford it.*

4. *A college scholarship fund will show pride in our school and in the achievements of its students.*

5. *Knowing that college scholarships are available will encourage students to work harder.*

Two facts my audience may not know:

1. *Only 15% of the students from our school who go to college receive financial help from their schools.*

2. *College tuition costs in our state have risen 50% over the last five years.*

Two objections and responses:

1. *Students who can't afford to go to college can get student loans from a bank.*

Response: *Not all students who need financial help qualify for student loans.*

2. *Most of the money would be spent on scholarships in only one year.*

Response: *If the money were deposited in a bank account, it would earn interest which could help pay for scholarships.*

EXERCISE TEN

Using your notes from Exercise Nine, write a persuasive letter. Begin your letter with a heading such as "Dear Members of the School Board," naming the audience you are addressing. From your list of facts and opinions, choose the one you feel is most persuasive. Turn that fact or opinion into a sentence to start your letter.

Complete the first paragraph of your letter by writing two or three more sentences to explain the reason you gave in your opening sentence. If your reason is a fact, the other sentences might explain the fact, or provide other details supporting the same idea.

After you finish your first paragraph, choose two or three more facts or opinions from your list. Use the same pattern to turn them into the second and third paragraphs of your letter.

Look back to the two possible objections and responses you wrote in your notes. Choose one of them, and turn the objection and response into a paragraph of two or three sentences. Put this paragraph next in your letter.

Look over what you have written and decide on an effective ending. In a single sentence, or in a short paragraph of three or four sentences, sum up the points you have made. Then add a final sentence asking your audience to take the action you desire.

Example: *Dear Members of the Parents' Organization:*

Last year, several good students from our school did not go to college because they couldn't afford it. Some of these students might have become doctors. Others might have become teachers, lawyers, or members of other professions important to our community. Only a lack of money stood in their way. This is why a college scholarship fund would be the best use of the money from our class treasury.

Here are some facts that will help to show why a college scholarship fund is needed. Last year, only 15 percent of the students from our school who went to college received financial help from their schools. And in the last five years, college tuition costs in our state have risen 50 percent. The average family in our community cannot pay these high costs alone.

In today's world, a college education is essential for success in a career. Businesses need employees with scientific training, an understanding of the society they live in, and the ability to communicate effectively. These skills can best be gained through a college education. The young people of our community should be given all the help they can to achieve such an education.

It is true that some students can get a loan from a bank to help with college costs. But not all students are able to obtain student loans. Today some banks no longer have the money for such loans. Student loans are not the whole answer to this problem.

A college scholarship fund will help students who graduate from our school in the future to attend college, even if they lack money. It will also benefit our town and show people the concern we feel for our community. The future depends on well-educated young people. I hope you will approve a college scholarship fund.

EXERCISE ELEVEN

Look over your letter. As you read it, answer the questions in the following Checklist. Make any changes necessary so that the answer to each question is yes.

Checklist

1. Does the letter present both facts and opinions?
2. Do all the ideas in the letter help support the gift choice?
3. Does the letter include facts that might help the audience understand the need for the gift?
4. Does the letter respond to a possible objection that the audience might raise?
5. Is the beginning of the letter clear, strong, and interesting?
6. Does the ending of the letter sum up the ideas effectively?

13

Using Verbs Correctly

Lesson One

Verb Tense

Imagine that you were able to travel through time. Would you travel to the past to see the famous events of history? You could be at the battle of Waterloo. You could watch the first power-driven airplane fly at Kitty Hawk. Or you could see what dinosaurs were really like.

Maybe you'd prefer to visit the future. Will space flight be common? Will people live to be 150 years old? Will robots do housework—or even homework? A time traveler could find out.

For now, this kind of time travel is pure fantasy. But in some ways, we're all time travelers. With every tick of the clock, we race into the future, at a speed of sixty seconds a minute. And every day, we visit the past: We remember events that happened years ago, or we look through a photo album and see ourselves, old friends, and relatives in situations we had forgotten. The past, the present, and the future are of interest to all human beings.

In order to communicate with others about what occurred in the past or what may happen in the future, you need words that express *time*. Verbs do this. The forms of verbs that express time are called *tenses*. Notice how the tenses express different times in these sentences:

I often **travel** through time with my homemade time machine.   (present tense)

Yesterday, I **traveled** to ancient Egypt.   (past tense)

Tomorrow, I **will travel** to the future.   (future tense)

I **have traveled** to several different periods in history.   (present perfect tense)

No one **had traveled** through time before.   (past perfect tense)

By tomorrow night, I **will have traveled** to the year 2090.   (future perfect tense)

290

The Principal Parts of Verbs

The tenses of verbs are formed from the principal parts of the verb. As you learned in Unit Three, Lesson Three, the principal parts of a verb are the *base form* (or the *infinitive*), the *present participle,* the *past,* and the *past participle.*

Here are the principal parts of the verb *travel:*

Base Form (Infinitive): **travel**
Present Participle: **traveling**
Past: **traveled**
Past Participle: **traveled**

Let's take a closer look at each of these principal parts.

The *base form* is also called the *infinitive.* It is the first form you see when you look up a verb in the dictionary. The base form is often used with *to:*

(to) **travel**
(to) **enjoy**
(to) **ask**

The *present participle* is the form of the verb that ends in *-ing.* As a verb, the present participle is always used with a helping verb that is a form of the verb *be:* for example, *am, is, are, was, were, had been.*

(am) **returning**
(had been) **remembering**
(was) **cooking**

As you learned in Unit Seven, Lessons Three and Four, the *-ing* form of the verb can also be used as an adjective or a noun (gerund).

The *past* form of the verb is usually formed by adding *-ed* to the base form:

look + ed = **looked**
want + ed = **wanted**
discover + ed = **discovered**

If the infinitive ends in *e,* just add *-d:*

hope + d = **hoped**

Many verbs have past forms that are formed in other ways. They are known as *irregular verbs.* You will learn about them in Lesson Two of this unit.

The *past participle* of regular verbs is formed in the same way as the past: by adding *-ed* or *-d* to the infinitive. (As you will learn in Lesson Two, the past participles of irregular verbs are formed differently.) As a verb, the past participle is always used with a helping verb that is a form of the verb *have* or *be:*

(have) **painted**
(had) **followed**
(is) **covered**

The past participle can also be used as an adjective, as you learned in Unit Seven, Lesson Three.

Conjugating a Verb

There are six commonly used verb tenses. All are formed from the principal parts of verbs. The six tenses are the *present,* the *past,* the *future,* the *present perfect,* the *past perfect,* and the *future perfect.*

Listing all the forms of a verb is called *conjugating the verb.* These forms include the first, second, and third person in both singular and plural for each of the six tenses. Here is the conjugation of the verb *turn.*

Principal parts: (to) turn, (is) turning, turned, (has) turned

Tense	Singular	Plural
Present		
First Person:	I turn	we turn
Second Person:	you turn	you turn
Third Person:	he, she, it turns	they turn
Past		
First Person:	I turned	we turned
Second Person:	you turned	you turned
Third Person:	he, she, it turned	they turned
Future		
First Person:	I will turn	we will turn
Second Person:	you will turn	you will turn
Third Person:	he, she, it will turn	they will turn

Present Perfect

First Person:	I have turned	we have turned
Second Person:	you have turned	you have turned
Third Person:	he, she, it has turned	they have turned

Past Perfect

First Person:	I had turned	we had turned
Second Person:	you had turned	you had turned
Third Person:	he, she, it had turned	they had turned

Future Perfect

First Person:	I will have turned	we will have turned
Second Person:	you will have turned	you will have turned
Third Person:	he, she, it will have turned	they will have turned

Notice that in the present and the present perfect tenses, the third person singular forms are different from the other forms.

PRACTICE A

Each of the following sentences contains a verb in italics. Number your paper from 1 to 10. Next to each number, write the tense of that verb. Write *present, past, future, present perfect, past perfect,* or *future perfect.*

Example: He *had hoped* to finish his project last week.
past perfect

1. I *will have finished* my paper by tomorrow afternoon.
2. Susan *had complained* about her broken bicycle for over two months.
3. John and Al *will follow* in Al's car.
4. They *have shared* a locker since ninth grade.
5. Jan *had used* all the eggs, so I couldn't make egg-drop soup.
6. By the end of next month, they *will have visited* Florida six times in the past two years.
7. Rick *will perform* in The Threepenny Opera with the local theater group.
8. Jessica *picked* a bunch of wildflowers for her mother's birthday.
9. When my favorite soccer team loses, I *feel* blue.
10. Before she was elected class president, Cynthia *had served* as treasurer.

PRACTICE B

The following sentences lack verbs. The words in parentheses tell what tense the missing verb should be. Rewrite each sentence on your paper, adding the verb in the correct tense.

Example: I _____ in London for a week. (future of *stay*)

I will stay in London for a week.

1. Karen _____ the invitations to the party. (present perfect of *mail*)
2. Mr. Huan _____ law before becoming an accountant. (past perfect of *study*)
3. You _____ in the school talent show, didn't you? (past of *dance*)
4. Janice _____ the cello for eight years. (present perfect of *play*)
5. They _____ to get in touch with you. (future of *try*)
6. My dog _____ at every noise he hears. (present of *bark*)
7. Joaquin _____ his cousins in Mexico this summer. (future of *visit*)
8. Stevie's sister _____ by dinnertime tomorrow. (future perfect of *arrive*)
9. The reporter predicts that the voters _____ Callahan mayor. (future of *elect*)
10. Marci _____ her brother's car before it began to rain. (past perfect of *fix*)

PRACTICE C

Choose two of the verbs on the following list. Write six sentences for each verb, using a different tense in each sentence. After each sentence, write the verb tense you have used: *present, past, future, present perfect, past perfect,* and *future perfect.* Try to write about a different topic in each sentence.

Example: try

I try to go to sleep by ten o'clock on school nights. (*present*)

We tried to find a birthday present for Harry. (past)
The mayor will try to come to our meeting. (future)
Julia has tried to make friends in her new neighbor-hood. (present perfect)
He had tried to get to work early, but his car stalled on Main Street. (past perfect)
By next week, Alma will have tried every recipe in the cookbook. (future perfect)

Verbs: wash walk finish cook play

The Continuous Form

Each of the six tenses has a *continuous* or *progressive* form. This form is used to show that an action is ongoing or continuing. It is formed from the verb *be* plus the present participle. Here are some examples of continuous verb forms:

Present Continuous Form: The leaves **are turning** red and gold.
Past Continuous Form: The car **was turning** up a side street.
Future Continuous Form: The students **will be turning** in their papers tomorrow.
Present Perfect Continuous Form: The weather **has been turning** colder lately.
Past Perfect Continuous Form: The dog **had been turning** over in its sleep.
Future Perfect Continuous Form: By tomorrow, the Ferris wheel **will have been turning** for seventy-two hours.

PRACTICE D

Below are five continuous verb forms. Use each one in a sentence of your own.

Example: has been waiting
Petey has been waiting over a month for the records he ordered by mail.

Verbs:
1. is climbing
2. was sleeping
3. will be appearing
4. has been barking
5. had been hoping

Lesson Two

Irregular Verbs

Glenn is a fine all-around athlete. He has just won a medal in the decathlon, a competition in which athletes must take part in several different events. A newspaper reporter has asked Glenn to explain his prize-winning performance. Here is Glenn's answer:

"It's simple. I just **performed** a little better than the other athletes. I **jumped** farther; I **vaulted** higher; I **runned** faster; and I **throwed** the javelin farther. That's how I **winned** the gold medal."

Luckily for Glenn, English grammar is not one of the skills needed for the decathlon. Most of the verbs Glenn used in his answer were past-tense verbs ending in *-ed*. However, some of them sound strange. Not all verbs have past-tense endings in *-ed*. A verb whose past tense is formed differently is known as an *irregular verb*.

● **The past and past participle of an irregular verb are not formed by adding *-ed* (or *-d*) to the base form.**

Three of the verbs Glenn used — *perform, jump,* and *vault* — are regular verbs. Here are their principal parts:

Base Form (Infinitive)	Present Participle	Past	Past Participle
perform	performing	performed	performed
jump	jumping	jumped	jumped
vault	vaulting	vaulted	vaulted

The other verbs Glenn used — *run, throw,* and *win* — are irregular verbs. They form their principal parts differently:

Base Form (Infinitive)	Present Participle	Past	Past Participle
run	running	ran	run
throw	throwing	threw	thrown
win	winning	won	won

Glenn should have told the reporter, "I *ran* faster, and I *threw* the javelin farther. That's how I *won* the gold medal." The words

296

in italics are the correct past forms of the irregular verbs *run*, *throw*, and *win*.

Below is a list of some other common irregular verbs. Verbs that change forms in similar ways have been grouped together. The last group in the list contains verbs that cannot be grouped with any other irregular verbs.

Base Form (Infinitive)	Present Participle	Past	Past Participle
(to) arise	(is) arising	arose	(has) arisen
(to) drive	(is) driving	drove	(has) driven
(to) fall	(is) falling	fell	(has) fallen
(to) give	(is) giving	gave	(has) given
(to) ride	(is) riding	rode	(has) ridden
(to) rise	(is) rising	rose	(has) risen
(to) shake	(is) shaking	shook	(has) shaken
(to) write	(is) writing	wrote	(has) written
(to) begin	(is) beginning	began	(has) begun
(to) drink	(is) drinking	drank	(has) drunk
(to) ring	(is) ringing	rang	(has) rung
(to) run	(is) running	ran	(has) run
(to) shrink	(is) shrinking	shrank	(has) shrunk
(to) sing	(is) singing	sang	(has) sung
(to) spring	(is) springing	sprang	(has) sprung
(to) swim	(is) swimming	swam	(has) swum
(to) blow	(is) blowing	blew	(has) blown
(to) fly	(is) flying	flew	(has) flown
(to) grow	(is) growing	grew	(has) grown
(to) know	(is) knowing	knew	(has) known
(to) throw	(is) throwing	threw	(has) thrown
(to) break	(is) breaking	broke	(has) broken
(to) choose	(is) choosing	chose	(has) chosen
(to) freeze	(is) freezing	froze	(has) frozen
(to) speak	(is) speaking	spoke	(has) spoken
(to) steal	(is) stealing	stole	(has) stolen
(to) burst	(is) bursting	burst	(has) burst
(to) cost	(is) costing	cost	(has) cost
(to) cut	(is) cutting	cut	(has) cut

(to) hurt	(is) hurting	hurt	(has) hurt
(to) put	(is) putting	put	(has) put
(to) shut	(is) shutting	shut	(has) shut
(to) split	(is) splitting	split	(has) split
(to) spread	(is) spreading	spread	(has) spread
(to) bring	(is) bringing	brought	(has) brought
(to) build	(is) building	built	(has) built
(to) buy	(is) buying	bought	(has) bought
(to) catch	(is) catching	caught	(has) caught
(to) fight	(is) fighting	fought	(has) fought
(to) forget	(is) forgetting	forgot	(has) forgot *or* (has) forgotten
(to) get	(is) getting	got	(has) got *or* (has) gotten
(to) keep	(is) keeping	kept	(has) kept
(to) leave	(is) leaving	left	(has) left
(to) lend	(is) lending	lent	(has) lent
(to) lose	(is) losing	lost	(has) lost
(to) send	(is) sending	sent	(has) sent
(to) sit	(is) sitting	sat	(has) sat
(to) sleep	(is) sleeping	slept	(has) slept
(to) spend	(is) spending	spent	(has) spent
(to) teach	(is) teaching	taught	(has) taught
(to) bind	(is) binding	bound	(has) bound
(to) find	(is) finding	found	(has) found
(to) lay	(is) laying	laid	(has) laid
(to) pay	(is) paying	paid	(has) paid
(to) say	(is) saying	said	(has) said
(to) hold	(is) holding	held	(has) held
(to) lead	(is) leading	led	(has) led
(to) stand	(is) standing	stood	(has) stood
(to) win	(is) winning	won	(has) won
(to) do	(is) doing	did	(has) done
(to) go	(is) going	went	(has) gone
(to) lie	(is) lying	lay	(has) lain
(to) see	(is) seeing	saw	(has) seen

If you are not sure of the principal parts of any irregular verb, look up the base form of the verb in a dictionary. The principal parts are usually listed before the definition.

The Verb *Be*

Be is the most frequently used verb in English. It is also a difficult irregular verb to conjugate. Here is the conjugation of *be:*

Principal Parts: (to) be, (is) being, was, (has) been

Tense	Singular	Plural
Present		
First Person:	I am	we are
Second Person:	you are	you are
Third Person:	he, she, it is	they are
Past		
First Person:	I was	we were
Second Person:	you were	you were
Third Person:	he, she, it was	they were
Future		
First Person:	I will be	we will be
Second Person:	you will be	you will be
Third Person:	he, she, it will be	they will be
Present Perfect		
First Person:	I have been	we have been
Second Person:	you have been	you have been
Third Person:	he, she, it has been	they have been
Past Perfect		
First Person:	I had been	we had been
Second Person:	you had been	you had been
Third Person:	he, she, it had been	they had been
Future Perfect		
First Person:	I will have been	we will have been
Second Person:	you will have been	you will have been
Third Person:	he, she, it will have been	they will have been

PRACTICE A

Number your paper from 1 to 10. Choose the correct verb form from the two in parentheses. Write the completed sentence on your paper.

Example: I (saw, seen) a deer in the woods.
I saw a deer in the woods.

1. The bell had (rang, rung) by the time I got to class.
2. Because of the heavy fog, the man (drived, drove) his car off the road.
3. When my friends got together, we (began, begun) to play basketball.
4. Dolores's mother (forgave, forgiven) her for breaking the dish.
5. An expensive vase has been (broke, broken).
6. I (was, been) away for three days.
7. Terry's father (sang, sung) in the choir for two years.
8. Sara wants to know where she can put the food she has (brung, brought).
9. The winners of the music contest were (chose, chosen) yesterday.
10. The bicycle is rusty because it (lay, lain) out in the rain all night.

PRACTICE B

The sentences below lack verbs. The words in parentheses tell what tense the missing verb should be. Rewrite each sentence on your paper, adding the verb in the correct tense.

Example: The temperature _____ three degrees in the last hour.   (present perfect of *rise*)
The temperature has risen three degrees in the last hour.

1. Until it started to rain, the Cohens _____ eager to go swimming.   (past perfect of *be*)
2. Mrs. McKinney _____ my brother and me for thirteen years.   (present perfect of *know*)
3. The mayor _____ about the need for more police.   (past of *speak*)

4. Linda _____ two miles before she got tired. (past perfect of *swim*)
5. I studied all night, but I _____ part of what I learned. (present perfect of *forget*)
6. During the January freeze, two water pipes _____ , cutting off the water supply to many homes. (past of *burst*)
7. The science club _____ a booth at the school fair for the last four years. (present perfect of *run*)
8. Junior _____ a story about the hockey game for the school paper. (past of *write*)
9. By the time Luis arrived, Mr. and Mrs. Trevino _____ already _____ . (past perfect of *eat*)
10. The earthquake _____ many houses in the valley. (past of *shake*)

PRACTICE C

Below are ten irregular verbs not covered in this lesson. Choose five of them. For each verb you choose, write the principal parts on your paper. If you are not sure of the correct forms, find them in a dictionary. Then write a sentence for each verb, using any tense you like.

Example: wear
         (to) wear, (is) wearing, wore, (has) worn
         The team members have worn their new uniforms only once.

Irregular Verbs:
sell   shine
bend   weep
feel   bleed
make   read
tell   grind

Lesson Three

Verb-Tense Consistency

You and several friends have just returned from separate summer vacations. You are telling one another stories about your adventures. One of your friends tells the following story:

I was staying for two weeks in a cabin in the mountains with my mom and dad. My cousins, Carrie, Phil, and Fran, had been staying in a cabin nearby at the same time. One day, we walk to a pond and rented two paddle boats. We decided to have a race. Carrie and I get into one boat, and Phil and Fran got into the other. In the middle of the race, Phil starts shouting, "We have been sinking!" Sure enough, there had been a hole in the bottom of their boat. We have tried to bail out the water, but the boat had kept sinking. Fran cried, "I can't swim!" She had been pretty scared. But when the boat finally will sink, we all started to laugh. The pond is only four feet deep.

If you think this story sounds strange, you're right. Phil and Fran aren't the only ones that are all wet. Your friend's use of verbs is "all wet," too.

Look at the story again. Notice how the tenses change from the past to the present and the future. As a result, the story is confusing. The tenses of the verbs in the story should be *consistent.* This means that actions that happen at the same time should be expressed by verbs that are in the same tense.

To make the verbs in this story consistent, put all the verbs in the past tense, since the actions in the story all took place in the past. Here is the story with verb-tense consistency:

I **was staying** for two weeks in a cabin in the mountains with my mom and dad. My cousins, Carrie, Phil, and Fran, **stayed** in a cabin nearby at the same time. One day, we **walked** to a pond and **rented** two paddle boats. We **decided** to have a race. Carrie and I **got** into one boat, and Phil and Fran **got** into the other. In the middle of the race, Phil **started** shouting, "We're sinking!" Sure enough, there **was** a hole in the bottom of their boat. We all **tried** to bail out the water, but the boat **kept** sinking. Fran **cried,** "I can't swim!" She **was** pretty scared. But when the boat finally **sank,** we all **started** to laugh. The pond **was** only four feet deep.

302

A story that took place in the past can also be told with verbs in the present tense. Using the present tense helps those who read the story feel that they are seeing the events as they happen. Here is an example:

One day, we **walk** to a pond and **rent** two paddle boats. We **decide** to have a race. Carrie and I **get** into one boat, and Phil and Fran **get** into the other. In the middle of the race, Phil **starts** shouting, "We're sinking!"

Using present-tense verbs to tell about events in the past can be effective. The one thing you must not do is jump back and forth between the past and present tenses.

There will be times when you need to use more than one tense in the same story. For example, you may need to show that one event happened before or after another event. You can use different tenses to show the order of the events. Read this sentence:

He **left** yesterday, but he **will return** tomorrow.

Left is in the past tense, to show that the action it describes happened in the past. *Will return* is in the future tense, to show that the action it describes will happen in the future.

Mae **remembered** that she **had seen** the movie.

Remembered is in the past tense, to show that the action it describes happened in the past. *Had seen* is in the past perfect tense, to show that the action it describes happened *before* Mae remembered that she had seen the movie. The past perfect tense is used to show that an action took place farther in the past than another action that is described in the past tense.

PRACTICE A

Each of the following sentences contains two verbs that are in different tenses. Copy each sentence on your paper, putting both verbs in the tense given in parentheses.

Example: Gems have long been considered precious; they were mined for thousands of years.   (present perfect)
Gems have long been considered precious; they have been mined for thousands of years.

1. There are many kinds of precious stones, and each had its own story. (present)
2. At one time, people believe that diamonds gave warriors strength in battle. (past)
3. Diamonds do not give strength to warriors, but they have been the hardest gems. (present)
4. Diamonds will usually be colorless, but some are blue, green, or red. (present)
5. Rubies have always been the most precious red gems, and they had been considered signs of love and happiness. (present perfect)
6. People once thought that rubies protect them from being poor. (past)
7. Others believe that emeralds brought riches to their owners. (past)
8. Amethyst is a purple stone which was a favorite of people born in February. (present)
9. Opals have varied in color, and seem to change color in different light. (present)
10. Unlike most gems, opals break easily because they will contain liquid. (present)

PRACTICE B

In the story below, the base form of each verb appears in parentheses. Rewrite the story on your paper, putting all the verbs in the past tense.

Example: Whenever my brother and I (pass) the old Alcott house, we (feel) nervous.
Whenever my brother and I passed the old Alcott house, we felt nervous.

Some of the people in town (say) that the Alcott house (be) haunted. Only old Mrs. Alcott (live) there, and few people ever (see) her.

Last Friday, Willie and I (go) past the Alcott house on our way to school. We (see) a light in a window on the second floor. We (be) surprised, for that room (be) usually dark.

As we (walk) past, a face with red eyes suddenly (appear) in the room. It (look) pale and slightly green. "A ghost!" I (think).

Suddenly old Mrs. Alcott (come) to the window and (see) us looking in.

Willie and I (be) about to run away when the front door (open). It (be) Mrs. Alcott. "You!" she (cry). "Come here, you two!" Nervously, we (obey).

"So, you're curious about my upstairs room, are you?" she (ask). "Well, come inside and see for yourself!" She (grab) our hands and (drag) us upstairs.

Mrs. Alcott (pull) us through the dark house to the door of the mysterious room. "Take a look!" she (laugh) as she (push) open the creaking door.

It (be) a big, new color television set. "Isn't it a beauty?" Mrs. Alcott (say) proudly. "I just can't seem to get the color right, though," she (sigh). "Everyone on TV seems to have a green face and red eyes."

PRACTICE C

Think of something scary that once happened to you. Tell about it in a paragraph of at least seven sentences. Put all the verbs in the past tense.

Then rewrite the paragraph. Put all the verbs in the present tense.

Lesson Four

The Subjunctive Mood

As you have seen in this unit, verbs show time through the use of different tenses. Verbs have another ability that you should know about: they can show mood. However, unlike people, who have many moods, verbs have only three. These three moods are called the *indicative*, the *imperative*, and the *subjunctive*.

● **The indicative mood is used to make ordinary statements of fact or belief. It is the most commonly used mood.**

You **need** a haircut.
My hair **grows** faster than yours.

- The <u>imperative mood</u> is used to express commands and informal requests.

Wipe your feet before entering.
Please **sit** down.

- The <u>subjunctive mood</u> is used to express formal requests and unreal conditions.

The announcer requested that we **hold** our applause.
If I **were** you, I wouldn't say that.

Formal Requests

The subjunctive mood is used to express formal requests, demands, or recommendations. The clause containing the request usually starts with the word *that*. The verb that expresses the request is in its infinitive form (base form). (If the verb consists of more than one word—if it is a verb phrase—the first helping verb in the phrase is in its infinitive form.)

I suggested that he **see** a doctor right away.
The law requires that a driver's vision **be** at least 20/40 with or without glasses.
Rick moved that the money **be donated** to charity.

Unreal Conditions

The most common use of the subjunctive mood is to express something that is contrary to fact or very doubtful.

If I **were** a millionaire, I would take a trip around the world.   (contrary to fact—I am not a millionaire.)

Harold wishes he **had** time to visit us.   (contrary to fact— Harold does not have time to visit us. A wish is always contrary to fact, because we wish for things that we don't have.)

Wouldn't you be happy if you **won** the next race?   (doubtful— You will probably not win the next race.)

The boldface verbs in these examples refer to unreal or doubtful conditions in the present or future. They are in their **present-subjunctive** form. As you can see, the present-subjunctive form is the same as the past-tense-indicative form.

Note: The verb *be,* which has two past-tense forms (*was* and *were*), uses *were* in the present subjunctive.

The boldface verbs in the next two examples refer to unreal conditions in the past. They are in their past-subjunctive form. As you can see, the past-subjunctive form is the same as the past-perfect-indicative form.

If Shirley **had seen** you, she would have stopped and talked.
Carl wishes that he **had finished** college.

A common error in spoken English is to use *would have* instead of *had* in sentences like these:

Incorrect: If Claire **would have tried** harder, she might have succeeded.
Correct: If Claire **had tried** harder, she might have succeeded.

Incorrect: I wish that we **would have met** sooner.
Correct: I wish that we **had met** sooner.

If-Clauses

Many contrary-to-fact statements begin with the word *if.*

If she **were** your sister, what would you do?
He would have behaved differently if he **had known** the truth.

However, not every clause that begins with *if* refers to something that is contrary to fact. Sometimes an *if*-clause refers to something that may or may not be true. In such a clause, the verb should be in the indicative mood, not the subjunctive.

Sue asked Angelo if he **was** on the swimming team. (Not: *if he were.* Angelo may or may not be on the swimming team. Since the facts are not known, the statement cannot be contrary to the facts.)

Use the subjunctive in an *if*-clause only if the clause refers to something that is contrary to fact.

Do not use the subjunctive in a clause that begins with *whether.* Use the indicative.

Incorrect: We kept wondering whether our cousin **were** still angry.
Correct: We kept wondering whether our cousin **was** still angry.

PRACTICE A

Number your paper from 1 to 10. Some of the italicized verbs are used correctly. Others are not. If a verb is correct, write C after the number of its sentence. If a verb is incorrect, write the correct form.

Example: John often wishes he *was living* on a desert island.
            were living

1. Park rules require that Ella *keeps* her dog on a leash.
2. We asked him whether he *was feeling* better.
3. Do you know if he *were* happy with his test score?
4. The defense attorney moved that the charges *be dropped*.
5. I wish that last summer *had* not *been* so cool.
6. The performers would be grateful if the audience *was* more attentive.
7. They asked that the date of the examination *would be changed* to November 15.
8. The child wishes that his mother *were* home from shopping.
9. I would have helped her if she *would have asked* me.
10. Julia's piano teacher recommends that she *practices* every day.

PRACTICE B

For each blank, choose the correct form of the verb in parentheses. Write the correct form on your paper.

Example: He talks as if he _____ the encyclopedia.
            (memorize)
            had memorized

1. The judge ordered that the courtroom _____ cleared. (be)
2. Stella wishes that the work _____ finished. (be)
3. If Kitty ever _____ on time, the whole class would applaud. (arrive)
4. The lamp would have worked if you _____ it in. (plug)
5. Sammy wishes that he _____ to the county fair with us yesterday. (go)
6. If I _____ a broom, I would sweep. (have)

7. The doctor recommends that my sister _____ sugar. (avoid)
8. Larry moved that the nominations _____ closed. (be)
9. They asked if the tour guide _____ willing to wait a few minutes. (be)
10. If he _____ early enough, he would have been admitted to camp. (apply)

Review Exercises

I. The sentences below lack verbs. The words in parentheses tell what tense the missing verb should be. Copy the sentences on your paper, adding the verb in the correct tense. (Lesson One)

Example: Jan _____ to become a dietician. (present perfect of *decide*)
Jan has decided to become a dietician.

1. The bride _____ a lace handkerchief from her aunt. (past of *borrow*)
2. I _____ the sound of that stereo before I buy it. (future of *test*)
3. Lisa _____ to get a set of golf clubs for her birthday. (past perfect of *hope*)
4. Sharon _____ the carousel more than any other ride at the fair. (past of *enjoy*)
5. Juan _____ on the 9:25 a.m. train to Boston. (future of *travel*)
6. Nico _____ San Francisco twice in the last year. (present perfect of *visit*)
7. The sonic boom from the planes _____ some windows near the airport. (past of *shatter*)
8. By the time we arrive, the game _____. (future perfect of *start*)
9. Conrad _____ the entire dinner for tonight. (present perfect of *prepare*)
10. Arnie _____ the surprise party two weeks in advance. (past perfect of *plan*)

II. Each sentence below contains an irregular verb in the present tense. Rewrite each sentence twice. First, change the verb to the past tense. Then, change the verb to the present perfect tense. Write the completed sentences on your paper. (Lesson Two)

Example: The school chorus sings at every assembly.
The school chorus sang at every assembly.
The school chorus has sung at every assembly.

1. The Seahawks lose about half of their games.
2. The wind blows from the north.
3. Shelley is vice-president of the sophomore class.
4. Erica gives talks about astronomy to her science class.
5. The Hansens eat dinner together.
6. The librarian puts away two books for Amy.
7. An emergency van brings a doctor to the scene of the accident.
8. Loose rocks fall from the top of the cliff.
9. Tryouts for the basketball team begin today.
10. Aaron goes to a speech teacher.

III. In the paragraph below, the base forms of the verbs are in parentheses. Rewrite the paragraph on your paper, putting all the verbs in the past tense. (Lesson Three)

Examples: My thirteenth birthday (be) a special one.
My thirteenth birthday was a special one.

For my birthday I (get) a portable stereo from my parents. It (be) not fancy, but it (give) me the chance to play my favorite music. Whenever friends (drop) in, I (put) on my records. I usually (play) them quietly — especially after my sister (complain) about the noise. I (use) the stereo every day. I (be) pleased that it (last) as long as it (do). Almost two years after my parents (buy) it, it (break). I (feel) lost without it. Guess what I (ask) my parents to buy me for my fifteenth birthday!

IV. In each sentence choose the correct verb from the two in parentheses. Write the verb on your paper. (Lesson Four)

Example: Kim wishes that her brother (was, were) not away at college.
were

1. If the book (was, **were**) available in paperback, I would read it.
2. Common sense dictates that he (**has**, have) the brakes fixed.
3. They wondered whether he (**was**, were) going to the concert.
4. I have often wished that I (**had**, would have) spoken to you sooner.
5. I would go to the movies every night if tickets (**were**, would be) cheaper.
6. The referee asked if Tom (**was**, were) hurt.
7. A new member moved that a welcoming committee (was, **be**) formed.
8. Elise wished that she (was, **were**) taller.
9. I wouldn't be so nervous if I (was, **were**) prepared.
10. If the cake (**had**, would have) been chocolate, I would not have eaten any.

V. Choose one of the topics below. Write a paragraph with seven to twelve sentences. Make sure that all the verbs you use are formed correctly and that the verb tenses are used consistently. (Lessons One to Four)

Topics:
A Perfect Weekend
Why I Would (or Would Not) Like to Be President
What Is a Friend?
A Narrow Escape
A topic of your own choice

Writing With Style

Bennie Burble had a problem. His high school's annual spring dance was coming up. He wanted to ask Karla Kute, the most popular girl in the class, to be his date. But Bennie was shy. He was afraid to ask Karla face to face, so he decided to write her a letter. Here is what Bennie wrote:

Dear Karla,

It so happens that spring has arrived now that April is here. I think that spring is the best, nicest, and most pleasant time of the year. It's as pretty as a picture. And with the arrival of spring, as regular as clockwork, comes the arrival of the annual Spring Fling, which occurs every year.

This year's Spring Fling will be quite nice. A very nice band will be performing, and there will be a dance contest, which will be nice. It sounds rather nice, doesn't it?

So because this event is, in fact, coming up faster than a speeding bullet, it would be nice if a decision was made by you about your plans for this gala festival. The fact is that I am writing to you, as a matter of fact, about the point of whether you have in reality already made a date for the Spring Fling. It's as sure as shootin' that I hope you decide upon a decision that will make me as happy as a clam.

Sincerely,

Bennie

Bennie Burble

Bennie dropped the letter into Karla's locker and waited eagerly for her answer. The next day he found this note taped to his locker:

Dear Bennie,

I received your letter yesterday, but I'm not sure what you were trying to say. I read it two or three times, and I'm still confused. If you were trying to ask me to be your date for the Spring Fling,

314

why didn't you just say so? I would have loved to go with you. But while I was trying to understand your letter, Clint Moosehead asked me to the dance. I'm going to the Spring Fling with him.

Yours,

Karla

Karla Kute

Bennie was upset and confused. He was sure he had asked Karla to be his date. He took a copy of his letter to his friend Rupert, who worked for the school paper. He hoped that Rupert could tell him where he had gone wrong.

Rupert read the letter. When he finished, he shook his head.

"Well," said Bennie, "is it confusing? I think Karla was just looking for an excuse not to go to the dance with me. Maybe she doesn't like my style — the way I dance or the way I dress."

Rupert smiled. "Bennie, my friend," he said, "your problem is style, all right. But it has nothing to do with the way you dress or dance. Your problem is your *writing* style. You use so many unnecessary phrases, empty sentences, and clichés that you don't communicate clearly. I don't blame Karla for being confused."

What exactly is writing style? How do you get it? And how can it be improved?

Style is a particular way of doing something — dressing, dancing, writing, singing, bowling, and so on. A baseball player who pitches with style has a unique way of handling the ball. And a person who dances or plays the piano with style does so in a way that is special and appealing. Through training and practice, these performers have sharpened their basic skills so that their own styles can shine through.

It is the same with writing style. There are basic skills that you can learn and practice. Mastering these skills will allow your own individual style to shine through. In this unit, you will learn about three basic writing skills that will help you develop your style:

1. eliminating unnecessary words
2. strengthening your sentences
3. using figures of speech effectively

No two writers have exactly the same style. The way you write will reflect some things about you — your taste and your personality. By learning some writing skills you will allow your own special style to show.

Lesson One

Be Concise

How many of these famous sayings do you know?

"Ask not what, in fact, your country can do or perform for you or for your benefit; ask what you can actually do for and on behalf of your country."

"Speak softly, quietly, and in a way that is mild, and carry a stick that is large in size."

"The only thing we have to fear, in my opinion, is the thing that is known as fear in and of itself."

If none of these "famous sayings" is familiar to you, it's because they have been changed. Unnecessary words and phrases have been added to each saying. As a result, they are no longer memorable. They are, instead, awkward, confusing, and dull.

In their original form, these sayings contain no unnecessary words. They are *concise*. And their conciseness helps to make them memorable:

"Ask not what your country can do for you; ask what you can do for your country."

— John F. Kennedy

"Speak softly and carry a big stick."

— Theodore Roosevelt

"The only thing we have to fear is fear itself."

— Franklin D. Roosevelt

To express your thoughts clearly, and in as few words as possible, is a valuable writing skill. In this lesson, you will learn some methods to help you develop this skill.

316

Omit Redundancies

Look again at Bennie's letter to Karla, page 314. Here's the last sentence of the first paragraph:

"And with the arrival of spring, as regular as clockwork, comes the arrival of the annual Spring Fling, which occurs every year."

What is Bennie trying to say? He wants to remind Karla that it's time for the Spring Fling. But he could have said it more simply. Here are some other ways that Bennie might have said the same thing:

"It's time for the Spring Fling again!"
"April is here, so the Spring Fling is coming."
"In April comes our school's Spring Fling."

Any of these sentences says, in seven to nine words, the same thing Bennie said in twenty-two words.

Bennie's letter contains *redundancies*. A *redundancy* is needlessly repeated information. To correct a redundancy, cross it out. If necessary, reword the sentence containing the redundancy.

Here are some other examples of redundant and concise sentences that say the same things:

Redundant: My school is large and has many students, since there are over 2,000 students who attend it.
Concise: My school is large, with over 2,000 students.

Redundant: Coach Wilson allowed every player on the team to play, so that everyone got a chance to take part in the game.
Concise: Coach Wilson gave every player on the team a chance to play.

Notice that the concise sentences express the same ideas as the redundant ones. Being concise does not mean omitting ideas; it means omitting unnecessary words.

Here is another kind of redundancy found in Bennie's letter:

"I think that spring is the **best, nicest, most pleasant** time of the year."

In this sentence, the three adjectives have almost the same meaning. As a result, the adjectives make the sentence wordy and awkward. Two of the adjectives should be removed.

"I think that spring is the best time of the year."

Look at these examples:

The fans **shouted** and **yelled** for the team.
A **cute, adorable** puppy ran up to us.
This rain is **miserable** and **terrible**.

Here are the same ideas expressed more concisely:

The fans shouted for the team.
An adorable puppy ran up to us.
This rain is miserable.

Using more than one adjective, verb, or adverb in a sentence is not always wrong:

A **heavy, gray** fog settled over the city.
Simon **sang** and **danced** for the variety show.

When you use more than one adjective, verb, or adverb in a sentence, be sure that each one expresses something different from the others. After you write, look over your sentences. Ask yourself if they contain any repetitious information. If so, rewrite the sentences to make them concise.

EXERCISE ONE

The sentences below include redundancies. Rewrite each sentence to make it concise.

Example:　Prices are higher, so food is more expensive now.
　　　　　Food prices are higher now.

1. Hank's job at the warehouse is boring, and he is tired of it.
2. Rob found a cheap, inexpensive watch at the store.
3. The movie I saw last night was exciting, and I found it thrilling.
4. Your car makes an awful, horrible sound when you start it.
5. The shipwrecked sailors found themselves on an island, completely surrounded by water.
6. My brother and his new bride danced and waltzed gracefully across the floor.
7. My parakeet is sick, so she's not feeling well.
8. The tiniest, smallest, littlest bird flew onto my windowsill.

9. Speaking French has always been easy for David, because he is good at that language.
10. Stewart pretended to be ill; although he was really in good health, he acted as if he did not feel well.

Omit Empty Expressions

Look at this sentence from Bennie's letter:

"The fact is that I am writing to you, as a matter of fact, about the point of whether you have in reality already made a date for the Spring Fling."

This sentence has so many unnecessary words that it is hard to tell what Bennie is trying to say. The sentence does not contain redundancies, but it does contain *empty expressions.*

Empty expressions add no information to a sentence. They simply make a sentence longer and harder to read. Empty expressions should be removed.

There are several empty expressions that appeared in Bennie's letter:

The fact is that
as a matter of fact
the point of
in reality

When they are removed from the sentence, it is easier to understand Bennie's meaning:

I am writing to ask you whether you have already made a date for the Spring Fling.

The sentence is now fourteen words shorter than before, yet it expresses the same meaning.

Here are other empty expressions to avoid in your own writing:

in fact
the fact that
the point is that
in my opinion, I feel that
it so happens that
what I think is that
what I feel is

it seems to me

as far as I am concerned

Here are some more examples of sentences containing empty expressions. Each one is followed by an example of how to correct it.

Wordy: **Because of the fact that there was** a blizzard, school was closed.

Concise: Because of a blizzard, school was closed.

Wordy: **As a matter of fact,** I bought the eggs **for the purpose of** making a soufflé.

Concise: I bought the eggs to make a soufflé.

The fewer words you use to express your meaning, the clearer your style will be.

EXERCISE TWO

The sentences below contain empty expressions. Rewrite them to make them concise. Don't change the meaning of the sentences.

Example: The reason that I'm late is because I locked myself out of the house.

I'm late because I locked myself out of the house.

1. Due to the fact that there will be a pep rally after school, I won't be home until five o'clock.
2. George was, in fact, in a state of being hungry and tired when he made his departure.
3. What I believe is that Olive should be president of our class.
4. That board game is one that I feel to be a difficult one.
5. The thing is, I'm sure I'm right.
6. Our sleighride party, which is an annual event, will take place this Sunday.
7. The reason that I ate all the cookies was the fact that I was sure you didn't want any of them.
8. What I think is that a piece of strawberry pie would taste delicious right now.
9. These songs were written in the South in the period of time that came just before the turn of the century.
10. Because of the fact that I have no money, I will have to borrow some from you.

Avoid Circumlocutions

Circumlocution is a long but useful word. It begins with the letters *circ*, which may remind you of the word *circle*. A writer who uses circumlocutions seems to be going around in circles. A circumlocution is a roundabout way of expressing an idea. When a writer uses four, five, or six words to express an idea that could be expressed in one or two, he or she is using a circumlocution. Unlike an empty expression, a circumlocution does add meaning to a sentence. However, it contains more words than are needed.

Here are some sentences containing circumlocutions, with concise sentences that say the same things:

Wordy: **In the event that** you decide to come with us, give me a call.
Concise: **If** you decide to come with us, give me a call.

Wordy: Susan went to the library **for the purpose of engaging in** study.
Concise: Susan went to the library **to** study.

Below are some other common circumlocutions, along with simpler ways to express the same ideas:

at that point in time	then
as a result of this fact	therefore
in spite of the fact that	although
some time in the near future	soon

When a circumlocution appears in your writing, cross it out and replace it with a more concise word or phrase.

EXERCISE THREE

The underlined phrases in the sentences below are circumlocutions. Rewrite the sentences to make them concise. Replace each underlined phrase with one or two words that express the same meaning.

Example: <u>At the moment at which</u> the game began, Ella was stuck in traffic.
When the game began, Ella was stuck in traffic.

1. <u>In spite of the fact that</u> it was raining, Marc didn't wear his raincoat.

2. The crime rate dropped <u>during the period of time that</u> Carol Jenkins was mayor.
3. My house is on Twelfth Street, and my aunt lives <u>in the same general area.</u>
4. <u>As a result of the fact that</u> the train was late, Cynthia was late for work.
5. The principal <u>made a statement to the effect</u> that classes would be held despite the snowstorm.
6. <u>At the present time</u> the water level in the lake is high.
7. Paula gave Carl a camera <u>on the occasion of</u> his birthday.
8. <u>In the event that</u> John is late, he will meet us at the restaurant.
9. <u>At a time prior to the time when</u> the movie started, a cartoon was shown.
10. Rafael borrowed his father's watch <u>in order that it might be possible to</u> time the race.

Lesson Two

Write Strong Sentences

Harry S Truman was the thirty-third president of the United States. Like all political leaders, Truman made some decisions that were popular and others that were not. But unlike some people, Truman never hesitated to say exactly what was on his mind, even if it was unpopular. "If you can't stand the heat," he said, "get out of the kitchen." Truman took "the heat" for his decisions more than once. But whether or not you agreed with him, you always knew where Truman stood.

To this day, Truman is remembered for his plain-speaking and plain-writing styles. He said exactly what was on his mind—no more and no less. When you have something to say, you want your ideas to come across, too. There are several techniques you can use to make your writing style strong. These techniques can help you communicate to your reader loud and clear.

Use Words That Are Specific

What picture comes into your mind as you read this sentence?

The animal ate some food and took a drink.

322

Perhaps you think of a dog eating a frankfurter and drinking water. Maybe you see a chicken eating yogurt and drinking orange juice. Or maybe you imagine a yak chewing on a piece of pizza and enjoying a soft drink. Whatever picture comes into your mind, it is probably different from that imagined by the person next to you. The words used in the sample sentence are *general* rather than *specific*. As a result, the meaning of the sentence is unclear.

When specific rather than general words are chosen, the sentence means the same thing to everyone who reads it:

The elephant chewed on some peanuts and guzzled a tubful of lemonade.

Now you know exactly what kind of animal was eating and drinking, what kind of food and drink it consumed, and the way in which the food was eaten (*chewed*) and the liquid was drunk (*guzzled*).

When you write, choose nouns, verbs, and adjectives that express exactly what you are trying to communicate. Here are some examples of general words, followed by words that are more specific in meaning:

Nouns

General	Specific
weather	drizzle, heat wave, hailstorm, downpour, blizzard, drought
person	fire fighter, bully, beachcomber, acrobat, professor, letter carrier
hat	beret, turban, straw hat, derby, beanie, ten-gallon hat

Verbs

General	Specific
move	scamper, plod, race, stumble, stride, lope
say	declare, whisper, mumble, hiss, chatter, roar
get	receive, accept, seize, discover, snatch, buy

Adjectives

General	Specific
nice	generous, hospitable, polite, modest, clever, humorous

323

| mean | cruel, dishonest, jealous, sarcastic, ruthless, arrogant |
| sad | despairing, disappointed, broken-hearted, depressed, gloomy, grave |

Sentences that contain only general words are dull to read.

General: The weather was bad for a while.
Specific: It drizzled for six days in a row.

General: The man prevented an accident by shutting off the machine.
Specific: The night-shift engineer prevented an explosion by shutting off the faulty fuel pump.

In each case, the second sentence gives more specific information and is more interesting than the first.

Bennie's Burble's letter (page 314) contains words that are too general in meaning. Look at these examples:

This year's Spring Fling will be quite nice. A very nice band will be performing, and there will be a dance contest, which will be nice.

Here is one way Bennie could rewrite these sentences:

This year's Spring Fling will be exciting. A six-piece combo will play golden oldies from the late fifties and early sixties, and a free night at the Moonbeams Disco will be awarded to the best dancers.

EXERCISE FOUR

Rewrite each of the sentences below, replacing the general words with more specific words.

Example: A person was moving quickly outside.
A woman in a jogging suit was racing through the wheat field.

1. Two people saw an accident.
2. A vehicle passed in front of a building.
3. Have you seen my new clothes?
4. The children were playing a game.
5. A girl and her friend listened to music.
6. Those people attended a sporting event today.

7. I like going to class to learn about things.
8. She was eating some food in a public place.
9. He wore an expression on his face.
10. He found the thing under a piece of furniture.

Omit Weak Adverbs

Another way to make your writing vivid is to avoid weak adverbs. Words like *somewhat, quite, rather, very,* and *fairly* weaken sentences. Crossing out these adverbs usually strengthens the sentence. Here are some examples:

It is **rather** easy to get from here to Boise.
Are you **quite** sure the house is on fire?
That was a **somewhat** strange thing to do.

Removing the weak adverbs results in stronger sentences:

It is easy to get from here to Boise.
Are you sure the house is on fire?
That was a strange thing to do.

Active and Passive Voices

What difference do you see between these sentences?

The carrot cake was gobbled by Les.
Les gobbled the carrot cake.

Both sentences tell you about Les and the carrot cake. Both sentences use the verb *gobble.* However, in the first sentence, the verb is in the *passive voice.* In the second sentence, the verb is in the *active voice.*

The active voice is used when the subject of the verb does something:

Linc hit the punching bag.

The subject *Linc* does the hitting.

The passive voice is used when the subject of the sentence has something done to it:

The **punching bag was hit** by Linc.

The subject *punching bag* has the hitting done to it.

In a sentence with a verb in the passive voice, the person performing the action is often mentioned in a prepositional phrase: *by Linc.*

Here are some examples of sentences with verbs in the active and passive voice:

Active: Sally **bought** a new ant farm.
Passive: A new ant farm **was bought** by Sally.

Active: We **sang** several old songs.
Passive: Several old songs **were sung** by us.

Active: The governor **made** a speech.
Passive: A speech **was made** by the governor.

Using the active voice instead of the passive usually results in a stronger sentence.

EXERCISE FIVE

Rewrite each of the following sentences, changing the verbs from the passive voice to the active voice.

Example: *The Spirit of St. Louis* was flown by Charles Lindbergh.
Charles Lindbergh flew The Spirit of St. Louis.

1. Radium was discovered by Marie and Pierre Curie.
2. The dinner was cooked by the Boy Scouts.
3. Jokes will be told by a comedian and her partner.
4. Paul's teeth will be cleaned by the dentist this afternoon.
5. A long speech on water safety was given by our gym teacher.
6. Several wooden houses were destroyed by the hurricane.
7. *The Sound and the Fury* was written by William Faulkner.
8. Was this picture taken by a member of your family?
9. The names of the players were announced by Howard Cosell.
10. A question was asked by a man with a long beard.

Positive and Negative Statements

Sentences are stronger when they are in *positive form* rather than *negative form*. Avoid overusing the word *not*. Saying what something *is* makes a stronger sentence than saying what something is *not*. For example, *I am not happy* is weaker than the positive statement *I am sad*.

Negative Form	Positive Form
Jake has **not** left yet.	Jake is still here.
These eggs are **not** fresh.	These eggs are spoiled.
The movie was **not** short.	The movie was long.

If you change a sentence from the negative to the positive form, be sure to express the exact meaning you want. Look at these examples:

Negative Form	Positive Form
Harry was **not relaxed.**	Harry was **tense.**
	Harry was **alert.**
	Harry was **excited.**

As you can see, each "positive" sentence expresses a slightly different meaning. First decide what you want to say, then make sure that your words express your thoughts precisely.

EXERCISE SIX

Rewrite each of the sentences below on your paper, changing the negative form to a positive one.

Example: The dog is not awake.
           The dog is asleep.

 1. You aren't full of energy.
 2. This book is not heavy.
 3. I did not pay attention to the clown.
 4. The teacher was not pleased by the noise.
 5. She does not play her records quietly.
 6. The lake was not warm.
 7. My father was not standing at the baseball game.
 8. The Sahara Desert is not wet.
 9. This train is not standing still.
10. Our six kittens are not big.

Lesson Three

Use Figures of Speech

Have you ever felt as *cool as a cucumber?* Have you ever been *proud as a peacock?* Have you ever felt *hungry as a bear* or *happy as a clam?* Even if you haven't, it's likely that you've heard the phrases in italics. They are all common *figures of speech.*

You use a figure of speech whenever you use words to mean something other than their literal, dictionary meanings. When you say you are *cool as a cucumber,* you don't mean that you have measured your temperature with a thermometer and compared it with the temperature of a cucumber. And when you are *hungry as a bear,* you don't have an urgent need to eat roots, berries, and bugs, like a bear. These figures of speech are colorful ways to express the ideas of coolness and hunger.

Well-chosen figures of speech can add force and drama to your writing. In this lesson, you will learn some techniques for using them appropriately, as well as some pitfalls to avoid.

Similes and Metaphors

In each of the italicized figures of speech above, one thing is compared to another. The purpose of the comparison is to describe something by mentioning something else that is similar. Two common types of comparisons are *similes* and *metaphors.*

A *simile* is a comparison which uses the word *like* or *as.* Here are some examples:

Reading this book is **like** swimming through tar.
The sun today looks **like** a yellow balloon.
Carolyn's smile is **as** refreshing **as** a cool drink on a hot day.

In the similes above, one thing is compared to another in order to show vividly what it is like. In the first simile, the difficult task of reading a hard book is made vivid by comparing it to swimming through tar, something else that is difficult. In the second simile, the sun is compared to a child's toy, which suggests a happy, playful mood. In the third simile, a person's smile is compared to a refreshing drink.

328

The second type of comparison is a *metaphor*. In a metaphor, the comparison is suggested, not stated. A metaphor doesn't say that one object is *like* another; it says that one object *is* another:

That child is a little devil.
The football player is a mountain of a man.
The sun is a yellow balloon.

The first metaphor above suggests that the child is like a devil, wild or mischievous. The second metaphor suggests that the football player is enormous, like a mountain. The third metaphor is like the second simile on page 328. It expresses the same idea without using the word *like*.

Similes and metaphors surprise your reader by describing familiar things in unusual ways. Similes and metaphors allow you to exercise your imagination. Here are some suggestions for using similes and metaphors effectively.

1. *Use comparisons that match the feeling you want to express.* For example, suppose you wanted to describe the pleasant feeling of relaxing in your room on a quiet afternoon. You could compare it to anything that is both quiet and pleasant:

The afternoon was as quiet as a walk on a shady country road.
The afternoon was as quiet as a nap in a gently swinging hammock.
The afternoon was as quiet as Sunday morning in a small town.

Here are some comparisons that would not be appropriate:

The afternoon was as quiet as a tomb.
The afternoon was as quiet as a desert.
The afternoon was as quiet as a classroom during a final exam.

A tomb, a desert, and a classroom during an exam are all quiet places, but most people do not find them pleasant. These comparisons could spoil the feeling you want to express.

2. *Use comparisons for emphasis.* Similes and metaphors draw the reader's attention to the ideas or feelings they express. Use them to emphasize the most important ideas or feelings you want to describe.

It is possible to overuse similes and metaphors. The paragraph on the next page is an example.

The day of the football game was a jewel. The week before, it had rained cats and dogs. But Sunday dawned as bright and shiny as a new dime. Because it was a championship game, the stadium was a madhouse. We were packed in the seats like sardines in a can. Our family was snuggled together as close as peas in a pod. Because the air was as crisp as lettuce, we were all as hungry as bears. We ate hot dogs and peanuts as if we had never seen food before. The spectators waited for the game like eager beavers.

This paragraph is so loaded with similes and metaphors that it could confuse a reader. With all the cats, sardines, peas, bears, and beavers, it's easy to forget that the paragraph is about a football game!

3. *Avoid clichés.* The paragraph about the football game has another problem. Expressions like *rained cats and dogs, as close as peas in a pod,* and *eager beavers* have been used again and again in writing and conversation. As a result, they are stale. Overused expressions are called *clichés.* Here are some familiar clichés:

> quick as a wink
> dry as a bone
> costing a small fortune
> running like a scared rabbit
> filthy as a pigsty

When these phrases were new, they were clever and dramatic. But now they have lost the power to surprise.

When you want to spotlight a description, search your imagination for a new comparison.

4. *Make metaphors and similes consistent.* When comparing two things, use only one metaphor or simile at a time. Otherwise, you may create a *mixed metaphor.* A mixed metaphor occurs when two or more different metaphors or similes appear in the same expression. For example, look at this sentence:

> As our team sails forth to battle, let's hope it doesn't take a nose dive.

The first part of the expression compares the team to a ship— *as our team sails forth to battle.* But the second part talks about the ship taking a *nose dive*. Airplanes take nose dives, but ships do not. Comparing the team to both a ship and an airplane in the same sentence results in a mixed metaphor.

The problem is easy to correct. Just change part of the sentence to make the comparison consistent:

As our team sails forth to battle, let's hope it is seaworthy enough to ride out any storms ahead.

Use figures of speech like decorations on a cake. A few of them, well chosen, will make the cake beautiful. Too many decorative touches detract from the overall effect.

EXERCISE SEVEN

Below are the beginnings of some familiar similes. On your paper, complete each one with a cliché. Then complete each one in a way that is new and different.

Example: As honest as _____
            Cliché: *As honest as the day is long*
            New expression: *As honest as a Supreme Court judge*

1. As fast as _____
2. As much fun as _____
3. As big as _____
4. As hungry as _____
5. As soft as _____
6. As old as _____
7. As pretty as _____
8. As quiet as _____
9. As easy as _____
10. As strong as _____

EXERCISE EIGHT

The sentences below contain mixed metaphors. Rewrite each sentence so that it contains one consistent comparison.

Example: Her voice rolled through the theater as clear as a bell.
            Her voice rang through the theater as clear as a bell.

1. If you want to climb to the top in life, paddle your own canoe.

2. A political campaign is like a marathon; you have to have stamina to knock out the other candidates.
3. If you don't stop acting like a baby, I'm going to get you a rocking chair.
4. My dreams of glory have faded, like soda gone flat.
5. Although he seems slow as a turtle, in the end he will win the battle.

EXERCISE NINE

The paragraphs below have many problems of style. Rewrite the paragraphs on your paper, improving the style as much as you can. The example shows one way in which the first three sentences could be rewritten.

Example: Cooking is a skill that is difficult to master. It isn't everyone's cup of tea. I learned this unpleasant fact when I faced the prospect of undertaking the task and job of cooking a meal for my friends.
Cooking is hard, and not everyone can do it. I realized this when I first cooked a meal for my friends.

Disaster in the Kitchen

Cooking is a skill that is difficult to master. It isn't everyone's cup of tea. I learned this unpleasant fact when I faced the prospect of undertaking the task and job of cooking a meal for my friends. It was no picnic! It was a disaster due to the fact that nothing went right. Everything went quite wrong.

First, I tried to cook fried chicken. But the fact is that no one had told me you had to put coating on it first. It looked rather awful and tasted somewhat worse. Hugo, who is my best friend, said that he would prefer to dine on the delicate taste of cardboard. Friends are sometimes not kind.

The rest of the meal wasn't much better. What I mean is, it was terrible. In other words, I wasn't pleased with the outcome of my culinary endeavors. My mashed potatoes were lumpy potatoes. The salad dressing did not taste good because it was sour and bitter, with an unpleasant flavor. My bread was as hard as the rock of Gibraltar. I was very disappointed and quite embarrassed.

Only my dessert was a success. It was not homemade and it was not cheap. But the point is that everyone ate it as if there was no tomorrow. After that, we ordered some takeout food. This food was enjoyed by my guests. I wish the same could be said by me about my dinner. But if at first you don't succeed, try, try again. I plan to make a foreign food next week.

EXERCISE TEN

Choose one of the topics below. Write a paragraph of eight to ten sentences about the topic. When you finish, read over your work. Answer the questions in the Checklist that follows the exercise. Make whatever changes you feel are necessary before writing a final draft.

Topics:
A Lucky Break
The Dullest Sport
A Day at the Circus
An Airplane Trip
A topic of your own choice

Checklist

1. Do any of the sentences contain redundancies?
2. Are there any general words that can be made more specific?
3. Are there any verbs in the passive voice that could be changed to the active voice?
4. Are there any negative statements that can be made positive?
5. Have you used metaphors or similes to make the paragraph more colorful?
6. Are there any clichés that should be changed?
7. Have you expressed yourself clearly and in as few words as possible?

Using Pronouns and Modifiers Correctly

15

Using Pronouns and Modifiers Correctly

Lesson One

Personal Pronouns — The Three Cases

"All the world's a stage," Shakespeare wrote, "... And one man in his time plays many parts." How many parts do you play in your life? With your parents, you are a son or a daughter. With other students at school, you are a friend. To your teachers, you are a pupil. If you have a job, you are an employee. In your life, you will probably play many more parts. In each part, you behave somewhat differently.

Just as you may play several different parts in life, a pronoun may play several different parts in a sentence. (As you learned in Unit Three, Lesson Two, a pronoun is a word that is used in place of one or more nouns.) A pronoun takes different forms for its different parts in the sentence. Look at these examples:

I got up early on the day of the parade.
Mom made **me** a big breakfast.
I grabbed **my** trumpet and hurried to school.

Each of the pronouns in boldface type in the sentences above refers to the person who is speaking. Each pronoun is different because each is used in a different way in the sentence. The three pronouns are in three different *cases.*

- The <u>case</u> of a pronoun is the form it takes because of the way the pronoun is used in a sentence.

Personal pronouns may be in any of three cases: *subjective, objective,* or *possessive.* In this lesson, you will learn to recognize and use pronouns in each of these three cases.

The Subjective Case

- A personal pronoun used as a subject or a predicate nominative is in the <u>subjective case.</u>

336

Here is a list of personal pronouns in the subjective case. A *first person* pronoun refers to the person who is writing or speaking; a *second person* pronoun refers to the person being addressed; a *third person* pronoun refers to the person or thing being written or spoken about.

	Singular	Plural
First Person:	**I**	**we**
Second Person:	**you**	**you**
Third Person:	**he, she, it**	**they**

Here are examples of sentences with subjective pronouns:

Subject:

After school **I** played tennis with Eileen.
She won three games in a row.
They asked Eileen to play in the tournament next week.

Predicative Nominative:

The best player in school is **she**.

When you use one pronoun as the subject of a sentence, it usually comes naturally to use the subjective case of the pronoun. However, when pronouns are part of a compound subject, it is easier to make a mistake. (See Unit One, Lesson Five, for a review of compound subjects.) Which of these sentences is correct?

Him and **me** rode on the roller coaster.
He and **I** rode on the roller coaster.

The second sentence is correct. The pronouns *he* and *I* form a compound subject. As parts of the subject of the sentence, they must be in the subjective case.

When you write a sentence with a pronoun or pronouns in a compound subject, you can check the case of the pronouns by dividing the sentence into two sentences. Use each part of the compound subject as the subject of one sentence. The pronoun that sounds correct when used as a subject by itself is also correct when used in a compound subject.

Robert and (**she, her**) went for a dip in the pool.

Divide the sentence into two sentences.

Robert went for a dip in the pool.
(**She, Her**) went for a dip in the pool.

Since *she* sounds correct in the second sentence, *she* should be used in the compound subject:

Robert and **she** went for a dip in the pool.

When a compound subject includes the first-person pronoun *I*, *I* should come last:

My sister and **I** flew a kite.

When a pronoun is used as a predicate nominative, it should be in the subjective case. Read aloud the sentences below. Each is correct.

Who is there? It is **I**.
The top students are Dwight and **she**.
The person who will drive you to school is **he**.

Subjective pronouns used as predicate nominatives sound awkward to many people. Therefore, some people do not use subjective pronouns after linking verbs in everyday speech. In the sentences above, they might say, "It's *me*," "The top students are Dwight and *her*," and "The person who will drive you to school is *him*."

In writing, however, you should use subjective pronouns after linking verbs. Follow this rule in your schoolwork and other formal writing.

PRACTICE A

For each sentence below, choose the correct personal pronoun from the two in parentheses. Write the completed sentences on your paper.

Example: Kim and (I, me) will meet you at the bus depot.
  Kim and I will meet you at the bus depot.

1. Mark and (her, she) are the two best chess players in our school.
2. (He, Him) and the other members of the band practice twice a week.
3. The tallest person in my family is (I, me).

4. (Them, They) and their children drove across the United States last autumn.
5. It was (she, her) who lost her class ring while playing badminton.
6. Lois and (him, he) built a huge sand castle on the beach last Saturday.
7. My parents and (me, I) seldom agree on which TV shows to watch.
8. The students who will use the computer terminal next are Barbara and (he, him).
9. The Kranepools and (they, them) take turns working in the garden.
10. The winner of the school photography contest was (her, she).

The Objective Case

● **A personal pronoun used as a direct object, an indirect object, or an object of a preposition is in the <u>objective case</u>.**

Here is a list of personal pronouns in the objective case:

	<u>Singular</u>	<u>Plural</u>
First Person:	**me**	**us**
Second Person:	**you**	**you**
Third Person:	**him, her, it**	**them**

Here are several examples of sentences with objective-case pronouns:

Direct Object:

Our pet dachshund usually obeys **me**.
My aunt's poodle sometimes obeys **her**.

Indirect Object:

The author read **us** three of her poems.
We gave **her** a round of applause.

Object of a Preposition:

Francisco went bowling with **her**.
The Dugan twins were bowling in the lane alongside **them**.

A pronoun may be used as part of a compound direct object,

a compound indirect object, or a compound object of a preposition. A pronoun used in this way must be in the objective case.

Lola invited Jack, Francine, and **us**.   (compound direct object)
I wrote my sister and **him** a letter from Montreal.   (compound indirect object)
Sit here with Danny and **me**.   (compound object of a preposition)

When you use a pronoun as part of a compound direct object, a compound indirect object, or a compound object of a preposition, you can check the form of the pronoun by dividing the sentence into two sentences. The pronoun that sounds correct when used as an object by itself is also correct when used in a compond object.

The gas-station manager hired **Rafael** and (**I, me**).

Divide the sentence into two sentences:

The gas-station manager hired **Rafael**.
The gas-station manager hired (**me, I**).

Me sounds correct in the second sentence. Therefore, *me* should be used in the compound direct object.

The gas-station manager hired **Rafael** and **me**.

PRACTICE B

For each sentence below, choose the correct personal pronoun from the two in parentheses. Write the completed sentences on your paper.

Example: The little boy's father carried (he, him) across the puddle.
The little boy's father carried him across the puddle.

1. Would you help Max and (I, me) with this puzzle?
2. Sue and Dale went skating with Michael and (her, she).
3. The author sent our teacher and (we, us) a personal letter of thanks.
4. Steve's aunt took (him, he) and his sister on a tour of downtown Chicago.
5. Mr. Hansen sold Jerry and (me, I) his second-hand bicycle.

340

6. The stage manager invited (she, her) and Kevin backstage after the play.
7. Officer Stanley gave (he, him) and Fran a parking ticket and a stern warning.
8. You can take a turn at bat after Sharon and (me, I).
9. Roger's dog Pogo followed Roger and (us, we) all over town.
10. Please pass this plate of cornbread to Daisy and (him, he).

The Possessive Case

● **A personal pronoun used to show possession or ownership is in the possessive case.**

Here is a list of personal pronouns in the possessive case:

	Singular	Plural
First Person:	**my, mine**	**our, ours**
Second Person:	**your, yours**	**your, yours**
Third Person:	**his, her, hers, its**	**their, theirs**

Some of these possessive pronouns can be used as adjectives to modify nouns: *my, your, his, her, its, our,* and *their.* (For this reason, they are sometimes called *possessive adjectives.* In this book, the term *possessive pronouns* is used.) Here are examples of sentences with possessive pronouns used as adjectives:

My book is in **his** locker.
The dog finished **its** dinner.
The voters dropped **their** ballots in a box.

Some possessive pronouns do not modify nouns: *mine, yours, his, hers, ours,* and *theirs.* They stand alone in a sentence. Here are examples of possessive pronouns that do not modify nouns:

That bicycle is **his.**
If your pen won't write, use **mine.**
The choice is **yours.**

Notice that the pronoun *his* can be used either as an adjective or by itself.

A possessive pronoun never has an apostrophe:

Incorrect: Is this hat **her's**?
Correct: Is this hat **hers**?

Incorrect: The dog hurt **it's** paw.
Correct: The dog hurt **its** paw.

PRACTICE C

For each sentence below, choose the correct personal pronoun from the two in parentheses. Write the completed sentences on your paper.

Example: When Ed's umbrella broke, Tina lent him (her, hers).
When Ed's umbrella broke, Tina lent him hers.

1. The car runs poorly because (it's, its) engine needs tuning.
2. If you like, you can have half of (mine, my) sandwich.
3. The McAllisters claimed that the land alongside the driveway was (theirs, their's).
4. Mr. Billingham can't tell my handwriting from (your, yours).
5. Paula was annoyed to find green stains all over (hers, her) favorite blouse.
6. Terry's report is almost six pages longer than (ours, our's).
7. Sarah and Sal have offered to let us ride in (their, theirs) jeep.
8. Although my radio is older than (her's, hers), it plays much better.
9. My little sister is hoping to find buried treasure in (our, ours) backyard.
10. The oak tree lost several of (its, it's) branches in the thunderstorm.

PRACTICE D

Number your paper from 1 to 10. Write the correct pronoun from the two in parentheses next to the number.

Example: Everyone knew that the person in the King Kong costume was (he, him).
he

1. Frank told Max, Louise, and (I, me) a funny story.
2. Diego and (she, her) have written a song.
3. That black sports car is (their's, theirs).
4. Is there a disagreement between you and (he, him)?
5. Linda's grandfather read Karen and (she, her) a story.

6. The coach and (we, us) need more time to practice before the game.
7. I asked Sal and (they, them) to come for dinner.
8. Believe it or not, the first to cross the finish line was (I, me).
9. Jack, Dino, and (he, him) left the party early.
10. Is this wallet (yours, your's)?

Lesson Two

Special Problems With Pronouns

"Who's on first?" is a question made famous by the old-time comedians Bud Abbott and Lou Costello. In their well-known "Who's on First" routine, Abbott played the manager of a baseball team. The players on this make-believe team had unusual names, such as Who, What, and I-Don't-Know. Costello wanted to find out the names of Abbott's players. The routine went something like this:

Costello: Okay, Bud, tell me the names of the players on the team.
Abbott: I'd be happy to. Who's on first base, What's on second, I-Don't-Know's on third —
Costello (interrupting): Wait a minute. I don't understand. What's the name of the first baseman?
Abbott: No, What's the name of the second baseman.
Costello: I don't know.
Abbott: He's the third baseman.

Costello never figured out the joke, so this routine went on for a long time. Poor Costello got more and more confused.

It is probably a good thing that Abbott's baseball team didn't include a player named Whom. Imagine how confused Costello would have become then!

Who and Whom

If a poll were taken to find out what two words people most often confuse, the answer would probably be the pronouns *who* and *whom*. However, using these pronouns correctly is not really

343

very hard. Once you've learned a simple rule, you'll be able to use *who* and *whom* correctly.

- **Who is a pronoun in the subjective case. Who must be used as the subject of a verb. Whom is a pronoun in the objective case. Whom must be used as the direct object of a verb or as the object of a preposition.**

Who and *whom* can both be used to introduce an independent clause that asks a direct question. Here are some examples:

Who is the president of Mexico?   (*Who* is the subject of the verb *is*.)

Whom did you invite to the party?   (*Whom* is the direct object of the verb phrase *did invite*. The subject of the verb is *you*.)

To **whom** did you send the letter?   (*Whom* is the object of the preposition *to*.)

Who and *whom* can also be used to introduce subordinate clauses in complex sentences. (See Unit Nine, Lessons Two and Three for a review of subordinate clauses.)

I enjoyed watching the actor **who** played the part of the clown.   (*Who* introduces the subordinate clause *who played the part of the clown. Who* is the subject of the verb *played*.)

The fine actress **whom** we saw was the star's understudy.   (*Whom* introduces the subordinate clause *whom we saw. Whom* is the direct object of the verb *saw*.)

We enjoyed meeting the guest of honor about **whom** we had heard so much.   (*Whom* is the object of the preposition *about*.)

There is an easy way to check whether you have used *who* or *whom* correctly. Reword the sentence or the clause containing *who* or *whom* and substitute *he* or *him; she* or *her; they* or *them* for *who, whom*. You may have to change the word order of the clause. Here are some examples:

(**Who, whom**) is the author of the book you just read?

Reword the sentence, substituting *she* or *her* for *who* or *whom*:

(**She, Her**) is the author of the book you just read.

Since the subjective-case pronoun *she* is correct in the reworded sentence, the subjective-case pronoun *who* should be used.

The candidate (**who, whom**) the voters elected was Robert Greene.

Reword the clause, substituting *he* or *him* for *who* or *whom:*

The voters elected **him.**

Since the objective-case pronoun *him* is correct in the reworded clause, the objective-case pronoun *whom* should be used.

PRACTICE A

Number your paper from 1 to 10. Write the correct pronoun of the two in parentheses in each sentence below.

Example: (Who, Whom) did you see at the concert?
           Whom

1. (Who, Whom) wrote the novel *David Copperfield?*
2. To (who, whom) should I report the accident?
3. The President introduced the woman (who, whom) he had nominated to the Supreme Court.
4. Coin collectors (who, whom) buy wisely can sometimes profit from their hobby.
5. (Who, Whom) is there?
6. The person (who, whom) wants the last sandwich may have it.
7. Clara was the only speaker (who, whom) the audience applauded.
8. At (who, whom) were the dogs barking?
9. Is this the officer (who, whom) saved your life?
10. Sarah is someone (who, whom) you will like.

Pronouns in Elliptical Clauses

A common shortcut in English involves adverb clauses beginning with the words *than* and *as*. (For a review of adverb clauses, see Unit Nine, Lesson Three.) Instead of saying or writing the whole clause, we often leave out words that are implied or understood. When words are left out of a clause in this way, the clause is known as an *elliptical clause*. Read the examples that follow. Can you tell what words are implied or understood in the adverb clauses?

Marge helped me more **than he.**
Marge helped me more **than him.**

These sentences have two different meanings. Here are the sentences containing the understood words.

Marge helped me more **than he** (helped me).
Marge helped me more **than** (she helped) **him.**

As these examples show, it is important to choose the correct pronoun to use in an elliptical clause. The meaning of the clause depends on the case of the pronoun.

● **A pronoun in an elliptical clause is in the subjective case (*I, he, she, we, they*) when the pronoun is the subject of an understood verb. Otherwise, the pronoun is in the objective case (*me, him, her, us, them*).**

Whenever you end a sentence with a pronoun after *than* or *as*, complete the clause in your mind by filling in any understood words. Then figure out whether the pronoun is a subject. If it is, use a subjective-case pronoun. If not, use an objective-case pronoun.

Here is an example. Is the pronoun in the right case?

Dwight is a faster runner **than me.**

The objective-case pronoun, *me*, is wrong. The pronoun is the subject of the understood verb *am*. The subjective-case pronoun *I* should be used:

Dwight is a faster runner **than I** (am).

PRACTICE B

Number your paper from 1 to 10. Write the correct pronoun of the two in parentheses in each sentence below.

Example: Dan washes the dishes more often than (I, me).
                 I

1. Wendy travels by plane more than (I, me).
2. Tony sings better than (he, him).

346

3. My dog barks at my sister as much as (I, me).
4. Franco drives faster than (she, her).
5. Bob and Sharon did a better job than (they, them).
6. Sandy plays soccer as well as (I, me).
7. I am taller than (he, him).
8. Al bakes brownies as well as (she, her).
9. Our neighbors have a larger apartment than (we, us).
10. Freddy will be as much help as (I, me).

Pronouns Ending in -*self* or -*selves*

Pronouns ending in -*self* or -*selves* are usually used in one of two ways:

- **A pronoun ending in -*self* or -*selves* is used when you want to show that the action of the verb is reflected back onto the subject.**

When a pronoun ending in -*self* or -*selves* is used in this way, it is called a *reflexive pronoun*. Look at these examples:

The cat washed **itself**. (The subject *cat* performs the action of washing and also receives the action of the washing.)

Gina hurt **herself** on the parallel bars. (The subject *Gina* performs the action of hurting and also receives the action of the hurting.)

- **A pronoun ending in -*self* or -*selves* can be used to emphasize a noun or pronoun in a sentence.**

When a pronoun ending in -*self* or -*selves* is used in this way, it is called an *intensive pronoun*. Look at these examples:

Carl fixed the car **himself**. (The intensive pronoun *himself* emphasizes that Carl alone fixed the car.)

I will complain to the mayor **herself** about this problem. (The intensive pronoun *herself* emphasizes that the mayor will personally receive the complaint.)

Notice that in the two sentences above the intensive pronouns could be omitted without changing the meaning of the sentences. An intensive pronoun strengthens a statement without changing its meaning.

Do not use *hisself, theirself,* or *theirselves.* These words, although used in the dialects of some parts of the United States, are not part of standard English. The correct forms are *himself* and *themselves.*

Incorrect: They dressed **theirselves** for the party.
Correct: They dressed **themselves** for the party.

Also, do not use a reflexive pronoun when a personal pronoun can be used instead.

Incorrect: Donna invited Frank and **myself** to her party.
Correct: Donna invited Frank and **me** to her party.

PRACTICE C

Number your paper from 1 to 5. Write the correct pronoun of the two in parentheses in each sentence below.

Example: The MacDowells said that they painted the house (theirselves, themselves).
themselves

1. Lou typed his twenty-page paper by (hisself, himself).
2. Is Lucy going with (you, yourself)?
3. Mrs. Walters helped Jimmy and (me, myself) fix our flat tire.
4. To save money, the Petersens painted their front porch (theirselves, themselves).
5. The lecturer bored his audience by talking only about (himself, hisself).

Lesson Three

Using Modifiers Correctly

Huey and Louie are a little-known comedy team. Here is one of the jokes that have kept them little known:

Huey: Say, Louie, do you know what I bought last week at the county fair? A goat without a nose!
Louie: (puzzled) A goat without a nose? How does it smell?
Huey: (holding his nose) It smells *bad*!   (There are groans and boos from the audience.)

If Huey's goat smells *bad*, it needs a bath. But if it has no nose and can't smell things, Huey's goat must also smell *badly*.

To understand the difference between smelling *badly* and smelling *bad*, you need to know the difference between two kinds of modifiers: adjectives and adverbs. As you learned in Unit Three, adjectives are used to modify nouns or pronouns, while adverbs are used to modify verbs, adjectives, or other adverbs. (See Unit Three, Lessons Four and Five, for a review of adjectives and adverbs.)

● **Use an adjective, not an adverb, after a linking verb.**

Linking verbs include *be, feel, look, seem, smell, sound,* and *become.* (For review of linking verbs, see Unit Three, Lesson Three.) A modifier that follows a linking verb describes the subject. Since the subject is a noun or pronoun, the modifier must be an adjective. As you learned in Unit Five, Lesson Five, an adjective that follows a linking verb is called a predicate adjective.

Note that *good* and *bad* are adjectives, and should be used after linking verbs:

Huey's goat is **bad**. (The adjective *bad* follows the linking verb *is* and modifies the subject *goat*.)

It looks **good** with a ribbon in its tail. (The adjective *good* follows the linking verb *looks* and modifies the subject *it*.)

● **Use an adverb, not an adjective, after an action verb.**

Badly is an adverb. Use *badly* after an action verb to modify the action verb.

The goat dances **badly**. (The adverb *badly* modifies the action verb *dances* by telling *how* the goat dances.)

Well may be used as an adjective or an adverb. The adjective *well* means *healthy*. It follows a linking verb and modifies the subject of the verb.

The goat had the flu, but now it is **well**.

The adverb *well* means *in a good way*. It follows an action verb and modifies the verb.

The vet treated the goat **well**.

Remember that some verbs may be used either as linking verbs or as action verbs. Use the correct modifier depending on whether the verb is being used as a linking verb or an action verb.

The goat smells **bad**. (*Smells* is being used as a linking verb. The adjective *bad* modifies the subject *goat*.)

The goat smells **badly**. (*Smells* is being used as an action verb. The adverb *badly* modifies the verb by telling *in what way* the goat uses its sense of smell.)

PRACTICE A

In each of the following sentences, a word is italicized. Six of the sentences contain an italicized word that is incorrect. Number your paper from 1 to 10. If a sentence is correct, write C. If a sentence contains an error, rewrite the sentence correctly.

Examples: Mary felt *good* because she had finished her homework.
C

Why did the dog behave so *bad*?
Why did the dog behave so badly?

1. Terri seemed surprisingly *well* after the operation.
2. The weather doesn't look too *good* today.
3. Lonnie is a *well* skier.
4. Marnie felt *badly* because she had not gone to the wedding.
5. Peach ice cream tastes *well*.
6. I acted *badly* when I hung up on you.
7. Judith Jamison dances *good*.
8. Your new haircut looks *well* on you.
9. Was she hurt *badly* in the accident?
10. My old car runs *bad* in wet weather.

Misplaced Modifiers

Can you find the error in each of the following sentences?

Flapping wildly, I watched the moth in the spider's web.
Because they had yellowed with age, the employees threw away the old letters.
Dan and Jean saw two diesel locomotives on their way to the beach.

Each of these sentences contains a *misplaced modifier*. The sentences are silly or confusing because the modifiers are not placed next to the word or words that they modify.

● **A modifier should be placed as close as possible to the word or words it modifies.**

Look again at the sentences on the opposite page.

Incorrect: **Flapping wildly,** I watched the moth in the spider's web. (Because *flapping wildly* is placed next to *I,* the sentence implies that *I* am *flapping wildly.*)

Correct: I watched the moth **flapping wildly** in the spider's web. (*Flapping wildly* should be close to the word it modifies, *moth.*)

Incorrect: Dan and Jean saw two diesel locomotives **on their way to the beach.** (The sentence implies that the *diesel locomotives* are *on their way to the beach.*)

Correct: **On their way to the beach,** Dan and Jean saw two diesel locomotives. (*On their way to the beach* should be close to *Dan and Jean,* since they are the ones who are on their way to the beach.)

Incorrect: **Because they had yellowed with age,** the employees threw away the old letters. (The sentence implies that *the employees had yellowed with age.*)

Correct: The employees threw away the old letters **because they had yellowed with age.** (The *letters had yellowed with age,* not the *employees.*)

In each of the last two examples above, the poorly placed modifier creates a pronoun problem. When a phrase or clause is misplaced, the antecedent of the pronoun in the phrase or clause is unclear. In the sentence about Dan and Jean, the misplaced modifier implies that the antecedent of *their* is *locomotives.* When the phrase is moved close to *Dan and Jean,* it is clear that *Dan and Jean* is the antecedent of *their.* In the sentence about the old letters, the misplaced modifier implies that *the employees* is the antecedent of the pronoun *they.* Moving the adverb clause makes it clear that the antecedent of *they* is *the old letters.*

351

Dangling Modifiers

Sometimes you may use a modifier in a sentence and leave out the word or words being modified. A modifier with no word or words to modify is called a *dangling modifier.*

● **Every modifier should modify a word or words that appear in the sentence.**

Incorrect: **While standing in the open field last night,** a meteor streaked overhead. (Who was standing in the field? The sentence doesn't say. It needs to be rewritten to include the word *I.*)

Correct: **While standing in the open field last night,** I saw a meteor streak overhead.

or

While I was standing in the open field last night, a meteor streaked overhead.

PRACTICE B

Rewrite the sentences that follow to correct the misplaced or dangling modifiers. You may have to add or take away words.

Example: We laughed as the polar bears played in the water, snapping pictures.
Snapping pictures, we laughed as the polar bears played in the water.

1. Joshua watched the high diver plunge one hundred feet from the first row of the bleachers.
2. As they quacked noisily, the children fed pieces of bread to the ducks.
3. Intent on getting home, the keys were carelessly locked in my car.
4. She hurried to the library for the reference book she needed, which is open only until 5 p.m.
5. Squeaking with fear, the cat pursued the mouse around the barn.
6. While waiting for the bus, the rain began to fall.
7. Quickly filling with water, the crew tried to bail out the boat.
8. Dressed in light clothing, the sudden change in the weather chilled her.

9. Enjoying a stroll in the garden, the birds sang softly overhead.
10. Because they were soggy, the customers returned the French fries.

Lesson Four

Comparison of Modifiers

Degrees of Comparison

How hot is it today?

There are many ways to answer this question. You could answer it with a statement of fact: "The temperature today is 101 degrees Fahrenheit." You could answer it with an expression of strong feeling: "It's so hot I can hardly stand it!" Or you could answer the question by making a comparison:

"Today is *hotter* than yesterday."
"Today is the *hottest* day since last August 21."

In the last two sentences, *hotter* and *hottest* are adjectives. As the sentences show, adjectives can be used in making comparisons. Both adjectives and adverbs have special forms that are used in making comparisons. These forms are the *degrees of comparison*.

● The positive degree of an adjective or adverb gives information about the word being modified. When the positive degree is used, no comparison is being made.

Adjective: Sandra is **tall**. (The adjective *tall* modifies *Sandra*. No comparison is being made.)
Adverb: Sandra runs **quickly**. (The adverb *quickly* modifies *runs*. No comparison is being made.)

● The comparative degree of an adjective or adverb is used to compare two persons, actions, or things.

Adjective: Sandra is **taller** than Jan. (The adjective *taller* compares the height of two persons: Sandra and Jan.)
Adverb: Sandra runs **more quickly** than Jan. (The adverb *more quickly* compares how quickly Sandra runs and how quickly Jan runs.)

- **The <u>superlative degree</u> of an adjective or an adverb is used to compare three or more persons, actions, or things.**

Adjective: Sandra is the **tallest** girl in the school. (The adjective *tallest* compares the height of Sandra to that of all the other girls in the school.)

Adverb: Sandra runs **most quickly** of all the members of the track team. (The adverb *most quickly* compares the running speed of Sandra to that of all the other members of the track team.)

Here are more examples of the three degrees of comparison:

Adjectives

Positive	*Comparative*	*Superlative*
dark	darker	darkest
delicious	more delicious	most delicious

Adverbs

Positive	*Comparative*	*Superlative*
slow	slower	slowest
eagerly	more eagerly	most eagerly

Notice that the comparative and superlative degrees may be formed in two ways. One way is to add *-er* and *-est* to the end of the adjective or adverb. The other is to place *more* and *most* in front of the adjective or adverb.

How do you know which way is correct? It usually depends on the number of syllables in the adjective or adverb.

- **Add *-er* and *-est* to form the comparative and superlative of one-syllable adjectives and adverbs.**

Positive	Comparative	Superlative
old	older	oldest
fast	faster	fastest

- **Add *more* and *most* to form the comparative and superlative of adjectives and adverbs that have three or more syllables.**

Positive	Comparative	Superlative
fabulous	**more** fabulous	**most** fabulous
commonly	**more** commonly	**most** commonly

Two-syllable adjectives and adverbs vary. Let sound be your guide. You will find that adding *-er* and *-est* to some two-syllable adjectives and adverbs sounds awkward. In those cases, use *more* and *most* instead.

Positive	Comparative	Superlative
angry	angr**ier**	angri**est**
nervous	**more** nervous	**most** nervous
quickly	**more** quickly	**most** quickly

If you are not sure whether to use *-er* and *-est* or *more* and *most* with a particular two-syllable adjective or adverb, look up the word in a dictionary. Some dictionaries, but not all, will tell you which form is accepted.

Note: If an adjective or an adverb ends in *-y*, change the *y* to *i* before adding *-er* or *-est*.

Positive	Comparative	Superlative
lazy	laz**ier**	laz**iest**
lonely	lonel**ier**	lonel**iest**

PRACTICE A

Rewrite the sentences below on your paper. Add the correct form of the adjective or the adverb in parentheses.

Example: The living room needs a _____ air conditioner than the bedroom does. (comparative of *large*)
The living room needs a larger air conditioner than the bedroom does.

1. Mrs. Van Horsen's car is the _____ car in town. (superlative of *large*)
2. The team won the trophy _____ this year than they did last year. (comparative of *easily*)
3. Einstein has been called the _____ scientist of this century. (superlative of *great*)
4. Tina is _____ than her twin sister Gina. (comparative of *slender*)
5. Richard speaks _____ than his brother. (comparative of *often*)

6. The water in the pool is _____ than it was yester-day. (comparative of *cold*)
7. My weight is the _____ it has ever been. (superlative of *high*)
8. I was the _____ person on the trip. (superlative of *nervous*)
9. That jeep is _____ than this sports car. (comparative of *expensive*)
10. Les is the _____ of the four boys in his fam-ily. (superlative of *young*)

Irregular Comparisons

A few adjectives and adverbs have irregular comparative and superlative forms.

Adjectives

Positive	*Comparative*	*Superlative*
bad	worse	worst
good	better	best
many	more	most
much	more	most

Adverbs

Positive	*Comparative*	*Superlative*
badly	worse	worst
much	more	most
well	better	best

Here are examples of some of these words in sentences.

Positive: The news that Jean received was **bad.**
Comparative: The news was **worse** than she had expected.
Superlative: But she hadn't heard the **worst** news.

Positive: You seem to be in **good** health.
Comparative: Your health seems **better** today than yesterday.
Superlative: You seem to be enjoying the **best** health.

Positive: Eric skates **well.**
Comparative: Beth skates **better** than Eric.
Superlative: Marc skates **best** of all.

356

PRACTICE B

Rewrite the sentences below on your paper. Add the correct form of the adjective or the adverb in parentheses.

Example: I think that orange juice is _____ than grapefruit juice. (comparative of *good*)
I think that orange juice is better than grapefruit juice.

1. Our high school track team scored _____ points than the team from Huxley High. (comparative of *many*)
2. Roberto sang _____ today than yesterday. (comparative of *well.*)
3. Brian is a _____ baseball player than Sid. (comparative of *good*)
4. Although Sharon was nervous, she raced _____ than Tina. (comparative of *well*)
5. Cesar read _____ books this year than he read last year. (comparative of *many*)
6. That was the _____ pizza I've ever eaten! (superlative of *bad*)
7. Anna won the blue ribbon for being the _____ rider in the tournament. (superlative of *good*)
8. Because Marissa sang_____, she won the leading role in the musical. (superlative of *well*)
9. These shoes cost _____ than any other shoes in the store. (comparative of *much*)
10. Which team has the _____ victories this season? (superlative of *much*)

PRACTICE C

Make three columns on your paper, headed *Positive, Comparative,* and *Superlative.* In the correct columns, list the three degrees of comparison of the following adjectives and adverbs.

Example: thoughtful

Positive	Comparative	Superlative
thoughtful	*more thoughtful*	*most thoughtful*

1. pretty
2. fierce
3. badly

357

4. reliable
5. quiet
6. good
7. determined
8. much
9. deserted
10. happily

Lesson Five

Special Problems With Comparisons

Double Negatives

As you may have learned in math, two negatives can sometimes equal a positive. For example:

$$(-2) \times (-2) = +4$$

What is true in math is not true in English. Two negatives in English do not equal a positive; they equal a mistake called a *double negative*. To avoid writing double negatives, remember the following rule:

● **Two or more negative words should not be used together.**

Some common negative words are *no, not, never, nothing, none, no one, nobody, neither,* and *nowhere.* The words *scarcely, hardly, rarely,* and *barely* are negatives. The contraction *n't,* which stands for the word *not,* is also a negative.

It is easy to correct a sentence that contains a double negative. Rewrite the sentence, removing one of the two negative words.

Incorrect: I don't **never** want to see you again.
Correct: I don't ever want to see you again.

or

I **never** want to see you again.

Incorrect: **Scarcely no one** knows what to do.
Correct: **Scarcely** anyone knows what to do.

PRACTICE A

The sentences below contain double negatives. On your paper, rewrite each sentence correctly.

Example: I don't know nobody at this party.
           I don't know anybody at this party.
                              or
           I know nobody at this party.

1. Karen didn't pay no attention to the noise.
2. Stan said his summer was boring because he didn't go nowhere.
3. The thunderstorm didn't damage nothing.
4. Hardly no one was on the bus.
5. There isn't nothing to do here.

Double Comparisons

As you learned in Lesson Four, the comparative and superlative forms of adjectives and adverbs are formed in two ways: either by adding *-er* or *-est* to the end of the word, or by placing *more* or *most* before the word.

A common error is to use both methods at the same time. The error that results is called a *double comparison.*

Incorrect: Tanya is **more** friendlier than Sonya.
Correct: Tanya is friendlier than Sonya.

Incorrect: Your dog's face is the **most** saddest I've ever seen.
Correct: Your dog's face is the saddest I've ever seen.

Adjectives That Cannot Be Compared

Certain adjectives cannot be compared because they express an absolute state.

● **The adjectives *first, last, equal, final, only,* and *unique* should be used only in the positive degree.**

Incorrect: This is the **most unique** painting.   (Because unique means *one of a kind*, something cannot be "more unique" or "most unique.")
Correct: This is a **unique** painting.

359

Seven of the sentences below contain errors. Number your paper from 1 to 10. If a sentence is correct, write *C*. If a sentence contains an error, rewrite it correctly on your paper.

Example: Rich Little is the most funniest man I know.
           Rich Little is the funniest man I know.

1. Which of the two finalists do you think performed more better?
2. Tom's rug is the most colorful one in the show.
3. Philadelphia is the most biggest city in Pennsylvania.
4. Karen's sculpture is very good, but Lana's is more unique.
5. The two cars are about equal in capacity.
6. To drive the ball even farther, swing the bat more faster.
7. Some historians say the Vikings were the firstest to reach the New World.
8. Mr. Garr is the only professional pianist I know.
9. The telegram contained Ms. Lansford's finalest offer.
10. When the moon set, the night sky became even more darker.

Review Exercises

I. Some of the sentences that follow contain pronoun errors. Number your paper from 1 to 10. If a sentence contains no pronoun error, write *C* after the number of that sentence. If a sentence contains a pronoun error, rewrite the sentence correctly. (Lesson One)

Examples: Jack invited Ted and me to visit him for the weekend.
            C

            Mark and her are planning to make their own movie.
            Mark and she are planning to make their own movie.

1. The long line at the ticket window discouraged Elsa and I from seeing the show.
2. Two hours after the party started, Jason and him showed up.
3. Arthur and I have known each other for the last twelve years.
4. Is this skateboard Paula's or your's?

5. The winners of the potato-sack race were Jan and her.
6. Me and my family always go away during the last week in August.
7. The detective revealed that it was she who had hidden the jeweled dagger under the mattress.
8. I'm sure that the bus won't leave without you and I.
9. Would the role of the old sea captain be better for Kevin or he?
10. You and she tell the funniest stories I've ever heard.

II. For each sentence below, choose the correct pronoun from the two in parentheses. Write the correct pronouns on your paper. (Lesson Two)

Example: Mark insisted on painting the dune buggy (himself, hisself).
himself

1. Mrs. Marsh, (who, whom) has taught English for thirty-two years, is retiring.
2. Bert is paid a higher hourly wage than (me, I), although we do the same work.
3. We were speaking about your sister and (you, yourself) just before you walked by.
4. This is my cousin Phyllis, (who, whom) you met once before.
5. Can you type as quickly as (he, him)?
6. The salesperson (who, whom) called did not leave his phone number.
7. Joe crossed the finish line three seconds later than (she, her).
8. Do you think that Barry is a better drummer than (me, I)?
9. Every student (who, whom) I know signed the petition.
10. Todd and Alex bought the old car and repaired it (themselves, theirselves).

III. The following paragraph contains ten errors in the use of modifiers. Rewrite the paragraph, correcting the errors. The first of the ten errors has been done for you. (Lessons Three and Five)

Example: A popular spot for hiking and camping, I spent a night last December on Hunter Mountain.
I spent a night last December on Hunter Mountain, a popular spot for hiking and camping.

361

A popular spot for hunting and camping, I spent a night last December on Hunter Mountain. My friend Frank Callahan and his dad, an experienced outdoorsman, served as my guides. When we started our hike in the early afternoon, the weather seemed well. But as the day wore on, it grew much more colder. I hadn't scarcely expected to hike in temperatures below zero. Soon, my feet were frozen stiff. Weighing about thirty pounds, I began to stagger under my backpack. I didn't complain, because I wanted Frank to think that I could "rough it" as good as he could. But I was relieved when we finally reached our campsite. Cooked over a small gas stove, we enjoyed delicious steaks and hot mugs of coffee. Frank's dad built a fire, and after warming my feet I didn't feel badly at all. That night, the sky was filled with thousands of stars. It was one of the most loveliest sights I'd ever seen. Admiring that beautiful view, I wouldn't have changed places with no one on earth.

IV. Some of the sentences that follow contain errors in the comparison of adjectives and adverbs. Number your paper from 1 to 10. If a sentence contains no error, write *C* after the number for that sentence. If a sentence contains an error, rewrite the sentence correctly. (Lesson Four)

Examples: Jesse is the luckiest person I know.
   C

   Mitch finished his homework quicklier than Evan.
   Mitch finished his homework more quickly than Evan.

1. Of all the musicians on the school band, Kerry is the more talented.
2. Henry's right hand is the strongest of the two.
3. Angela's green eyes look well when she wears her red blouse.
4. The liveliest piece of music was the last one played by the orchestra.
5. Janice's garden is even beautifuller than I had expected.
6. Ms. Nelson is the best teacher in our school because she is the more experienced.
7. Which of the twins runs fastest?
8. The old Tyler farmhouse is the peacefullest place I know.

9. You will feel much better than you do now after a good night's sleep.
10. In Ontario, the summer is shorter and cooler than in Maryland.

V. Choose one of the following topics. Write a paragraph with ten to fifteen sentences. Make sure that every pronoun is in the correct case, and that all the modifiers are used correctly. (Lessons One to Five)

Topics:
The Funniest Person I Know
My Future Life as a Famous _____ (You fill in the blank.)
My Most Embarrassing Moment
My Message to the World
A topic of your own choice

Writing a Review

Imagine that you are reading your school newspaper, the *Weekly Flash*. Your eye is caught by the following advertisement:

Help Wanted

Movie reviewer for the *Weekly Flash*. Receive free tickets to new movies. No experience necessary, but you must have clear standards and be able to write a good review. Apply at the *Flash* office, Room 216.

You love movies, and the thought of free tickets makes you want to apply for the job. But what does a movie reviewer do?

A movie reviewer (sometimes called a *critic*) writes about movies, usually for a magazine or newspaper. A movie review includes a description of the movie and the reviewer's opinion of it. A good reviewer usually has clear standards that he or she uses in judging the quality of a movie. A *standard* is a basis on which a particular movie — or anything else — is judged.

There are critics who review many things other than movies: books, records, restaurants, television shows, plays. The opinions of a good critic can be valuable in helping readers to decide how best to spend their time and money.

Reviews can be fun to read. Reading someone else's opinion of a movie you've seen or a book you've read is a good way of developing your own standards of judgment. You may agree with the opinions of the reviewer, or you may disagree. Either way, you will learn something about what you like and don't like in a movie or a book.

In this unit, you'll learn how to write a review. You will learn how to develop standards for judging things, and how to back up your opinions. You may want to try your hand at writing a review for your school's newspaper. But even if you don't, you'll enhance your enjoyment of movies, books, and many other things if you learn to judge them with the care and thoughtfulness of a good reviewer.

Lesson One

Standards

Your friend Toby has just eaten at the Pot o' Gold, a brand-new restaurant in your neighborhood. You like to try new places to eat, so you ask Toby if he would recommend it. "In some ways I would," he replies, "and in some ways I wouldn't." Here is his explanation:

"Well, the Pot o' Gold is very dark. I hate that; I like to be able to see what I'm eating. And the waiters are too talkative; my food got cold before they stopped chatting with me. But the food is very good — rich, heavy, with lots of thick sauces. And there's no music or entertainment going on while you're trying to eat. I hate having music blasted at me while I'm chewing."

Toby has given you a brief restaurant review of the Pot o' Gold. As you can tell, he has mixed feelings about the restaurant. You can also tell something more: you can tell why he likes and dislikes the Pot o' Gold. Toby's answer tells what *standards* he uses to judge a restaurant.

Here are the reasons Toby gave for liking and disliking the Pot o' Gold, and the standards that Toby's reasons imply:

1. Toby thinks the Pot o' Gold is too dark. He likes to be able to see what he's eating. This suggests that one of Toby's standards in judging a restaurant is *bright lighting*.

2. The waiters are too talkative. Another of Toby's standards is *quiet service*.

3. Toby likes the food at the Pot o' Gold because it is rich and heavy, with thick sauces. This tells you that *rich, heavy food with thick sauces* is another standard by which Toby judges a restaurant.

4. Toby prefers eating in a restaurant where there is no music. Another of Toby's standards is *quiet*.

Will you eat at the Pot o' Gold the next time you go out? It depends on your own standards. Perhaps you like dim lights in a restaurant; you feel they give a place "atmosphere." And perhaps you like waiters who talk to you; restaurants where the waiters are silent strike you as snobbish. If you prefer food that is light

367

on calories, you might not choose a place where the food is rich and heavy. And if you like to be entertained while you eat, you might not like the Pot o' Gold. In short, your standards may differ from Toby's. Because Toby's "review" explained his standards, you can decide whether or not your standards are similar, and so decide whether your opinion of the Pot o' Gold is likely to agree with Toby's.

Discovering your own standards is the first step in writing a review that expresses your opinion of anything, whether it is a restaurant, a movie, a book, or something else. And although you may not have thought much about your standards before, you probably have standards for almost everything.

Here is an example. If you wanted to discover your own standards for judging books, you could begin by thinking of a book you like and one you don't like. First, list your reasons for liking and not liking the two books, like this:

A book I like: *The Hound of the Baskervilles,* by Arthur Conan Doyle.
The reasons I like it:
1. It's filled with action.
2. It is suspenseful and spooky.
3. The characters are interesting and believable.
4. The story ends happily.

A book I don't like: *Slime City,* by Hugo Z. Fish.
The reasons I don't like it:
1. It's too long.
2. It has too much unnecessary violence.
3. The characters are unrealistic.
4. The ending is depressing.

These two lists reveal some of the standards you use in judging books.

1. You like the fact that *The Hound of the Baskervilles* is filled with action. This shows that *a lot of action* is one of your standards.
2. *Believable, realistic characters* are needed for you to enjoy a book.
3. The lists show that you prefer a book with a *happy ending.*

4. You don't like *Slime City* because it's too long. One of your standards for books is that it be *not too long.*
5. You like a book that has *no unnecessary violence.*

From these lists of likes and dislikes, you can develop five general standards that you use in judging books. There may be other standards you apply to books. To develop your list of personal standards further, you might need to think about other books you like or dislike.

EXERCISE ONE

Choose two of the following five categories. For each category you choose, list an item in that category that you like and an item that you don't like. Then, for each item, write three to five reasons for your opinion.

Example: Category: *Indoor Games*
An Item I Like: *Checkers*
Reasons:
1. It requires only two players.
2. It can be played in a short time.
3. It is challenging.
4. Almost everyone knows how to play it, so you don't have to spend time explaining the rules.
5. It is quiet.
An Item I Don't Like: *Charades*
Reasons:
1. There is too much physical activity in the game.
2. It requires too many people.
3. Many people don't know how to play it, so you have to spend time explaining the rules.
4. It's too noisy.
5. It takes a long time to play.

Categories:
Sports
Hobbies
Television Shows
Foods for Lunch
Pets

Look over the lists of reasons you wrote for Exercise One. Decide what general standards they represent. List your standards for the two categories you used. Each list should include at least three standards. Keep your lists for use later in the unit.

Example:　Category:　*Indoor Games*
　　　　　　Standards:
　　　　　　1. small number of players needed
　　　　　　2. challenging
　　　　　　3. known to most people
　　　　　　4. quiet
　　　　　　5. can be played in a short time

Lesson Two

Using Specific Details

One Saturday night, you go out to eat at the Blue Turnip restaurant. You've never eaten there before, but your friend Ruthie has recommended it. "I'm sure you'll like it," she said. "It's not expensive, the food is good, and the atmosphere is unusual and fun." You head for the Blue Turnip, expecting a great time.

However, your night out is a disaster. The food at the Blue Turnip turns out to include all the dishes you hate. The atmosphere is silly and uncomfortable. Worst of all, you find that the meal costs more than you expected, and you spend your whole allowance to pay the bill.

Your friend Ruthie meant well. But her advice did not prepare you for your experience at the Blue Turnip. Why not? You can tell from her recommendation that three of her standards for restaurants are *low price, good food,* and *unusual atmosphere.* But Ruthie's ideas of low price, good food, and unusual atmosphere aren't the same as yours. Ruthie didn't clarify her opinion by supporting it with *specific details.*

If Ruthie had used details in describing the Blue Turnip, her opinions would have been more useful to you. Here is an example of what Ruthie could have said:

370

"Try the Blue Turnip. It's inexpensive. You can get an entire plate of alfalfa fritters or seaweed and beans for only $5.95. And soft drinks are only 65¢. The food is delicious. The house specialty, a turnip casserole, is made with tomatoes, garlic, cucumbers, and kidney beans — topped with blue cheese. Yum! And the atmosphere is very unusual. All the seats are in the shape of vegetables — you can sit in a big, soft squash or a tufted green pepper."

Now you have a better idea of what Ruthie means by "inexpensive," "good food," and "unusual atmosphere." You may not agree with her that $5.95 is inexpensive; you may feel that a turnip casserole sounds terrible; and you may not think that sitting on a big green pepper is fun or comfortable. But because Ruthie has used specific details to explain her opinions, her "review" is helpful to you. At least you know that the Blue Turnip is *not* the restaurant for you.

EXERCISE THREE

Look at the lists of standards for two different categories you wrote for Exercise Two. Think of a specific item in one of the two categories. Write three paragraphs explaining why you like or don't like the item. Each paragraph should follow this pattern:

1. Write a sentence that describes one of your standards for judging something in this category.
2. Then write two or three sentences that give details showing how the item does or does not measure up to your standard.

Your three paragraphs should use three of the standards from your list.

Example: *Category: Indoor Games*
Item: Charades
I prefer a game that requires only a small number of players. Charades needs at least four people, and it's better with six or more. It's often difficult to find that many people who know the game and are willing to play. A game that requires only two players, like chess or Chinese checkers, is easier to organize and play.

I also like a game that challenges my mind. Charades can be challenging if the players take it seriously, but usually everyone just starts laughing at the funny faces and gestures used in the game. When I try to get others to play more seriously, they call me a wet blanket.

I like a quiet game that can be played anywhere at any time. Charades usually gets noisy, especially if a large group is playing. When my friends and I are playing charades at my house, my grandfather or my aunt usually asks us to quiet down, which often breaks up the game.

Lesson Three

Summarizing the Plot

On your way to school each morning, you pass the Beverly Theater. One Friday, you notice that a new movie has opened at the Beverly. The name of the movie appears in big letters on the marquee: *The Black Stallion*. You've never heard of that movie before; you haven't heard any of your friends or family members talking about it. How can you decide whether you'd like to go to the Beverly Theater to see *The Black Stallion*?

As you've learned in this unit, reading a review of the movie could probably help you to decide whether you would enjoy *The Black Stallion*. A review could also help you in another way: It could tell you what the movie is about. The title alone does not explain this. *The Black Stallion* could be about a rodeo performer and a bucking bronco, or about a medieval knight and his favorite steed, or about a farm girl and the horse she loves. Without knowing what the movie is about, it is impossible to tell whether it might interest you. A good review will tell you what the movie is about by including a *summary of the plot*.

The *plot* of a movie, book, play, or other work is the series of events that make up the story. In other words, the plot is what happens. (You will learn more about plots in Unit Eighteen.) A *summary* is a brief description of the plot. A review of a movie, book, play, or any other work with a story usually includes a summary.

A summary doesn't include every detail of a plot. Telling everything that happens might bore the reader or spoil any surprises the movie might have. If you're reviewing a mystery movie, you shouldn't end your summary by saying, "And it turns out that the butler did it." If you do, you will spoil the suspense of the movie for those who haven't already seen it.

To write a summary, outline the major events of the movie. Be sure they are in chronological order. Go over the events you have listed and cross out any that are not necessary to let the reader know what the movie is about. Be sure that you don't reveal the ending or any surprises along the way.

Here is a possible list of the major events of the movie *The Black Stallion*:

1. A boy and his father are on a ship.
2. The ship goes down in a violent storm.
3. The only survivors of the shipwreck are the boy and a beautiful black horse.
4. They are washed ashore on a deserted island.
5. The horse is wild, but gradually he and the boy become friends.
6. They are finally rescued and return home, where the boy keeps the horse.
7. The boy enters the horse in a race, which provides the most exciting part of the movie.

This list can be used as the basis for a paragraph that summarizes the plot of the movie. When summarizing a plot, use verbs in the present tense. Notice how present-tense verbs are used throughout the following summary paragraph:

The Black Stallion, now playing at the Beverly Theater, is an exciting drama of a boy and a horse. When the movie begins, both are aboard a steamship headed for the United States. The boy, played by Kelly Reno, is traveling with his father, but the two are separated when a violent storm causes the ship to sink. The boy and the horse, the only survivors of the shipwreck, are washed ashore on a deserted island. The horse is wild, and seems untameable, but little by little he and the boy become friends. The two are finally rescued, and the boy returns home to his mother, played by Terri Garr. She allows him to keep the horse, and with the help of an old trainer, played by Mickey Rooney, the boy rides the horse in a big race. The race provides the movie with its exciting conclusion.

Notice that the summary gives some details, but not all. It mentions, for example, that the horse gradually becomes tame, but it doesn't say how. And it says that there is a race at the end of the film, but it doesn't give away the outcome. The summary gives enough details to let you know what the movie is about. If you aren't interested in horses, remote islands, or races, you probably won't want to see the movie. But if you like any or all of these things, you might think the movie is worth seeing.

When reviewing a movie, a book, a play, a television show, or any other work that tells a story, it is useful to give a summary in the first paragraph. You should also give the name of the work being reviewed and any other important information, such as the name of the author.

EXERCISE FOUR

Choose a movie to review. It could be a movie you have seen recently, or one that you will see especially for this assignment. If you want, you can review a television movie.

Write a one-paragraph summary of the plot of the movie. Include the major events of the story, but don't reveal any of the movie's surprises. Be sure that the events are in chronological order and that your verbs are in the present tense. Include the name of the movie or show, as well as any other information you think is important. Your summary should be six to ten sentences long. Keep this paper. You will use it when writing the rest of your review later in this unit.

Lesson Four

Writing and Revising

Imagine that you've been given the job of movie reviewer for the *Weekly Flash*. The readers of the school newspaper will be turning to your reviews for a thoughtful opinion of the latest movies. It's up to you to write the best reviews you can.

In this lesson, you'll put together the skills you've learned in this unit as you write the first review in your "career" as a movie critic.

Judging a Movie

Do you know what your own standards are for movies? Do you like excitement, comedy, or romance? Are you most interested in good acting, spectacular special effects, or a strong musical sound track? Perhaps you've never thought about what makes you like or dislike a movie. Here is a list of questions that will help you discover your standards for a good movie. It includes questions you might ask yourself about the movie you are reviewing. The questions cover four general areas: *plot, characters, technical quality,* and *audience appeal.*

Plot

1. Was the plot believable? Why or why not?
2. Was the plot developed clearly, or was it confusing?
3. Did the movie have a special feeling? Was it funny, sad, exciting, or did it have some other feeling?
4. Was the movie always interesting, or was it boring at times? Why?

Characters

1. Were the characters in the movie interesting or thought-provoking? Why or why not?
2. Were the characters believable? Why or why not?
3. Was there one character toward whom you felt especially sympathetic? Why?
4. Was the acting good or bad? Why?
5. Was there any one actor whose performance was better or worse than the others? Why?

Technical Quality

1. Were the camera angles and lighting used in the movie interesting and attractive? Why or why not?
2. Were the settings and costumes interesting? Were they appropriate to the movie?
3. Did the music enhance the story, or did it distract your attention from what was happening on the screen?

4. Was the movie's sound clear, or did you have trouble hearing at times?
5. Were there any special effects in the movie, such as unusual stunts, floods, earthquakes, or flying saucers? Were the effects believable, or did they seem fake?

Audience Appeal

1. Do you think the movie would appeal only to a certain audience—children, adults, teenagers, sports fans—or would it appeal to almost anyone? Why?
2. Is there a certain kind of person to whom you would recommend this movie? Who and why?

These questions may help you identify your own standards for judging a movie. They may suggest other points of special interest or importance to you.

EXERCISE FIVE

Look at the summary of a movie you wrote for Exercise Four. Reread the questions in the list on pages 375–376. Answer them on a piece of paper. If there are questions that don't apply to the movie you are reviewing, ignore them. Then use your answers to the questions about Plot, Characters, and Technical Quality to describe your standards for judging movies. Write a few words to describe each of your standards.

Example: Question: *Was the plot believable? Why or why not?*
Answer: *The plot of The Black Stallion was far-fetched, since the average person never gets ship-wrecked on a desert island, tames a wild horse, or takes part in a horse race. However, I didn't mind this, because I like movies that contain fantasy and unusual adventures.*
Standard: *I prefer movies that contain fantasy and unusual adventures.*

EXERCISE SIX

Now it's time to put together your review. Begin with the introductory paragraph summarizing the plot that you wrote for Exercise Four.

Next, write three or four paragraphs giving your opinion of the movie. If you want, you can write one paragraph on each of the first three topics in the list on pages 375–376: Plot, Characters, and Technical Quality. In each paragraph, describe one or two of your standards. Then tell how the movie did or did not measure up to that standard. Include details to explain and support your opinion.

Add a brief concluding paragraph in which you tell whether you would or would not recommend the movie to your readers, and why. You can use your answers to the questions on Audience Appeal (list, page 376) in this paragraph.

When you finish, check your work by consulting the Checklist below.

Checklist

1. Does the review begin with a brief summary of the plot?
2. Does the summary tell enough of the plot to give the reader an idea of what the movie is about, without giving away any surprises?
3. Are all verbs in the summary in the present tense?
4. Does the review explain the standards used in judging the movie?
5. Does the review include details to support and explain the opinions?
6. Does the review include a concluding paragraph that tells why you would or wouldn't recommend the movie?

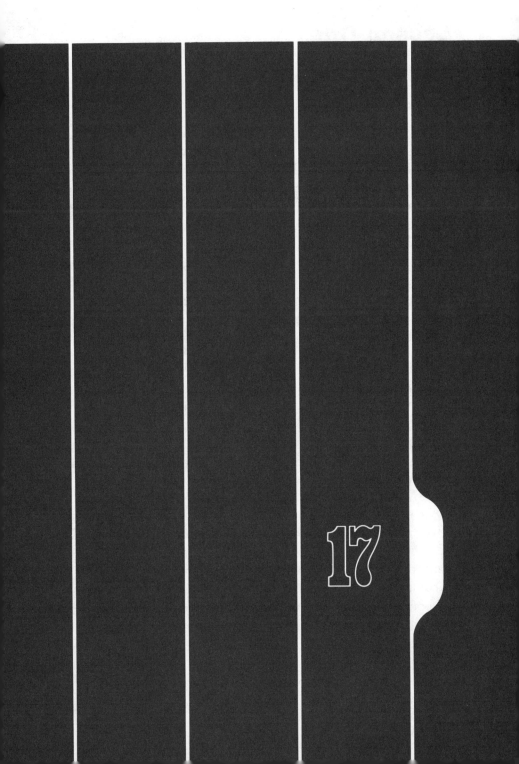

Unit Seventeen
Punctuation

17

Punctuation

Lesson One

End Punctuation

Try to read the following paragraph:

are you afraid of heights do you get seasick can you imagine driving across a tossing, twisting bridge more than two hundred feet above the water on the morning of November 7, 1940, some people had this experience when they tried to cross the Tacoma–Narrows Bridge in the state of Washington a forty-two-mile-per-hour wind was blowing the slender bridge began to rise and fall violently the authorities closed the road, and the few motorists inched off the bridge by this time the bridge was twisting forty-five degrees from side to side a reporter had gotten one third of the way across he deserted his car and crawled to safety just before a six-hundred-foot section of the bridge fell into the water ten minutes later, the entire roadway collapsed what a narrow escape

If you found the paragraph hard to read, it is because the paragraph has not been divided into sentences. The first word of each sentence has not been capitalized, and the end of each sentence has not been marked with an end punctuation mark.

Here is the same paragraph with the correct capitalization and end punctuation:

Are you afraid of heights? Do you get seasick? Can you imagine driving across a tossing, twisting bridge more than two hundred feet above the water? On the morning of November 7, 1940, some people had this experience when they tried to cross the Tacoma–Narrows Bridge in the state of Washington. A forty-two-mile-per-hour wind was blowing. The slender bridge began to rise and fall violently. The authorities closed the road, and the few motorists inched off the bridge. By this time, the bridge was twisting forty-five degrees from side to side. A reporter had gotten one third of the way across. He deserted his car and crawled to

380

safety just before a six-hundred-foot section of the bridge fell into the water. Ten minutes later, the entire roadway collapsed. What a narrow escape!

As you can see, the end punctuation marks help to make the paragraph easier to read.

There are three kinds of end punctuation marks: periods, question marks, and exclamation points. Different kinds of sentences call for different end punctuation marks. (See Unit One, Lesson Two for a review of the different kinds of sentences.)

1. A period (.) follows a declarative sentence.

In 1940, the Tacoma–Narrows Bridge was the third longest bridge of its type in the world.
It is dangerous to travel during a bad storm.

2. A question mark (?) follows an interrogative sentence.

Did the weather bureau predict today's high winds?
Can you find the Tacoma–Narrows Bridge on a map of Washington?

3. An exclamation point (!) follows an exclamatory sentence.

Whew! That was a close call!
What a frightening experience that must have been!

4. A period or an exclamation point follows an imperative sentence. A period follows a sentence that expresses a polite request. An exclamation point follows an order or a command.

Stay tuned for tonight's weather report.
Hurry and get off that bridge!

Abbreviations

Abbreviations are shortened forms of words. Most abbreviations are followed by periods. Here are examples of some common types of abbreviations:

Units of Measurement

| inch | **in.** |
| pound | **lb.** |

Note: Abbreviations for units of measurement in the metric system are usually not followed by periods.

centimeter   **cm**
kilogram   **kg**

Parts of Addresses

Street   **St.**
Avenue   **Ave.**

Days and Months

Monday   **Mon.**
September   **Sept.**

Abbreviations are not usually used in compositions or other formal writing. Here are some abbreviations that are correct in formal writing:

1. The following titles are abbreviated when used with a person's name: **Ms., Mr., Mrs., Dr., Jr.,** and **Sr.** The titles *Ms., Mr., Mrs.,* and *Dr.* come before the name; *Jr.* and *Sr.* come after the name.

Ms. Rodriguez   **Dr.** Chan
Mr. Seletti   Whitney M. Young, **Jr.**
Mrs. Helen Henderson   Preston Hughes, **Sr.**

Note: Miss is not an abbreviation.

2. Titles of government officials, military personnel, and professors are abbreviated when used with a person's full name.

Gov. Alfred E. Smith   **Sen.** Hubert H. Humphrey
Gen. Benjamin O. Davis   **Prof.** Yolanda Diaz

When only the person's last name is given, these titles should be written out.

Governor Smith   **Senator** Humphrey
General Davis   **Professor** Diaz

3. Initials used in place of part of a person's name are a form of abbreviation. Use a period after each initial.

O. J. Simpson   **B. B.** King
T. S. Eliot   **J. D.** Salinger

4. When the time of day is written in numbers, the abbreviations **a.m.** and **p.m.** can be used. Use *a.m.* with times between midnight and noon; use *p.m.* with times between noon and midnight.

The Wilcox brothers worked on the car from 9:00 **a.m.** to 7:30 **p.m.** on Saturday.

5. The abbreviations **B.C.** and **A.D.** can be used with historical dates. *B.C.* means "before Christ"; *A.D.* is an abbreviation for the Latin phrase *anno Domini,* which means "in the year of the Lord."

Rome was founded in 753 **B.C.**
The Vikings roamed the seas from about **A.D.** 750 to **A.D.** 1000.

Note that the abbreviation *B.C.* follows the year; the abbreviation *A.D.* comes before the year.

6. Well-known corporations, government agencies, and other organizations may be referred to by initials. Such abbreviations are usually written without periods. Notice that small words, such as *and, of,* and *for* are not included in the abbreviation.

NASA	National Aeronautics and Space Administration
NOW	National Organization for Women
AFL–CIO	American Federation of Labor–Congress of Industrial Organizations

7. When used in addresses, names of states may be abbreviated. The official two-letter United States postal abbreviations for states are written without periods.

AZ	Arizona
IN	Indiana
MS	Mississippi

If you are in doubt about whether to use an abbreviation in your writing, it is usually better to spell the word out.

PRACTICE A

The sentences in the following paragraph lack end punctuation marks. Rewrite the sentences on your paper, adding the correct end punctuation. The first sentence has been done for you.

Example: *Chuck's date with Isabella was one he'd love to forget.*

Chuck's date with Isabella was one he'd love to forget He took her to a fancy restaurant When the waiter brought the check, he realized that his wallet had fallen out of his pocket What an embarrassing moment He left Isabella in the restaurant, dashed back to the car, and found the wallet under the front seat However, his clothes got grimy as he looked for the wallet Can you imagine Isabella's face when she saw him After they left the restaurant, Chuck decided to take a shortcut home What a mistake Within five minutes he was lost Once Chuck found the highway again, the car sputtered to a stop The gas tank was empty How was Chuck to know that the gas gauge wasn't working He finally got Isabella home at three in the morning That was the worst date that Chuck has ever had

PRACTICE B

Below is a list of ten words. Choose four of them. For each word you chose, write four sentences. One sentence should be a statement. One sentence should be a question. One sentence should express a strong emotion. One sentence should be a request or a command. Be sure to use the correct end punctuation for each sentence.

Example: sandwich
My father made me a delicious tuna and olive sandwich for lunch.
Do you realize that you just sat on my sandwich?
That's the biggest sandwich I've ever seen!
Please make me a peanut butter and banana sandwich.

tiger	fire
telephone	motorcycle
game	banana
magician	lighthouse
camera	diamond

Lesson Two

Commas

Howard is applying for a summer job as a lifeguard. He has written a letter of application to the director of recreational programs in his town. Here is part of Howard's letter:

I have the experience training and personal qualities to be a good lifeguard at the Eastwood Pool this summer. I have been swimming since I was five and three years of water polo and competitive swimming have made me an expert swimmer. Last summer I passed my life-saving test and first aid was one of my electives last year at school. As my swim coach will verify I am reliable quick-thinking and calm in an emergency. In addition I am familiar with the programs and rules at Eastwood Pool. I hope Ms. Greenbaum you will consider me for the job.

Howard is probably qualified to work as a lifeguard, but his punctuation skills need some sharpening. Howard's letter would be easier to read if commas were placed where needed.

A comma marks a short pause within a sentence. When used correctly, commas help to make the meaning of a sentence clearer. See how much easier it is to read and understand Howard's letter when commas are used.

I have the experience, training, and personal qualities to be a good lifeguard at the Eastwood Pool this summer. I have been swimming since I was five, and three years of water polo and competitive swimming have made me an expert swimmer. Last summer I passed my life-saving test, and first aid was one of my electives last year at school. As my swim coach will verify, I am reliable, quick-thinking, and calm in an emergency. In addition, I am familiar with the programs and rules at Eastwood Pool. I hope, Ms. Greenbaum, you will consider me for the job.

To make your writing clear and easy to read, learn these rules for using commas.

● **Use a comma to separate the items in a series of three or more. The items can be single words, phrases, or clauses.**

385

Ruth, Gehrig, and DiMaggio are members of the Baseball Hall of Fame.

Carla and Pam raced across the parking lot, down the beach, and into the icy water.

Reginald may buy a new stereo system if he works after school, if he saves half of his earnings, and if he keeps up his grades.

Some writers do not use a comma before the conjunction (usually *and*) before the last item in a series. However, if you include the comma, you can avoid confusion:

The musical acts in the school talent show included Jeff Healy, the Anderson Twins, Maria Collins and Barbara Lindsay.

With no comma before the conjunction *and*, it sounds as if Maria Collins and Barbara Lindsay together were one act.

The musical acts in the school talent show included Jeff Healy, the Anderson Twins, Maria Collins, and Barbara Lindsay.

The comma before the conjunction makes it clear that four different acts have been listed.

A comma is not used after the last item in a series.

Incorrect: Gina made strawberry tarts, coconut chews, and baklava, for the party.

Correct: Gina made strawberry tarts, coconut chews, and baklava for the party.

Commas are not needed when items in a series are separated by conjunctions.

Weeds **and** moss **and** tiny wildflowers filled the cracks in the granite.

We will play volleyball **or** hunt for shells **or** build a castle in the sand.

● **Use a comma to separate two or more adjectives that come before and modify the same noun. Do *not* put a comma between the last adjective and the noun it modifies.**

Loud, lively music floated down the block.

The dark, damp, windswept tunnel made Gary shiver.

A tall, thin, sad-eyed stranger stood in the open doorway.

When two or more adjectives precede a noun, they do not always need a comma between them. Here is a simple test to tell whether a comma is needed: If the sentence sounds good when you put the word *and* between the adjectives, separate the adjectives with a comma. If the sentence sounds awkward with *and* between the adjectives, don't use a comma.

The friendly playful dogs tried to lick Sara's face.

Say: "The friendly *and* playful dogs tried to lick Sara's face." The sentence sounds good, so a comma should be used between the adjectives:

The friendly, playful dogs tried to lick Sara's face.

The two angry dogs nipped fiercely at Sara's ankles.

Say: "The two *and* angry dogs nipped fiercely at Sara's ankles." The sentence sounds awkward, so no comma should be used.

● Use a comma before the conjunction *and, or, but, nor, for,* or *yet* when it joins the independent clauses in a compound sentence.

(For a review of compound sentences, see Unit One, Lesson Six.)

The marching band practiced formations, and the cheerleaders worked out their routine for the halftime show.

Compound sentences that are made up of two short clauses may be clear enough without a comma.

Karen walked home and Kevin took the bus.
The car stopped but the truck didn't.

PRACTICE A

Copy the following sentences on your paper, adding commas where they are needed.

Example: We planted peas corn beans and lettuce in our garden.
    We planted peas, corn, beans, and lettuce in our garden.

1. Jim wanted to try skydiving but his father thought it was too dangerous.

2. My sister got home from the hospital and found carnations two boxes of chocolates three paperback novels and a thick stack of get-well cards.
3. Kerry's silky black hair hung in braids to her waist.
4. The City Council bought the old house and converted it into a museum library and bookstore.
5. The powerful sweet smell that filled the yard came from the honeysuckle bush.
6. The starting gun went off with a bang and twelve sprinters dashed madly toward the finish line.
7. There was a power failure last summer but operations at the local hospitals were not affected.
8. Dead leaves were inside the drain pipes behind the shutters and under the front porch.
9. Black clouds of thick foul-smelling smoke came from the old car's exhaust.
10. Aaron can speak English French Italian and Polish.

More Rules for Using Commas

● Use a comma after certain words, phrases, and clauses that come at the beginning of sentences.

1. Use a comma after introductory adverbs such as *however, nevertheless, instead, moreover, meanwhile,* and *furthermore.*

> Furthermore, you should clean your room before you go out.
> Meanwhile, it had begun to rain.
> However, the accident was not serious.

2. Use a comma after a mild exclamation that begins a sentence, such as *wow, why, oh, say,* and *hey.* Also use a comma after *yes* or *no* at the beginning of a sentence.

> Wow, there must be a hundred guests at this party.
> Why, haven't you heard the news about Mrs. Callison?
> Say, these tacos taste delicious.
> Yes, I'd like to go to the movies with you.

Note: If an exclamation expresses a strong emotion, it should be followed by an exclamation point.

> Wow! What a catch!

3. Use a comma after a prepositional phrase at the beginning of a sentence if the comma is needed to make the meaning of the sentence clear.

After the dance we went out for hamburgers and ice cream. (No comma is needed.)

After the dance, contests were held for the best and most unusual costumes. (Without the comma, the sentence would seem to begin, "After the dance contests. . . .")

4. Use a comma after an adverb clause that begins a sentence. (See Unit Nine, Lesson Three for a review of adverb clauses.)

After we had climbed the face of the cliff, we had to find a way to get down.
Because solar heating saves money, the Gilfords decided to install a solar heating system.
If you like jazz, you'll like my uncle's band.

● **Use commas to set off nonessential phrases or clauses from the rest of the sentence.**

A nonessential phrase or clause is one that gives information about the noun or pronoun it modifies, but is not needed to identify the noun or pronoun. (See Unit Seven, Lesson Six, and Unit Nine, Lesson Two, for a review of nonessential phrases and clauses.)

Alan Alda, the television and movie actor, spoke at our high school graduation. (nonessential appositive phrase)

Words that are essential to identify the noun or pronoun they modify should not be set off with commas.

The actor Alan Alda was born in New York City.

● **Use commas to set off a word in direct address.**

Cheryl, would you like to bring the records for the party?
You certainly deserved that award, Daisy.
I saw your name, Everett, in the story about surfing.

● **Use commas to set off parenthetical expressions such as *in fact, after all, for instance, for example, as you know, if possible, in my opinion,* and *I think.***

The club members, after all, have the right to choose the activities they prefer.

In my opinion, Abraham Lincoln was our nation's greatest president.

A roller skating rink, for example, is a good place to spend a Saturday afternoon.

● **Use commas to separate the day of the week from the month and the year in a date; to separate the parts of an address; after the salutation of an informal letter; and after the closing of all letters.**

Friday, August 13
October 14, 1066
212 McDougall Street, Murfreesboro, Tennessee
Dear Katie,
Sincerely,

Do not put a comma between the state and the zip code in an address. Leave a space between the state and the zip code.

Alhambra, California 91801

PRACTICE B

Copy the following sentences on your paper, adding commas where they are needed.

Example: Whenever you drive the other cars on the highway aren't safe.
Whenever you drive, the other cars on the highway aren't safe.

1. Yes operator I would like to make a collect call to Jackson Mississippi.
2. If you send in two dollars and five box tops you will receive a canvas bicycle bag.
3. My aunt Jenny who is a scuba diver saw a twelve-foot barracuda while diving off the coast of Mexico.
4. On January 26 1531 a major earthquake struck Lisbon Portugal.
5. Oh I didn't know that this seat was already taken.

390

6. Terry's car which was expensive four years ago is worth a lot more today.
7. Nevertheless Philip is the most highly qualified person for the job.
8. The next book on the reading list *Winesburg, Ohio* is about life in a small midwestern town.
9. Before the movie stars began arriving in limousines.
10. Marjorie I'd like you to finish painting the back porch by tomorrow morning if possible.

PRACTICE C

The informal letter below lacks commas. Copy the letter on your paper, adding commas where they are needed.

40 Lexington Avenue
Livingston New Jersey 07039
August 24 1983

Dear Felicia

I enjoyed your letter telling about your summer. I have spent the last two months working in the library going to the beach and taking short trips with my family. In June and July we went to Busch Gardens in Williamsburg Virginia to Six Flags Over Georgia in Atlanta and to Walt Disney World in Orlando Florida.

On these trips I discovered how much I love roller coasters. When the roller coasters dropped down those high steep slopes my stomach seemed to drop down into my toes. The wind blew in my face and my eyes began to water. You may think it all sounds awful but I thought it was wonderful! On the first ride I always kept my eyes closed but by the second ride I could force myself to watch.

The Loch Ness Monster which is the big roller coaster in Busch Gardens had some fast scary corkscrews. The Great American Scream Machine in Georgia was thrilling but I liked Space Mountain at Walt Disney World best. How would you like to go with us next time Felicia? Write soon.

Your friend

Denise

Lesson Three

Semicolons

Here are three versions of a couplet by the poet Ogden Nash. (A *couplet* is two lines of poetry that rhyme.) Can you find the differences among them?

1. I love the Baby Giant Panda.
   I'd welcome one to my veranda.
2. I love the Baby Giant Panda,
   And I'd welcome one to my veranda.
3. I love the Baby Giant Panda;
   I'd welcome one to my veranda.

All three versions of this couplet express the same meaning, and each version contains two independent clauses. But in each version, the clauses are written and punctuated differently. In the first, the two independent clauses are written as two sentences. In the second, they are joined by a comma and the conjunction *and* to form a compound sentence. And in the third version — the version that Ogden Nash actually wrote — they are joined by a semicolon (;).

Ogden Nash's couplet is an example of the most common use of the semicolon.

- **A semicolon is used between the independent clauses in a compound sentence if the clauses are not joined by the conjunction *and, but, or, nor, for, so,* or *yet.***

Here are some compound sentences containing semicolons:

The clouds grew dark overhead; big drops of rain began to fall.
The starter's flag fell; the fifteen cars roared down the track.

Note: Only closely related clauses may be joined by a semicolon.

There are three other common uses for the semicolon:

- **A semicolon is used in a compound sentence between independent clauses that are joined by adverbs such as *however, nevertheless, instead, moreover, meanwhile, furthermore,* and *otherwise.***

392

A comma usually follows these adverbs.

They had planned to see the movie at eight o'clock; however, the tickets for that show were already sold out.

Ed didn't bother to repair the broken sofa leg; instead, he propped up the sofa on a pile of old newspapers.

● **A semicolon is used between the independent clauses in a compound sentence when there are commas within the clauses.**

The shower, the refrigerator, and the television were all broken; but the travelers, who had driven all day, decided to stay there anyway.

Maurice, a sophomore, is the best player on the team; and Coach Gilmore, a fine judge of athletic talent, expects Maurice to be even better next year.

● **A semicolon is used between the items in a series when there are commas within the items.**

For breakfast you may have bacon, eggs, and toast; sausages, flapjacks, and cereal; or grapefruit, a muffin, and orange marmalade.

Major battles of the war in the Pacific included the Battle of the Coral Sea, on May 7, 1942; the Battle of Midway, on June 4, 1942; and the Battle of the Philippine Sea, on October 21, 1944.

PRACTICE A

The following sentences lack commas and semicolons. Copy the sentences, adding commas and semicolons where they are needed.

Example: I ran across the yard and down the street to the bus stop however the bus had already left.
I ran across the yard and down the street to the bus stop; however, the bus had already left.

1. Stanley changed the topic for his report three times consequently it took him two weeks to write it.
2. The handlebars on Francisco's bicycle were loose he had forgotten to check them before leaving home.

3. Cecilia made a perfect dive from the high board she entered the water in one smooth gliding motion.
4. The door to Troy's locker was jammed however the maintenance worker was able to pry it open with a screwdriver.
5. For the costume party my little brother wore large bulging clown shoes thick baggy pants a green orange and red shirt with pink stripes a fake gold pocket watch black plastic glasses with a huge rubber nose and a bushy curly beard.

PRACTICE B

Below are five pairs of sentences. Combine each pair to form one sentence with two independent clauses. Use a semicolon to separate the clauses. Add or subtract words if you want to.

Example: J. R. Richard was a fine pitcher for the Houston Astros. His career was interrupted when he suffered a stroke.
J. R. Richard was a fine pitcher for the Houston Astros; however, his career was interrupted when he suffered a stroke.

1. The eerie howling of the coyotes could be heard all night. Our dog barked nervously at the sound.
2. Kevin worked all day putting up wallpaper in the living room. The paper peeled off because of the humid weather.
3. The airline had sold too many tickets for the flight. The plane remained on the ground until some passengers agreed to take a later flight.
4. The campers brought warm sleeping bags and heavy sweaters on the trip. They expected cool weather in the mountains.
5. The brown jacket and the beige slacks were the wrong size for Mark. The gray sports coat and the navy slacks fit him perfectly.

Lesson Four

Colons

A colon (:) is used to call attention to the words that follow it. Here are the most common uses of the colon:

● **A colon is used before a list of items.**

Ms. Lum purchased the following supplies for the art classes: modeling clay, water-color paints, drawing paper, and a roll of canvas.

To earn money for his camping trip, Bob tackled some big after-school projects: he cleaned out Mr. Katz's garage, he weeded the Eislers' garden, and he chopped a pile of wood for the Demuths' fireplace.

Note: Do not use a colon immediately after a verb or a preposition.

Incorrect: The kinds of music Sabrina enjoys are: rock and roll, blues, jazz, and country and western.
Correct: Sabrina enjoys the following kinds of music: rock and roll, blues, jazz, and country and western.

● **A colon can be used to introduce a quotation.**

In his speech, the governor referred to these words of Shakespeare: "Some are born great, some achieve greatness, and some have greatness thrust upon them."

Ambrose Bierce defined a bore in the following way: "A person who talks when you wish him to listen."

Note: Do not use a colon if a verb comes immediately before the quotation.

Incorrect: It was Shakespeare who wrote: "Uneasy lies the head that wears a crown."
Correct: It was Shakespeare who wrote, "Uneasy lies the head that wears a crown."

● **A colon is used between the hour and the minute in writing the time.**

The next flight leaves from Terminal C at 9:15 a.m.

By 7:45 p.m. the roads near the site of the accident had been cleared.

● **A colon is used after the salutation of a formal or a business letter.**

Dear Governor Brown:
To the Editor:
To Whom It May Concern:

PRACTICE

The following paragraphs lack semicolons and colons. Copy the paragraphs on your paper, adding semicolons and colons where they are needed. Not every sentence needs a semicolon or colon.

Example: There have been many great feats of exploration in the twentieth century the discovery of the North and South Poles, the climbing of Mount Everest, and the first space flights. Of these, perhaps the most heroic was the climbing of Everest, the highest mountain in the world it was a feat of amazing courage and skill.

There have been many great feats of exploration in the twentieth century: the discovery of the North and South Poles, the climbing of Mount Everest, and the first space flights. Of these, perhaps the most heroic was the climbing of Everest, the highest mountain in the world; it was a feat of amazing courage and skill.

There were many obstacles to climbing Everest a short six-week climbing season, blizzards, mists, high winds, avalanches, and the dangerously thin air. The British climber George Leigh Mallory was one of the first to make the attempt however, in 1924, his quest came to a tragic end. He and another climber disappeared in the mist 800 feet below the summit only Mallory's ice-ax was ever recovered.

In 1953, another British climbing team attempted to scale Mount Everest. By that time, seven unsuccessful expeditions had clarified the main problems the strain of physical exertion at 20,000 feet above sea level and the extremely cold, thin air. To combat these problems, the British team climbed slowly they hoped to adjust their bodies to the extreme temperature gradually. On the morning of May 29, two climbers from the expedition approached the summit of Everest Tenzing Norkay and Edmund Hillary. They carried with them only a few things tanks of oxygen, a camera, and the flags of Nepal, Britain, India, and the United Nations. At 9:00 a.m. they began the last 400 feet of the ascent around 11:30 a.m. they reached the summit, 29,028 feet above sea level.

Lesson Five

Dashes and Parentheses

The dash (—) is a punctuation mark that is often overused. If your sentences contain too many dashes — like the sentence you are now reading — they will be awkward — hard to read — and perhaps confusing — as you can see.

The sentence you just read would be less awkward if most of the dashes were changed to commas: If your sentences contain too many dashes, like the sentence you are now reading, they will be awkward, hard to read, and perhaps confusing — as you can see.

Use dashes sparingly. Here are some rules that will guide you in their use.

- **Use a dash to set off an abrupt change or break in the thought expressed in a sentence.**

  The jazz band — what a talented group of students — thrilled the audience with song after song.

  April answered the phone — what else could she do? — after it had rung thirty times.

- **Use a dash to precede an explanation.**

  Battered cartons, stacks of records, shopping bags filled with old clothes — these filled every inch of the back seat of his car.

  Author, statesman, scientist, architect, educator — Thomas Jefferson was all these, and more.

- **Use a dash to set off parenthetical information.**

Mr. and Mrs. Gonzales — they own a grocery store down the block from my house — have just bought the house next door.

The poet Hilda Doolittle — usually known simply as H. D. — was the author of *Red Shoes for Bronze* and *Sea Garden*.

- **Use parentheses ( ) to set off short explanations or comments that are not a grammatical part of the sentence.**

Kate Chopin (1851–1904) and Willa Cather (1876–1947) wrote thought-provoking stories about women struggling to find their identities.

The camera manual tells the user how to set the shutter speed (page 3), how to change lenses (page 5), and how to use the flash attachment (pages 9–10).

With some kinds of explanations or comments, either parentheses or dashes can be used. The choice is up to you. If you use dashes, the break in the sentence will probably seem more abrupt to the reader.

Parentheses, like dashes, should be used sparingly. If you find that you have used parentheses several times in one paragraph, look over your sentences again. You may be able to rephrase them to eliminate some of the parentheses.

PRACTICE A

Copy the following sentences on your paper, adding dashes where they are needed.

Example: The contraption you could hardly call it a car sounded like a dozen garbage-can lids rattling along the street.
The contraption — you could hardly call it a car — sounded like a dozen garbage-can lids rattling along the street.

1. Cindy asked in fact, she practically begged Tony to accept the job.
2. The young lawyer I think he was an unsuccessful actor told jokes in court and did imitations of famous people.
3. Wearing a hat with a feather two feet long what a sight! Barbie strutted onto the stage.

4. Maya promised her brother how could she refuse? to bring him souvenirs from every country she visited.
5. The accident some said it had been deliberate forced the referee to interrupt the game.

PRACTICE B

Number your paper from 1 to 5. Copy the following sentences, adding parentheses where they are needed.

Example: The time it takes each planet to orbit the sun varies from 88 days Mercury to two hundred years Pluto.
The time it takes each planet to orbit the sun varies from 88 days (Mercury) to two hundred years (Pluto).

1. Two great leaders of nineteenth-century Italy were Mazzini 1805–1872 and Garibaldi 1807–1882.
2. "Jody Twist" Josephine Adamo began her musical career as the lead singer in a group at our high school.
3. Lionel ordered three items from the catalog: a pair of leather gloves item #619, a nylon windbreaker item #1130, and a cotton shirt item #336.
4. Among the small associations listed in the directory are the National Cartoonists' Society 450 members, the Byron Society 275 members, and the Pilgrim Society 700 members.
5. The first three moon landings were made by the Apollo 11 mission July, 1969 the Apollo 12 mission November, 1969 and the Apollo 14 mission February, 1971.

Lesson Six

Hyphens and Apostrophes

Hyphens and apostrophes are used within words.

Hyphens

There are four common uses for the hyphen (-):

● **Use a hyphen to divide a word between syllables at the end of a line.**

When the wrestling meet was over, the principal telephoned to congratulate the winners.

Because of the high winds, several small fishing boats had to be called into port.

If you are not sure where a syllable break occurs in a word,
look up the word in a dictionary.
Never divide a word of one syllable at the end of a line.

Incorrect: About noon on Friday, we drove through a brief rainstorm.

Instead of dividing a one-syllable word, end the line before or
after the one-syllable word.
Never divide a word so that only one letter appears at the end
of a line or the beginning of a line.

Incorrect: The kitten batted a fallen a-
corn across the lawn.

Instead of dividing a word this way, put the whole word on one
line.

● **Use a hyphen in certain compound words.**

sister-in-law	life-size
self-portrait	jack-o'-lantern
ex-president	great-grandmother

As you learned in Unit Three, Lesson One, some compound
words are written as one word (**grasshopper, highway**); some are
written as two words (**rain forest, French fries**); and some are
hyphenated. If you are not sure whether to use a hyphen in a
compound word, look up the word in a dictionary.

● **Use a hyphen in all compound numbers from twenty-one to
ninety-nine.**

My grandfather came to America **sixty-six** years ago.
Twenty-two guests attended my sister's birthday party.

● **Use a hyphen in a fraction that is used as an adjective or an
adverb.**

400

The chairperson of the committee was elected by a **two-thirds** majority.

The bookcase in the corner of the classroom is **three-quarters** full.

PRACTICE A

Copy the following sentences on your paper, adding hyphens where they are needed. If you are not sure whether a word needs a hyphen, look the word up in a dictionary.

Example: My aunt was thirty four years old when she learned to drive.

My aunt was thirty-four years old when she learned to drive.

1. Carrie's little sister played for two hours with her new jack in the box.
2. After working as a reporter for twenty two years, Mr. Bailor was named editor in chief.
3. Eli's mother in law planned a surprise graduation party for him.
4. The job of painting the school auditorium is only one third finished.
5. Martin lacks the self discipline to stay in training through out the football season.

Apostrophes

Here are the two common uses of the apostrophe (').

● **An apostrophe is used to form the possessive case of many nouns. The possessive case is used to show ownership or relationship.**

Anita's pet lizard lives in a glass tank.

The coach's advice was that Tammy should run about two miles three times a week.

The city's problems are serious but not impossible to solve.

There are certain rules you should know for forming the possessive case of nouns.

1. To form the possessive case of a singular noun that does not end in *s*, add an apostrophe and an *s*.

Lionel's motorcycle is in his father's garage.
The plumber's mistake was not serious.
A bird's feathers are similar in function to a reptile's scales.

2. To form the possessive case of a singular noun ending in *s*, add either an apostrophe and an *s* or only an apostrophe. If the noun has only one syllable, add an apostrophe and an *s*. If the noun has more than one syllable, use your judgment. Avoid writing a word that is awkward to pronounce.

The boss's briefcase could not be found.
The chorus's second performance went smoothly.
Narcissus' story is one of the legends of ancient Greece.

3. To form the possessive case of a plural noun ending in *s*, add only an apostrophe.

The foxes' den was hidden under a thick clump of bushes.
A cry for help interrupted the two lifeguards' conversation.
The Harrises' vacation lasted two weeks longer than they
had planned.

4. To form the possessive case of a plural noun that does not end in *s*, add an apostrophe and an *s*.

The children's toys were scattered all over the yard.
The men's locker room has just been repainted.
The geese's honking awoke me early this morning.

5. Personal pronouns in the possessive case have no apostrophe.

I can hear **his** voice through the window.
The blouse is missing two of **its** buttons.
This dog is **ours**.

● **Use an apostrophe to form a contraction.**

A contraction is a word made by shortening and joining two or more words. An apostrophe shows where a letter or letters have been left out in forming the contraction.

| are not | **aren't** |
| she will | **she'll** |

you have   **you've**

they are   **they're**

PRACTICE B

Copy the sentences below on your paper, adding apostrophes where they are needed.

Example: Franco couldnt move his fathers desk by himself.
Franco couldn't move his father's desk by himself.

1. Its hard to imagine why anyone wouldnt like apple pie.
2. The womens roles in the play were more demanding than the mens roles.
3. Maureen shouldnt take her boat out when the weather is stormy.
4. Whos in charge of depositing the clubs money in the bank?
5. The Moores party lasted for three hours on Saturday.

Lesson Seven

Quotation Marks

Read the following paragraph. Do you find it difficult to understand?

Gilbert said, Hurry up! You're wasting time. Just roll the ball down the alley as straight as you can. I can't! Felix replied. Just swing your arm toward the pins and let go, Gilbert ordered. Come on! Everyone is watching us. I told you I can't, Felix said. My thumb is jammed in the hole. You've got to be joking, Gilbert groaned. The knuckle is swollen, Felix said, and my thumb really hurts. I hate bowling. Now I'll have to carry this ugly ball around with me forever. What's the problem here, boys? the manager demanded.

Quotation marks (" ") could make this paragraph easier to read. Quotation marks are used to set off the exact words spoken by a person. See how much clearer the paragraph is when quotation marks are used. Of course, beginning a new paragraph each time the speaker changes also helps.

Gilbert said, "Hurry up! You're wasting time. Just roll the ball down the alley as straight as you can."

"I can't!" Felix replied.

"Just swing your arm toward the pins and let go," Gilbert ordered. "Come on! Everyone is watching us."

"I told you I can't," Felix said. "My thumb is jammed in the hole."

"You've got to be joking," Gilbert groaned.

"The knuckle is swollen," Felix said, "and my thumb really hurts. I hate bowling. Now I'll have to carry this ugly ball around with me forever."

"What's the problem here, boys?" the manager demanded.

Here are some rules for using quotation marks in your writing:

● **Use quotation marks to enclose a direct quotation.**

A *direct quotation* is the exact words someone has said or written. Put quotation marks before and after the words quoted.

"Let's eat outside on the lawn," Licia said.

"I can't," I said. "The coach wants to talk to the team about last week's game."

If a conversation is reported without using the exact words of the speakers, the description of the conversation is an *indirect quotation*. Do not use quotation marks with an indirect quotation.

Licia suggested that we eat outside on the lawn. I told her I couldn't because the coach wanted to talk to the team about last week's game.

Here are the rules for capitalizing and punctuating direct quotations:

1. Begin the first word of a direct quotation with a capital letter.

The man said angrily, "You dialed the wrong number — again."
Sondra asked, "Do you see those mysterious red and yellow lights?"

2. If a sentence in a direct quotation is divided by an interrupting expression, such as *he said, she asked,* or *I replied,* use a small letter to begin the second part of the quoted sentence.

404

"You can't buy a new bicycle," she said, "until you sell your old one."

"According to the polls," shouted the reporter, "your opponent has a substantial lead in the race for the Senate."

If the second part of a broken quotation is a new sentence, capitalize the first word.

"I have the tickets you asked for," Eric said. "Where would you like me to send them?"

3. Use a comma, question mark, or exclamation point to separate a direct quotation from the rest of the sentence.

Commas that set off a quotation come before the quotation marks.

"I saw some fish jump," Mitch said.
Terry said, "I saw them, too."
"The fish in this pond," Sonny said, "are practically begging to be caught."

A question mark or exclamation point goes inside the closing quotation marks if the quotation itself is a question or an exclamation.

"Do you want to dance?" he asked.
"You were sensational!" Dad yelled.

A question mark or exclamation point goes outside the closing quotation marks if the quoted material is not a question or a exclamation, but the entire sentence is a question or an exclamation.

Why did Esther say, "See you Monday"?
What a mistake it was for Mr. Herrick to say, "I don't care"!

4. When quoting two or more speakers, begin a new paragraph each time the speaker changes.

"Do you have my name listed?" the man asked.
"Yes, Mr. Arthur, your name is right here," the receptionist replied. "Your appointment is for 11:15."
"It's 11:25 right now. The doctor is in her office, isn't she?" the man snapped angrily.

"Just take a seat, Mr. Arthur," the receptionist replied. "I'm sure that Dr. Nakamura will see you soon."

5. When a quoted passage is longer than one paragraph, put quotation marks at the beginning of each quoted paragraph and at the end of the final paragraph only.

> Ellen stepped to the podium and said, "Fellow students, today we will elect our class president for the coming school year. This is an important decision, and it calls for careful thought. I'd like to tell you why I think I deserve your vote.
>
> "I will work hard for the good of our school. I will support the kinds of after-school activities you ask for. And I will do my best to get all students involved in school programs."

6. Use single quotation marks (' ') to enclose a quotation within a quotation.

> "Why did Anna say, 'I don't want to talk about it'?" Marge asked.
>
> Lenny said, "Now I understand why you said, 'Cleaning the basement will take days.' "

● **Use quotation marks to enclose words used in unusual ways, slang words, and technical terms.**

> The young pitcher had a strong arm, but he did not have good "location." (In baseball, a pitcher's "location" is the ability to throw the ball exactly where he wants it.)

> After the party, Sharon and Steve agreed that it had been a "blast."

> The printer used a set of metal "quoins" to lock the type in place.

● **Use quotation marks to enclose the titles of short stories, chapters of books, essays, poems, magazine and newspaper articles, songs, and radio and television programs.**

> The best story we read in class was Katherine Mansfield's "The Garden Party."

> "The Child's Need for Magic" is the most important chapter in Bruno Bettelheim's book *The Uses of Enchantment.*

Tricia recited Naoshi Koriyama's poem "Unfolding Bud."

The article from *Newsweek* entitled "France's Close Election" was hanging on the bulletin board.

Neil Diamond's "Shiloh" is my brother's favorite song.

PRACTICE A

Copy the following sentences on your paper, adding quotation marks where they are needed.

Example: The customer said to Warren, You must have made a mistake.

The customer said to Warren, "You must have made a mistake."

1. I would prefer, she answered, not to sleep in the attic by myself.
2. Are you free for lunch Thursday afternoon? Errol asked.
3. I saw a fish that looked like a baby barracuda, Tish said.
4. Tish's remark, Stan said, frightened me away from the water.
5. Vince said, You should try sky diving. I'm sure you'd like it.
6. Who said, I wish I had lived four hundred years ago?
7. The ceiling of our kitchen leaks, Mom said, whenever the people upstairs use their dishwasher.
8. I'd fix the leak myself, she continued, if I had the tools.
9. Why did Zeke say, I quit? Iris asked.
10. We need a touchdown! Norman yelled.

PRACTICE B

On the next page is a conversation among three people: an apartment manager, Mr. Hatch, and Mrs. Hatch. The quotation marks have been left out, and the conversation is not written in paragraphs. Rewrite the conversation correctly.

Example: Here is the one-bedroom apartment advertised in the newspaper, the apartment manager said. I see that it has a back door and a porch, Mrs. Hatch said. What a fine view of the valley! Mr. Hatch added.

"Here is the one-bedroom apartment advertised in the newspaper," the apartment manager said.

"I see that it has a back door and a porch," Mrs. Hatch said.

"What a fine view of the valley!" Mr. Hatch added.

Oh, I'm sure you'll be happy here, the apartment manager said. By the way, do you two have any pets? Well, we have a small cat, Mrs. Hatch said. She's very gentle. Do you have only one cat? the apartment manager asked. We also have a bull mastiff, Mr. Hatch admitted. How do the dog and the cat get along? the apartment manager inquired. Mrs. Hatch said, They get along fine, but they don't seem to like the rabbits and the parakeet. It's not that, Mr. Hatch broke in, I think they just get bored. You know how playful animals can be. Mrs. Hatch added, Fortunately, we keep the rabbits in a pen and the parakeet in a bird cage. Do you have any other pets? the apartment manager demanded. We keep our rattlesnake in a glass tank, said Mr. Hatch. He's had his fangs removed. Wait until you meet him — you'll love him! Then there's the tarantula, Mrs. Hatch continued. He lives in an aquarium with a fine mesh screen on top. Wait a minute! the apartment manager interrupted. This sounds like a zoo. May I suggest that you take a little drive about five miles due east. What for? Mr. Hatch asked. I happen to know there's a farm for rent there, the apartment manager answered, as he gently pushed them toward the door.

Lesson Eight

Italics

Italic is a kind of type that leans to the right. Words printed in italics look different from the words around them: *Italics stand out.* In handwriting or typewriting, underlining is used to stand for italics.

Here are some rules to help you know when to use italics or underlining in your writing.

● Use underlining *(italics)* to indicate the titles of books, magazines, newspapers, plays, movies, works of art, and the names of ships and planes.

Keith carries his copy of *The Hobbit* with him everywhere.

Have you seen the latest issue of *Sports Illustrated*?

Shakespeare's *Macbeth* will be performed at the Smythtown Theater next week.

Humphrey Bogart and Ingrid Bergman are the stars of the movie *Casablanca*.

Rodin's *The Thinker* is a famous modern sculpture.

Charles Lindbergh flew his plane *The Spirit of St. Louis* across the Atlantic Ocean in 1927.

- **Use underlining *(italics)* to indicate words, letters, and numbers referred to as such, and for foreign words.**

Jason won the spelling bee by correctly spelling *chrysanthemum*.

In the word *night,* the letters *g* and *h* are silent.

Lou Gehrig wore a *4* on the back of his New York Yankee uniform.

Paula enjoys being called *mademoiselle* by the waiters in the French restaurant.

PRACTICE

Copy the following sentences on your paper, adding underlining where it is needed.

Example: While I was sick, I read Dorothy Sayers' mystery novel The Nine Tailors.

While I was sick, I read Dorothy Sayers' mystery novel <u>The Nine Tailors</u>.

1. Prints of two famous paintings, Renoir's Boating Party and Monet's Water-Lilies, hung in the living room.
2. I recommend that you see the play The Pirates of Penzance when it comes to our local theater.
3. Some of Ursula's favorite movies are Dr. Jekyll and Mr. Hyde, starring Fredric March; Dr. Zhivago, starring Omar Sharif and Julie Christie; and Dr. Strangelove, starring George C. Scott.
4. The steamboat Sultana exploded in the Mississippi River in 1865.
5. In our English class, we studied Thomas Hardy's novel Far from the Madding Crowd.

6. All that Burt remembers from his first class in French is the phrase bon jour.
7. I don't recognize the woman on the cover of this week's issue of Time.
8. The battleships West Virginia, Helena, and Tennessee were all docked at Pearl Harbor, Hawaii.
9. Does Carl spell his name with a C or with a K?
10. George Orwell's book Down and Out in Paris and London tells what living in poverty is like.

Review Exercises

I. The following paragraphs lack end punctuation marks. Copy the paragraphs on your paper, adding end punctuation marks where they are needed. (Lesson One)

Example: Have you ever tried surfing If you have, you know that it takes skill, coordination, and lots of practice
Have you ever tried surfing? If you have, you know that it takes skill, coordination, and lots of practice.

The Polynesians who first settled the Hawaiian Islands invented the sport of surfing Their kings surfed on long, narrow boards made from *wiliwili* wood Some of these boards were sixteen feet long and weighed over a hundred pounds Although certain beaches were reserved for royal surfing, other Hawaiians also surfed, using smaller, heavier boards When the British captain James Cook sailed to the Hawaiian Islands in 1778, he was startled to see people skimming along the tops of waves What an amazing sight Unfortunately, the missionaries who arrived in 1821 discouraged the sport

In the early twentieth century, an Olympic swimmer from Hawaii named Duke Kahanamoku encouraged the rediscovery of surfing and the growth of surfing clubs Before World War I, surfing spread to California Surfing exhibitions at Redondo Beach drew the attention of Californians to the sport Do you think Kahanamoku would be surprised at the popularity of surfing today

410

II. The following paragraphs lack commas. Copy the paragraphs on your paper, adding commas where they are needed. (Lesson Two)

Example: Surfing is no longer an exotic little-known sport.
Surfing is no longer an exotic, little-known sport.

As surfing grew in popularity during the early years of this century the problem of developing a strong lightweight easy-to-carry surfboard was addressed. An improved surfboard was greatly needed and modern technology was brought to the problem. Tom Blake Pete Peterson and Bob Simmons all played parts in the invention of the modern surfboard. Blake designed the first hollow surfboard Peterson created surfboards made of light strong balsa wood and Simmons experimented with foam and fiberglass. Most surfboards are now made of polyurethane foam or fiberglass.

Surfing is popular all over the world. People surf in Australia South America Mexico South Africa France and Indonesia — in fact almost anywhere the waves are strong enough. In the United States the American Surfing Association founded in 1966 unites surfers surfing clubs and competitive teams in the pursuit of the sport. More and more people are taking up surfing to get close to nature to enjoy the thrill of competition and to experience the excitement of one of the world's most dynamic thrilling sports.

III. The following paragraphs lack semicolons. Copy the paragraphs on your paper, adding semicolons where they are needed. (Lesson Three)

Example: Figure skating has long been popular in Europe it has recently grown in popularity in the United States.
Figure skating has long been popular in Europe; it has recently grown in popularity in the United States.

As a team, Tai Babilonia and Randy Gardner have trained long and hard to achieve the excellence they display on ice. They have studied skating techniques; skills drawn from the world of dance, including ballet, jazz, and modern dance; and the unique skating routines designed to make use of their own special style. Working so closely together, Tai and Randy have developed a strong friendship; they respect each other and enjoy a real partnership both on and off the ice.

Skating in pairs competition is demanding; it requires physical strength, grace, skill, and coolness under pressure. In national and international competitions, Tai and Randy have performed many dazzling routines. Their programs feature both fast skating and graceful ballet-like movements; they also include spectacular lifts, jumps, spins, dips, and splits. Randy and Tai's programs have won them numerous medals in world competition. Because of Randy's injury, they were unable to compete in the 1980 Winter Olympics; however, their talent and determination seem likely to bring them more success in the future.

IV. The following sentences lack colons. Copy the sentences on your paper, adding colons where they are needed. (Lesson Four)

Example: The recipe calls for the following seasonings thyme, sage, paprika, red pepper, sweet basil, and oregano.
The recipe calls for the following seasonings: thyme, sage, paprika, red pepper, sweet basil, and oregano.

1. My neighbor goes to work at 812 a.m. and returns home at 540 p.m.
2. In her English class, Wendy read the following a historical novel, a Greek tragedy, a science-fiction film script, and a collection of short stories.
3. During her walk on the deserted beach, Deirdre found several unusual objects a Mexican coin, a small conch shell, a piece of petrified wood, and a rusty skeleton key.
4. Remember Benjamin Franklin's wise advice "He that goes a borrowing goes a sorrowing."
5. The garden at the old mansion was filled with all sorts of flowers daffodils, tulips, geraniums, chrysanthemums, and roses.
6. Because of bad weather, the 830 p.m. flight to Chicago didn't arrive until after 200 a.m.
7. Please go to the hardware store to buy these items a pound of nails, a gallon of paint remover, a spool of wire, and a small screwdriver.
8. A sense of humor has many benefits it eases the pressures of life, it helps to strengthen one's friendships, and it helps keep worries under control.

9. The Highway Department needs money for many projects the completion of the Ramsey Street Bridge, the repair of the fences along Route 12, and the filling-in of potholes on several side streets.

10. The play *Richard III* begins with these famous words "Now is the winter of our discontent."

V. Some of the sentences in the following paragraphs lack parentheses or dashes. Copy the paragraphs on your paper, adding parentheses and dashes where they are needed. (Lesson Five)

Example: Few athletes perhaps none have played as dramatic a role in American history as Jackie Robinson.
Few athletes — perhaps none — have played as dramatic a role in American history as Jackie Robinson.

Jack Roosevelt Robinson 1919–1972 was a superb all-around athlete. During his college years, Robinson played for Pasadena City College and the University of California in track, football, basketball, and baseball. After coaching and playing baseball with the Kansas City Monarchs of the Negro National League now no longer in existence Robinson got his big chance. He became the first black player at least, the first in modern times to play with a team in the all-white "organized" leagues.

In his first year with the Montreal Royals of the International League 1946, Robinson was voted the league's Most Valuable Player. The following season, he joined the Brooklyn Dodgers of the National League. Robinson was an immediate success. Hitting, fielding, base-stealing Robinson did it all. Robinson's competitive zest he was a fiery, exciting ballplayer won the respect of teammates, opponents, and fans everywhere.

When he was named the Most Valuable Player in the National League in 1949, Robinson led the league in batting average .342 and stolen bases 37. He helped the Dodgers win six National League pennants and one World Series 1955. In his first year of eligibility 1962, Robinson was elected to the Baseball Hall of Fame.

VI. Copy the following sentences on your paper, adding hyphens and apostrophes where they are needed. (Lesson Six)

Example: Im sure your aunt would enjoy receiving two tickets
            to the theater for her twenty fifth birthday.
            *I'm sure your aunt would enjoy receiving two tickets
            to the theater for her twenty-fifth birthday.*

1. Chester announced proudly that he had finished reading his
   forty third mystery novel yesterday.
2. I tried to follow Pattys advice about keeping my head down,
   but my golf swing seemed as awkward as ever.
3. Youll enjoy this movie, Im sure; one of your favorite actors
   is in it.
4. The museums most popular exhibit is the wax figures of the
   Apollo 11 astronauts.
5. My great great grandparents came to this country toward the
   end of the nineteenth century.
6. It isnt easy to walk across a room while balancing an egg on
   a spoon.
7. Representative Bauman was re elected by a margin of only
   sixty six votes.
8. Havent your brothers finished their go cart for the big race
   yet?
9. Dont try diving into the swimming pool; its only about one
   third full.
10. Marthas new store specializes in sleepware for pets; its known
    as "Cats Pajamas."

VII. The paragraphs that follow lack quotation marks and italics
(underlining). Copy the paragraphs on your paper, adding quotation marks and underlining where they are needed. (Lessons
Seven and Eight)

Example: In February, Butler High's drama club staged Agatha
            Christie's play Ten Little Indians and an original play
            based on Edith Wharton's short story Roman Fever.
            *In February, Butler High's drama club staged Agatha
            Christie's play* <u>Ten Little Indians</u> *and an original play
            based on Edith Wharton's short story "Roman Fever."*

Last week, Butler High's drama club packed the Blount Auditorium for all three performances of the school's spring play, West
Side Story. The musical, loosely based on Shakespeare's play

Romeo and Juliet, calls for skill in both singing and dancing. On both counts, the Butler High production was a success.

Lola Andrews was a spirited Maria. Her strong, clear soprano was especially effective in the lovely song I Feel Pretty. Phil Zucotti was attractive and believable as Tony. His singing of the ballad Tonight thrilled the audience with its vitality.

Both the Valley Tribune and the Springfield Gazette praised the show. Rex Rollins, in the Tribune, said, The students of Butler High have put on a production that some professional companies couldn't equal. In the Gazette, Judith Kirsch wrote, Butler High's West Side Story is one of the best shows I've seen this year. How many high schools, Kirsch added, could put on such a remarkable production? What a thrill it must have been for Lola and Phil to see themselves mentioned by Judith Kirsch as, in her words, future Broadway performers!

Writing an Autobiographical Narrative

Have you ever looked through an old family photo album? In its pages you can glimpse moments from your past. Perhaps there's a picture of you on the day your Little League team won the county championship. You might come across a picture of a family barbecue or the Halloween party when you dressed up as a pumpkin. Pictures of the past can remind you of events and feelings that you might have forgotten.

Photographs are not the only windows to the past. Memories can be captured without a camera and film. The only tools you need are a pen and some paper. You can use these tools to write an *autobiographical narrative,* a story based on an incident in your life.

In this unit, you will write an autobiographical narrative. You will start by browsing through the "photo album" in your mind to choose one memory you would like to share with a reader.

Lesson One

Choosing an Incident

Imagine that one evening you are sitting and talking with friends. People are telling interesting or funny incidents from their lives. One friend tells about the time she hit a baseball that went two hundred miles (it landed in a passing freight train). Another friend tells about the time he won a dance contest by performing on roller skates.

When it's your turn, you begin, "I was born on August 14, 1966, in a small town outside of Des Moines, Iowa. My parents' names are Ida and Maurice. They met at an amusement park in Sydney, Australia in 1953, and after deciding to get married, they . . ." By this time, one of your friends says, "Wait a minute. We don't have time to listen to your life history. Just tell us one story, please!"

You think for a minute and decide to tell your friends about the time you rode a mule to the bottom of the Grand Canyon. Here is what you say:

"Two summers ago, my family and I visited the Grand Canyon. We rented some mules from a tour guide, who showed us how to ride them. We rode the mules to the bottom of the canyon. We stayed there awhile. Then we rode back up to the top of the canyon."

"Well, go on with the story," one of your friends says. "Did someone get lost at the bottom of the canyon? Did one of the mules break a leg? Did you find a 500-million-year-old fossil? What happened?"

"That's all there is," you reply. "Didn't you enjoy hearing the story?"

"Let's just say that I wouldn't stay up to watch it on the late night movie," your friend replies. "That story doesn't have any point!"

Your friends' comments might have taught you two important facts about telling a story:

1. A good story focuses on one incident.
2. A good story has a point.

Choosing an Incident With a Point

An autobiographical narrative can be based on many different kinds of incidents. Perhaps there was a time in your life when you made a difficult choice, such as deciding whether to take a certain job. Perhaps you remember an incident that was especially funny — a camping trip that turned out to be a disaster, or a role in a school play that made you vow never to appear on stage again. There might have been a time in your life when you faced danger or learned to accept a disappointment or witnessed an exciting event. Any of these experiences could be the basis for an interesting autobiographical narrative.

To choose an incident to write about, spend some time thinking about the memorable incidents in your life. As you browse through your "photo album" of memories, think about the following questions. They can help you decide whether a particular incident has a point that makes it worth writing about.

1. Do you have strong feelings about the incident?
   a. Was it especially funny?
   b. Was it scary, exciting, or sad?
   c. Did you do something that you are proud to remember?
2. Did you learn something about yourself or others from the incident?
3. Did the incident lead to an important change in your life?
4. Did the incident reveal something about your character?
5. Did the incident have an unexpected result?
6. Was the incident part of the best day you can remember — or the worst?

If you can answer yes to one or more of these questions about an incident you remember, that incident might be a good basis for an autobiographical narrative.

EXERCISE ONE

Using the questions above to give you ideas, make a written list of at least five incidents in your life that could be the basis for an autobiographical narrative. Save this list for use later in the lesson.

Example: *1. the day my little sister got lost at the beach, and my friends and I had to find her*
2. the day it started to rain in the middle of an outdoor concert by my rock band
3. the time I unfairly accused my best friend of taking my radio, which I had misplaced
4. the time my family's car ran out of gas while we were crossing the Sonoran Desert
5. the day I struck out my own brother to win a big baseball game for my team

The Elements of a Good Plot

To be interesting, a narrative must have a *plot*.

● **The plot is the series of events that take place in a narrative. A good plot includes a *conflict*, a *climax*, and a *resolution*.**

Not every incident is the basis for a good plot. For example, if you and your friends go on a picnic, the picnic could be considered an incident. It might include a number of separate events: you arrive at the picnic grounds, you cook the hot dogs, you play softball, and you leave. But although this is a series of events, it is not a good plot. A narrative that related these events would probably be dull. A good plot needs a *conflict*.

- **A conflict is a disagreement or struggle over some thing or some idea.**

Conflict can make a series of events memorable. For example, if you and your friends went on a picnic and were challenged to a softball game by a group of bigger, stronger teenagers from another school, the conflict between the two groups might make an interesting plot. If two of your friends went off exploring and fell into an old, dried-up well, your efforts to rescue them might be the basis for a good plot. Conflict can come in many forms, but some kind of conflict is necessary for a good plot.

Here are some kinds of conflicts that occur often in life and in stories:

1. *A conflict between people.* If you and a friend have an argument, there is a conflict between you. If you are held up at gunpoint, there is a conflict between you and the criminal.

2. *A conflict within a person.* If you can't decide whether to try out for the basketball team or take an after-school job to help your family make ends meet, there is a conflict within you. If a teacher accidentally leaves a copy of next week's test on his desk, there may be a conflict within you as you wrestle with temptation.

3. *A conflict between a person and nature.* If you are lost in the woods without food, or adrift in the middle of a river in a small rowboat, there is a conflict between you and the forces of nature.

4. *A conflict between a person and society.* If you decide to fight for a cause that most people disagree with, there is a conflict between you and society.

These and other kinds of conflict can all be part of a good plot.

The series of events that make up the plot should move toward a *climax*.

- **The climax is the point in a narrative at which the most important event occurs. The climax is usually the turning point in the conflict.**

The climax of a narrative about an argument between you and a friend might occur when your friend declares, "I never want to see you again." The climax of a story about being lost in the woods might come with the discovery of some dry wood that permits you to light a signal fire.

Someone who reads or hears a narrative wants to know how the conflict was settled. How were you rescued from the rowboat? Did you win in your fight for an unpopular cause? The way the conflict is finally settled is called the *resolution*.

● **The _resolution_ is the action that follows the climax of a narrative. The resolution is how the conflict is settled. It also includes the results of the conflict, if any.**

In his book *Good Old Boy,* writer Willie Morris tells of his boyhood in Yazoo, Mississippi. One incident that Morris describes involves a bet he and his friends made with some boys who were visiting Yazoo from another town. The arrival of the visitors starts the conflict in Morris's story:

> In the summer of our eleventh year, a group of five or six boys from Greenwood, a town about fifty miles up the River, came to Yazoo for a two-week visit with their rich relatives. They were extremely obnoxious visitors, and since Greenwood was a somewhat larger town, they lorded it over us, calling us country bumpkins and the like, and acting for all the world as if they were from Paris or Constantinople or the lost underwater world of Atlantis. I have met many snobs in my lifetime, but, to date, these boys from Greenwood, Mississippi, still rank as the biggest.

The conflict between Morris and his friends and the "snobs" from Greenwood is the basis for the plot. It is because of the new boys' attitude that the Yazoo boys make a bet with them that becomes the core of the story. Without the conflict, Morris would not have a story to tell, only a series of memories. (You will see how the conflict of Morris's story reached its climax and was resolved later in this unit.)

When you choose an incident from your life to write about, you should choose one with the elements of a good plot. The incident should include a *conflict* of some kind; the events should lead up to a *climax*; and the conflict should be settled in a *resolution*.

Look again at the five incidents you listed in Exercise One. Copy them on another piece of paper. Leave at least three lines under each incident. Then, for each incident, briefly describe the conflict, the climax, and the resolution.

Example: *The time my family's car ran out of gas while we were crossing the Sonoran Desert*
Conflict: There was a conflict between my father and my uncle over whether we should stay in the car or send one person on foot to try to get help.
Climax: The climax came when my uncle set off with a tin can to try to find a gas station.
Resolution: Three hours later, a passing truck driver picked us up, and we found my uncle almost ready to collapse ten miles down the road.

Use this information to choose the best incident to write about. If there's one incident with a strong conflict, you might choose that incident to write about. If no incident on your list has a clear conflict, a real climax, and a resolution, think of another incident to write about. You can look at the list of types of conflicts on page 421 for ideas. Keep your paper for use later in this unit.

Lesson Two

Writing a Plot Outline

Imagine that you and your friends are once again exchanging stories about your lives. You decide that you'd like to tell about the time your little sister got lost during a beach party. You think this will make an interesting story because of its clear conflict — you and your friends racing against time to find your little sister before she got hurt. And the point of the story, you feel, is that it shows how you reacted in a dangerous situation. Here is how you tell the story:

"Well, the whole thing turned out fine because we finally found my little sister. If it hadn't been for the raisins, the whole thing might never have happened. But we really felt scared when the lifeguard warned us about the strong tides at the beach that day. So, anyway, on our way home that evening . . ."

One of your friends interrupts you. "What's going on?" he asks. "How did your little sister get lost? What do raisins have to do with it? What about the tides? Please begin at the beginning!"

Your friend's suggestion — begin at the beginning — is good advice. If the events of a story are not told in the order in which they happened, the story is likely to be confusing. As you learned in Unit Two, Lesson Five, the order in which a series of events happened is called *chronological order*. For most narratives, chronological order is best. A *plot outline* will help you organize the events of an autobiographical narrative in chronological order.

● A <u>plot outline</u> is a list of the main events in a narrative, written in the order in which they occurred.

Here is a plot outline for an autobiographical narrative about your five-year-old sister's getting lost at the beach. The events are numbered in the order in which they happened.

1. I took my sister Kathy to a beach party with my friends.
2. We ate sandwiches and hot dogs, played ball, swam, and danced all afternoon, while Kathy played in the sand.
3. Around five o'clock, the lifeguard ordered everyone out of the water because strong tides were pulling swimmers out to sea.
4. Suddenly, I realized that Kathy was nowhere to be seen.
5. I organized my friends into five search parties and sent each group to a separate part of the beach.
6. After half an hour of searching, Paula and George found Kathy sitting behind some big rocks eating raisins.
7. Kathy explained that she'd gone there to be alone so that she wouldn't have to share her raisins.
8. On our way home, I vowed that I'd never let Kathy out of my sight at the beach again.

When writing a plot outline, start by listing all the events that might be part of the story. Don't worry if you can't remember them in the exact order in which they occurred. Just list everything that happened as you remember it. After listing all the events you can remember, number them to show what happened first, second, third, and so on. If you think of other events that should be added, put them in. Copy your outline over in chronological order.

Below is a plot outline for an autobiographical narrative. The events are not in chronological order. Read all the sentences. Then copy them on your paper in chronological order and renumber them.

1. The train waited at the Los Angeles station for one hour.
2. By the time we reached San Diego, my eardrums were almost shattered.
3. He cried all the way to the first stop, Los Angeles.
4. I began to sing along to make the trip go faster.
5. As soon as the train left San Francisco, a baby in the seat behind me began to cry.
6. Two years ago, I took my first long train trip, from San Francisco to San Diego, and I was excited.
7. After we left Los Angeles, two kids ahead of me began to sing Linda Ronstadt songs.
8. Before the trip, while I waited in the station, I made sure I had my ticket.
9. As I walked off the train, I realized that what I would most remember about my first train trip would be a crying baby!
10. But our singing started the baby's crying again.

EXERCISE FOUR

Write a plot outline for the incident from your life that you chose in Exercise Two. Be sure the events are listed in chronological order. Save this paper. You will use it later in the unit.

Lesson Three

Setting

Suppose you are telling your friends the story of your sister Kathy's adventure at the beach party (outlined on page 424). You've told about Kathy's getting lost and about your organizing five search parties to look for her. Which of the following two ways of telling what happened next is more effective?

Version A

My friends and I searched up and down the beach for half an hour. There was no sign of Kathy. The longer we searched, the more worried we became. We knew that she might have wandered off into the ocean.

Version B

My friends and I searched up and down the beach for half an hour. The beach was nearly deserted now; for almost a mile in each direction I could see only barren, gray sand, with no sign of Kathy. The longer we searched, the more worried we became. We knew that she might have wandered off into the ocean. We could hear the waves crashing on the shore and against the sharp, jagged rocks that jutted into the water.

If you think that Version B is more effective, it is probably because of the descriptive details that make the *setting* of the story vivid.

The setting of the story — the place where the events take place — should be described as clearly as possible. A vividly described setting can help your reader understand your feeling about the story. In the story about Kathy's getting lost, the details about the "barren, gray sand," the "waves crashing on the shore," and the "sharp, jagged rocks" show the dangers that Kathy could have been facing. The description adds to the tension of the story.

Here is another example of how a setting can help set the mood for a story. In telling the story of the boys who visited the town of Yazoo, Willie Morris gives the feeling of life in a small Mississippi town by describing the setting vividly. Here is a part of the story that shows how Morris went about it:

We were close to growing plants, to the earth, and to nature's wilder moods. Many times I would go off by myself into the fields and woods that surrounded the town. I loved the little creeks and streams that trickled out of the hills into the delta, and most of all I loved the old Yazoo River. . . . How many boys must have been claimed over the generations by the murky, swirling Yazoo? It was a river not to be tampered with, but we loved it nonetheless: the way it opened up and wound around, the decaying houses along its banks, the moss hanging over it from the cypress trees. . . .

In the Mississippi Delta there was nothing gentle about nature. It came at you violently, or in a rush; sometimes it was just plain lazy and at others crazy and wild. In the spring, when the muddy waters overflowed the Yazoo into town, and the shacks on stilts in the bottoms were covered over, we would see the open trucks with convicts crowded in the back, their black-and-white stripes somber under the gray sky. Or a tornado would twist down and do strange tricks to the things it hit, carrying someone 50 yards and leaving him barely hurt, or driving straws into car tires like needles, or sending our garage across the alley into a field of weeds.

As you learned in Unit Four, a good description uses *sensory details*. Sensory details are those that appeal to the five senses: sight, smell, hearing, taste, and touch. Notice how Willie Morris uses sensory details to make his setting come to life. There are details that appeal to the sense of *sight:* "We would see the open trucks with convicts crowded in the back, their black-and-white stripes somber under the gray sky." There are details, like the trickling creeks, that appeal to the sense of *hearing*. There are details that appeal to the sense of *touch,* too: "the murky, swirling Yazoo," the moss hanging from the trees, and the way nature "came at you violently, or in a rush." All of these details help the reader form a vivid picture of Willie Morris's boyhood home.

EXERCISE FIVE

Each of the following sentences could begin a description of the setting of a story. Choose two of them. Use your imagination to picture the setting. For each setting you choose, list six to eight details that could be included in a description of that setting. Try to appeal to all the senses. After each detail, write the sense to which it appeals.

Example: I'll never forget the December night I spent in a lean-to on top of Smoky Mountain.
There was no wind, but the air was icy cold. (touch)
The branches of all the trees were bare. (sight)
Our boots made a crisp crunching sound in the snow. (hearing)
My uncle Frank built a fire with sweet-smelling pine branches. (smell)

He made scalding hot cups of cocoa for us.   (touch)
The cocoa tasted sweet.   (taste)
There was no sound but the rustling of tiny animal feet.   (hearing)
The sky was clear and filled with thousands of stars.   (sight)

1. The auditorium was crowded with people, eager to see and hear the greatest rock concert ever to take place in our town.
2. Watching a thunderstorm from a house that overlooks a lake in the mountains is a breathtaking experience.
3. I hate shopping at the supermarket on a busy Saturday morning!
4. The abandoned farmhouse was a spooky place.
5. It was a hot, humid August afternoon when the two baseball teams met on our school field to battle for the town championship.

EXERCISE SIX

Think about the incident you chose for Exercise Two. Try to remember its setting as clearly as you can. List six to eight details to describe the setting. Use as many sensory details as possible.

Lesson Four

Characters

When you are sharing a story about your life, your audience wants to know more than *what* happened. They also want to know *who* was involved. The people in a story are called the *characters*. Describing them clearly will help the reader become involved in the story.

In *Good Old Boy*, Willie Morris describes two characters who are important to the plot of his story:

There was a pair of twins who lived in the town; their names were Paul and Pinky Posey. They looked so completely alike that at times even their parents could not tell them apart. They both had long red hair, they were identically bowlegged, they had the same floppy ears and squeaky voices, and they wore the same

428

clothes, which usually consisted of blue jeans and white T-shirts, minus shoes. They even got warts in the same places at the same time. Paul was slightly more intelligent than Pinky, but that was not saying much. The only way we could tell them apart was that Pinky had four toes on his left foot, but seldom did anyone want to get close enough for a thorough examination.

Notice the many details that Morris uses to describe the twins. The description helps you see the characters clearly. You realize that the twins are unusual, and you begin to be curious about what will happen to them.

As you write your autobiographical narrative, you have a choice to make about the characters. You can describe the people that were involved in the incident exactly as they were, or, if you want to keep the names of the people private, you can make up new names and faces for them. Whichever method you choose, you should have a clear picture of your characters in mind and write enough details to help the reader get the same picture.

Here are some questions that will help you think of details to use in describing characters.

1. What do the characters look like? Are they young, old, short, tall, bald, overweight, beautiful, or frightening? Do they have any interesting or unusual physical features, like the four toes of one of the Posey twins in Morris's story?

2. What do the characters wear? Do they wear overalls, a fur coat, a business suit, a leather jacket, or an evening gown?

3. How do the characters speak? Are some voices high and squeaky and others low and rumbling? Does a character stutter? Does a character have an accent?

4. How do the characters behave? Are they nervous, calm, full of energy, or tired? Are some lazy and others hardworking, some brave and others cowardly?

5. What habits do the characters have? Are they always yawning, snapping gum, kicking the ground, pulling on hair, or folding their arms? Do they stand, sit, or walk in special ways?

You don't have to answer each of these questions for all of the characters in your story. Only the most important characters should be fully described. Too many details can clog the flow of the story. A skillful writer chooses the details that are most interesting, important, or typical, and uses them. A few strong, meaningful details will impress the reader more vividly than a long list of unimportant ones.

EXERCISE SEVEN

Look at the four photos on page 435. Choose two that you find interesting. For each photo you pick, write six to eight details that could be used to describe that person. The details should include those that you see in the photo (such as hair, eyes, and facial expression) as well as details that you make up (voice, habits). The details that you make up should fit the person in the photo.

EXERCISE EIGHT

Write the names of two or three characters you would include in an autobiographical narrative based on the incident you chose for Exercise Two. (You may change their names if you wish.) Then write six to eight details to describe each character. Save this paper for use later in the unit.

Lesson Five

Dialogue

Describing the setting and the characters of a story vividly is one way to bring the story to life. Another way is by using *dialogue.*

Dialogue is conversation between two or more people in a story. Dialogue allows the reader to hear what the characters say and how they say it.

In *Good Old Boy,* Willie Morris tells of a bet he and his friends made with the stuck-up boys who were visiting Yazoo from another town. Each of the groups claims that it has the faster runner. Here is the way Morris uses dialogue to bring the argument to life:

430

Finally one of the Greenwood boys said, "And you see this big fellow right here? He can outrun anybody in this hick town."

"That's true," Marsh said. "I can outrun anybody in town, and I can do it runnin' backward!"

"Well, can you now?" Spit McGee suddenly exclaimed, jumping up from his game of marbles. "Here's bettin' you five dollars and ten moonpies that we know somebody who can run around this here block in 30 seconds, and it'll take your man at least three minutes to do it by Bubba Barrier's daddy's stopwatch."

"Thirty seconds around *this* block?" the leader of the Greenwood gang laughed. "That's impossible. Let's just walk around this here block and see how big it is." So we all started from the front of the high school building, turned left on College Street, left on Calhoun, left again on Jackson, and a final left on Canal, arriving after a good eight or 10 minutes' walk in front of the school again. It was not only a long block, it was the longest in town.

"Your man can't do it in 30 seconds," the Greenwood leader said. "Ol' Marsh can do it in three minutes, though, and your man can't do it in five."

"Meet us right here in front of the school this time tomorrow," Spit McGee said, "and bring your five dollars and enough extra spendin' money for the moonpies."

"We'll be here," the boy said, "and we'll make you look mighty silly."

By quoting the exact words that were said, Morris gives the reader a sense of "being there."

(If you are curious, here is how the conflict between the Yazoo boys and the Greenwood boys is settled: The Yazoo boys win the bet by pitting Paul Posey, one of the twins, against Marsh. The Greenwood boys don't know that Paul's identical twin Pinky is hiding halfway around the block. Paul disappears, and Pinky finishes the race well ahead of the astonished Marsh.)

Here are some things to remember when writing dialogue:

1. Be sure to let the reader know who is speaking. This is especially important if there are more than two people in the conversation. Every time a different character begins to speak, begin a new paragraph. Use *tags — he said, she asked, Don exclaimed,* and so on — to show who is speaking.

2. Vary the tags and where you place them. If all your tags are the same — *he said, she said, they said* — the effect will be boring. Put the tags in different places, too. You can put them at the beginning, middle, or end of a line of dialogue:

> Petunia complained, "There's a fly in my soup."
> "I see it," said the waiter.
> "Well," demanded Petunia, "what's it doing there?"
> "The backstroke, I believe," sneered the waiter.

3. If your tag is in the middle of a sentence of dialogue, be sure that the sentence is broken in a place that sounds natural. Here is an example of a poorly placed tag:

> "Here, take," screamed Petunia, "back the soup!"

There is no natural pause where the tag is inserted. The tag is better placed elsewhere in the line:

> "Here," screamed Petunia, "take back the soup!"

Reading your dialogue aloud will help you to place the tags where they sound most natural.

4. Make sure that your dialogue sounds realistic. Read it aloud to yourself or a friend. Does it sound real?

5. Try to make the dialogue fit the character who is speaking. If one of your characters is your five-year-old sister, she should speak differently from a thirty-year-old bus driver or a fifty-year-old college professor. Try to use words and phrases that sound like that character.

EXERCISE NINE

Below are five situations. Each one could be part of a story. Choose one of them. On your paper, write from ten to twelve lines of dialogue that the characters might say. Be sure that a reader can tell who is speaking at all times. Vary the tags and where they are placed.

1. You have a chance to talk to your favorite movie or television star. What will the two of you say to each other?
2. You are riding your bicycle and accidentally bump someone who doesn't like you. How will the conversation go?

3. You try to persuade a sister or brother to lend you some money.
4. Your two favorite sports figures meet and have a discussion.
5. A cab driver and a rider argue about the size of the tip.

EXERCISE TEN

Think again about the autobiographical incident you chose for Exercise Two. Find one or more places in the incident where dialogue could appear. Write at least five lines of dialogue that the characters actually spoke or could have spoken. Be sure that the reader can tell who is speaking.

Lesson Six

Writing and Revising

In this unit, you have chosen an incident from your life to use as the basis for an autobiographical narrative. You have outlined the plot and listed details describing the setting and the characters. And you've written some lines of dialogue you might use. Now it is time to put together all the elements in an autobiographical narrative.

EXERCISE ELEVEN

Write an autobiographical narrative that is two to four pages long. (A written page usually holds about 250 to 300 words.) Follow these suggestions for putting together your narrative.

1. Begin your story in a way that you think is interesting. If the setting of the story is important, you can start with a description of it. A description of one of the characters may be a good way to begin. Or you may want to start by telling the reader why the story is important to you.

If you are not sure which way of starting will be best for your story, try writing two or three opening paragraphs. Choose the one you like the best.

2. Make sure the setting and the characters are clear to the reader early in the story. Include at least three or four sensory details to describe the setting and each important character.

3. Tell the events of the plot in chronological order. Use the plot outline you wrote for Exercise Four as a guide.

4. Use dialogue at one or two points in the story where conversation takes place. Be sure to make it clear who is speaking. Vary your tags and where you put them.

5. You can end your story in any of several ways. You can simply end with the last event in the plot. If something important happened as a result of the incident — if you learned a lesson, or if you made a decision — you can tell about it in the last paragraph. Or you can tell how you feel about what happened. Try writing two or three endings, and choose the one you like best.

EXERCISE TWELVE

When you have finished your first draft, use the Checklist that follows to improve your story. If the answer to any of the questions in the Checklist is *no*, revise the story until the answer is *yes*.

If you wish, you may exchange papers with a classmate. Point out parts of the stories that are especially good. Discuss areas that could be improved further.

Checklist

1. Are the events told in chronological order?
2. Is it easy for the reader to follow what happened?
3. Is the setting of the story described through sensory details?
4. Are sensory details used to describe the important characters?
5. When dialogue is used, is it clear which character is speaking?
6. Does the dialogue sound realistic?